Also by Robert Kurson
available from Random House Large Print

Shadow Divers

CRASHINGTHROUGH

CRASHING

THROUGH

A TRUE STORY OF RISK, ADVENTURE, AND THE MAN WHO DARED TO SEE

Robert Kurson

RANDOM HOUSE
LARGE PRINT

All rights reserved.
Published in the United States of America by Random House
Large Print in association with Random House, New York.
Distributed by Random House, Inc., New York.

This book is based, in part, on an article written
by the author entitled "Into the Light," which appeared
in **Esquire** in June 2005.

Library of Congress Cataloging-in-Publication Data
Kurson, Robert.
Crashing through : a story of risk, adventure, and the man
who dared to see / by Robert Kurson.—1st large print ed.
p. cm.
Originally published: New York : Random House, © 2007.
ISBN-13: 978-0-7393-2722-7
1. May, Mike, 1953– 2. Blind—United States—
Biography. 3. Eye—Surgery—Patients—United
States—Biography. 4. Blind—Rehabilitation—
United States—Case studies. I. Title.
HV1792.M39K87 2007b
362.4'1092--dc22
[B]
2007012302

Illustration credits appear on pages 465–466

www.randomhouse.com/largeprint

FIRST LARGE PRINT EDITION

10 9 8 7 6 5 4 3 2 1

This Large Print edition published in accord with
the standards of the N.A.V.H.

TO AMY, NATE, AND WILL:
YOU ARE WHEREVER I LOOK.

TO DARE IS TO LOSE ONE'S FOOTING
MOMENTARILY.
NOT TO DARE IS TO LOSE ONESELF.

—SØREN KIERKEGAARD

CRASHINGTHROUGH

CHAPTER ONE

Mike May's life was near perfect when, on February 11, 1999, he made his way to the dais in the ballroom of San Francisco's St. Francis Hotel.

The forty-six-year-old businessman had been invited to present the prestigious Kay Gallagher Award for mentoring the blind, an award he'd won himself the previous year. Dozens in the audience knew his history: blinded at age three by a freak accident; three-time Paralympics gold medalist and current world record holder in downhill speed skiing; entrepreneur on the verge of bringing a portable global positioning system (GPS) to the blind; coinventor of the world's first laser turntable; mud hut dweller in Ghana; husband to a beautiful blond wife (in attendance and dressed in a tight black top, short black skirt, and black high heels); loving father; former CIA man.

People watched the way May moved. He walked with a quiet dignity, effortlessly negotiating the obstacle course of banquet tables and chairs, smiling at those he passed, shaking hands along the way. There was more than mobility in his step; his gait seemed free of regret, his body language devoid of longing. Most of the people in this room worked with the blind every day, so they knew what it looked like for a person to yearn for vision. May looked like he was exactly who he wanted to be.

He was accustomed to public speaking, and his messages were always inspiring. But every so often a member of the audience would turn on him, and it usually came at the same part of his talk, the part when he said, "Life with vision is great. But life without vision is great, too." At that point someone would stand and jab his finger and say, "That's impossible!" or "You're not dealing with your inner demons," or "You're in denial." The objections came from both the blind and the sighted. May was always polite, always let the person finish his thought. Then, in the warm but definite way in which he'd spoken since childhood, he would say, "I don't mean to speak for anyone else. But for me, life is great."

That, however, would not be the message for this evening. Instead, the tall and handsome May spoke glowingly about the award winner, about how much it had meant to him to win the Gallagher, and about the importance of mentoring. He seasoned his talk with jokes, some tried and true, others off the cuff, all to good effect. Then he presented the honoree with a plaque and a check and returned to his seat. When he sat down, his wife,

Jennifer, told him, "You made me cry. You look beautiful in that suit. That was a lovely talk."

May and Jennifer stayed at the hotel that night. Ordinarily, they would have awoken and made the seventy-five-mile drive to their home in Davis, California, each needing to return to work. But Jennifer's contact lenses had been bothering her, so she had scheduled an appointment with a San Francisco optometrist—not her regular eye doctor, but a college friend's husband who had been willing to see her on short notice. Though May was itching to get back to his home office, he agreed to accompany Jennifer to the appointment. The morning was glorious as the couple strolled San Francisco and enjoyed that rarest of pleasures, an unhurried weekday breakfast at a streetside café.

The optometrist's office was nearby, so May and Jennifer, along with May's Seeing Eye dog, a golden retriever named Josh, walked up Post Street to make it to the morning appointment. Jennifer assured him that the visit would take no more than thirty minutes. May had never accompanied his wife to an eye appointment and was pleasantly surprised to learn that they would be out so quickly.

The waiting room grabbed Jennifer's attention straightaway. An interior designer, she lived in a world of color and flow, and she began describing it to May: the direction the chairs faced, the narrowing of the hallway that led to the exam rooms, the taupe of the wall behind the receptionist—"whose cheekbones are stunning, by the way." It intrigued May that he had married a woman whose universe was so dominated by the visual, and it delighted him that she felt so passionate about sharing it all with him, even about the beautiful women.

A few minutes later Mike Carson, the optometrist, greeted May and Jennifer and led them to an office. Carson examined Jennifer, recorded some measurements, and told her he would write her a new contact lens prescription. May was glad that things had gone so quickly—this would allow him to get home in time to pick up their sons from school.

Carson finished making his notes and flipped on the light. He looked at May for a few seconds, made another note in Jennifer's file, then looked back at May. He asked how long it had been since May had seen an eye doctor.

"At least ten years," May replied.

"How about if I take a look?" Carson asked. "That's a long time to go without seeing a doctor."

"You want to examine me?" May asked.

"Just for a second," said Carson. "Let's just make sure everything is healthy in there as long as you're here."

May thought about it for a moment, then said, "Sure, why not?"

May and Jennifer switched places so that May now was in the examining chair, the one with the chin holder and instrument that looks like the pay-per-view binoculars on top of the Empire State Building.

"I think you're going to find that I'm blind," May joked.

The doctor leaned in and immediately saw that May had a blue-colored prosthetic left eye. His right eye, his natural eye, was nearly opaque and all white, evidence of dense corneal scarring. No pupil or color could be seen at all. Some blind people wear dark glasses to conceal such an eye, but May had never felt the need to do so. His eyelid drooped a bit, leaving his eye mostly closed, so no one reacted badly to it.

Carson stepped away and sat on a stool.

"Mike," he said, "I wonder if you'd mind if my partner, Dr. Dan Goodman, takes a look at you. He's an ophthalmologist, one of the best in the country. I think he'd be interested."

May glanced toward Jennifer with just the slightest quizzical look. Jennifer was already wearing the same expression.

"I guess it can't hurt," May said.

Carson left the room. For a moment neither May nor Jennifer said anything. Then each said to the other, "That's interesting."

A moment later Carson returned with his partner. Dr. Goodman, age forty-two, introduced himself and asked May how he'd lost his vision.

"It was a chemical explosion when I was three," May replied.

"Do you have an ophthalmologist?" Goodman asked.

"He died about ten years ago. He'd been my doctor since the accident," said May.

"What did he tell you about your vision?" Goodman asked.

"He tried three or four corneal transplants when I was a kid," May said. "They all failed. After that, he told me that I would never see, I'd be blind forever. He was supposed to be a great ophthalmologist. I knew he was right."

"Who was he?" Goodman asked.

"Dr. Max Fine," May replied.

Goodman's eyes lit up.

"Dr. Fine was a legend," Goodman said. "He was my teacher. I sought him out when I was young and asked to do surgery with him on Wednesday nights. He was one of the great ophthalmologists in the world."

May and Goodman spent a minute reminiscing about Dr. Fine. Then Goodman asked, "Mind if I take a look?"

"Not at all," May replied.

Goodman dimmed the lights, stepped forward,

and, using the thumb and forefinger on one hand, opened the lid of May's right eye. The stillness of the touch startled May. Goodman's hand stayed motionless, absent the vaguest hint of tremor. May had felt that kind of touch only once before, from Dr. Fine, who had held his eye open in just the same way.

Goodman peered into May's eye. He saw the massive corneal scarring that trademarks a chemical explosion. He shone a penlight into May's eye, which May could barely detect (most blind people have some vague light perception). But when Goodman waved his hand in front of the eye May could not perceive the movement. Goodman conducted a few more tests, then looked through the same biomicroscope Carson had used. It took only moments for him to see that May was totally blind.

The exam lasted perhaps five minutes. Goodman turned on the lights and pulled up his stool.

"Mike," Goodman said. "I think we can make you see."

The words barely registered with May.

"There is a very new and very rare stem cell transplant procedure," Goodman continued. "It's indicated for very few types of cases. But a chemical burn like yours is one of them."

Jennifer leaned forward. She wasn't sure whether to look at Goodman or her husband. What was Goodman saying?

"Despite your horrible corneal disease, it looks like there's good potential for vision in your eye, and that it can benefit from a stem cell transplant," Goodman said. "I've done maybe six of these procedures. Most ophthalmologists in the world haven't done any. It's not something anyone specializes in. And I don't know of anyone who has done one on a patient who has been blind for as long as you've been. But it could work."

All May could think to say was "That's interesting."

"If you're interested you need to come back for something called a B-scan," Goodman explained. "That's an ultrasound designed to look into the back of the eye to make sure there's no gross pathology or abnormality. But if the B-scan is clean, there's a good chance this could work."

Goodman's words sounded surreal to May. His body and brain agreed simultaneously that it was impossible, that once Goodman ran the tests he would see what Dr. Fine had seen—a patient beyond repair. Still, the newness of the science intrigued May—he'd never before heard the term "stem cell" used in connection with vision—and he fashioned this thought: "I'm in the technology business, and technology changes all the time. Why can't vision technology change, too?"

"Is it complicated?" May asked.

"The stem cell transplant is complicated," Goodman said. "By itself it provides no visual benefit. But it sets the stage for a cornea transplant three or four months later. If all goes right, the two surgeries add up to vision."

May appreciated that Goodman spoke clinically and directly, and without trying to inspire him. To Jennifer, something seemed amiss. Vision had always been impossible for May, not because science hadn't caught up to him but because something fundamental was missing or unfixable.

Jennifer watched May for his reaction. There was no hallelujah. There were no cries of "Oh, my God!" Rather, May pursed his lips slightly and gazed up and to the right a bit, the way he always looked when he was considering the theoretical rather than the wonderful.

"I'd like to think about it, if that's okay," May said.

"Of course," Goodman said. "Take your time. Call my office if you'd like to go ahead with the B-scan. It was very nice to meet you."

Goodman shook hands with May and Jennifer. And with that he was out of the room. The encounter had lasted less than ten minutes.

After the appointment May and Jennifer were walking back to their red Dodge Caravan, which was still parked near the St. Francis Hotel. The weather was bright and brisk, and reminded Jennifer of the couple's newlywed days living in San Francisco, when they walked miles for just the right Chinese takeout and talked about their future on the way.

"Do you and Wyndham have soccer practice tonight?" Jennifer asked, unlocking the Caravan's doors.

"Not tonight," May said. "Good thing, too. I'm already behind on a bunch of business calls. It's amazing—just one day and the whole world seems to rush out from under your feet."

Josh climbed in and sat on the floor of the passenger side, between May's feet. Jennifer found her sunglasses, started the ignition, and pulled out onto Post Street. With good traffic they would be in Davis in an hour and a half. May opened his cell phone and began to return business calls, simultaneously making certain that Jennifer didn't miss the turnoff to Route 80. Though May could not see, he possessed a collection of uncannily accurate mental maps—it was that kind of skill, and others, that caused many to consider him a kind of super–blind man.

Once across the Bay Bridge, the couple relaxed a bit. For a few miles neither said anything. Then Jennifer looked over at May and remarked, "Well, that was fascinating."

"It sure was," May said. "It doesn't sound real, does it?"

Jennifer hesitated for a moment. She hadn't had time to begin to sort out the implications of Goodman's offer, but she knew this much: something big had happened, and whatever it meant it was certain to be an intensely personal issue for her husband. For that reason she wanted to say nothing, to simply let him process it for himself. But she also needed to hear him talk.

"So, hypothetically," Jennifer finally said, "and we don't know if this would even work, but just for fun, what would it be like? What might you like to see?"

In twelve years of marriage they had never discussed what it might be like for May to see, not even in the playful way in which they allocated imaginary lottery winnings. Since early childhood, May himself had not thought about what it might be like to see, a fact that struck many who met him as inconceivable. The concept of vision simply was not part of his existence. Just the sound of Jennifer's question felt otherworldly to him.

"Well, Dr. Fine made it very clear that I would never see in my lifetime, so it's probably not possible," May said. "But just for fun . . ."

Jennifer kept her eyes on the road.

"I think I'd like to see panoramas, especially

at Kirkwood," May said, referring to the family's favorite ski resort. "And I'd like to see beautiful women."

"That makes sense," Jennifer said. "You're always thinking about those things anyway."

"Panoramas and women are two things I love but can't go around touching. They can't really be adequately described to me. Those are two things you really have to touch with your eyes in order to fully appreciate."

"Where might you go to see these beautiful women—other than your own home, of course?" she asked.

"Saint-Tropez. Straight to the topless beaches."

"I need a tan," Jennifer said. "Mind if I go with you?"

"If you don't mind me gawking."

"You've been gawking since I met you. What else?"

May thought further. He told Jennifer he might like to see the Eiffel Tower or the Statue of Liberty or the Galápagos Islands, all places to which he'd already traveled. Definitely the Golden Gate Bridge.

Jennifer nodded and kept driving, past rolling hills and sprawling strip malls. Neither she nor May spoke for a time, each of them content to paw at and then retreat from this new idea. Finally Jennifer asked May if he might like to see their boys.

"Of course I would," May said. "I would love

to share the experience with them—it would be like stepping on the moon with them. But it's interesting, Jen. I think about seeing them and I don't feel like I'll see anything I don't already see. I feel like I already know exactly what those boys look like, not just physically but their entire beings. So in a certain way I can't imagine vision making any difference. That sounds strange, doesn't it? But I can't imagine vision or anything else adding anything to how much I love or feel like I know those guys."

The van rolled along in silence for a few seconds.

"And, of course, I feel exactly the same about you," May said. "I already know you."

"What if you didn't like how I looked?" Jennifer asked.

"You're beautiful," May said. "I think I know exactly what you look like. What would I see that I don't already see? You're gorgeous."

For a while May and Jennifer said nothing. At the halfway point they compared hunger levels and debated whether to stop for lunch. The consensus was to press forward in order to make it home in time to pick up the kids from school.

"Saint-Tropez, huh?" Jennifer asked.

May laughed. Jennifer took the Davis exit, telling her husband about a new client she had lined up, listening to his ideas for a new driving route to Kirkwood. He appreciated this hour with his wife. She had never mentioned the myriad practical benefits that would accrue to her if he could see—his ability to drive, fill the gas tank, read his own mail, sort the laundry, pick up groceries.

"Imagine seeing the panoramas at Kirkwood," May said. "This really has been an interesting day."

Jennifer pulled her van into the two-car garage of the Mays' three-bedroom house, which sat at the elbow of one of the town's shady, tree-named streets.

Inside, the couple thanked Jennifer's mother, who had watched five-year-old Wyndham and seven-year-old Carson, and kissed her good-bye. May threw a tennis ball to Josh in the backyard, fixed himself a sandwich, and continued the day-long process of returning business calls. When the boys' school let out, he strapped the tan leather harness on Josh and walked over to pick them up. Kids called out, "Hi, Mr. May! Can we pet Josh?" As always, May said, "Sure thing, Tyler" or "Is that you, Emily?" On the walk home his sons competed to describe the bugs they'd found during recess.

The rest of May's day moved like every other: business calls, wrestling with the boys, feeling a new fabric Jennifer had picked for a client, drafting a business letter, doing the dishes, telling bedtime stories. It had been ten hours since May had returned from his meeting with Dr. Goodman. In that time he had not thought once about new vision.

And that is how quickly life returned to normal

for May. His start-up business was primary in his mind. In a risky move, he had resigned his executive position at a major adaptive technology company in order to design, manufacture, and market a portable GPS system for the blind—the first of its kind. By linking May's receiver and mapping software to a laptop computer contained in a backpack, a customer could tune in the global positioning satellites that orbited the earth. Then, with the push of a button, that customer could receive real-time, turn-by-turn directions to whatever location he desired: home, work, grocery store, restaurant, park, Starbucks—anywhere. May saw his product as liberating. It gave a kind of vision to the blind.

But he needed funding, so much of May's life centered on pitching potential investors. He had bet it all on this company (which was still without a name), drawing on personal savings to support both business and family. Neither he nor Jennifer was of independent means, which meant that he had maybe a year to make the business work. After that, he would need to return to the corporate world. The restraint on freedom that came with a traditional executive position was discordant with May's DNA.

He worked eighteen-hour days, testing the GPS between coffee shops in Davis, on the ferry to San Francisco, in airplanes as the unit's cables spaghettied onto the shoulder of the person seated beside him. In Anaheim he raced a group of blind cane users from their hotel to Disneyland. Even though he had to stop along the way to hot-glue some loose wires, he still won. May believed in his product.

And he was able to work from home, a godsend in allowing him the time with his family he so deeply desired.

When Wyndham's soccer coach quit before the team's first practice, parents gathered at May's house to determine what to do next. He told them that he would coach the team, practices and all, and that he would mail them schedules immediately. The parents applauded. When May got up to adjourn the meeting and reached for his cane, some of the mothers said, "Wait a minute—you're blind?" May said, "Yep."

He ran drills like Sharks and Minnows, set up orange cones in a mostly symmetrical field shape, and taught the five-year-olds (Jennifer called them "widgets") to run together in packets toward the correct goal. They loved his stories about playing soccer in college, like the one where he made the other team use his beeping ball for an entire half, and how he got a bloody nose when the silent ball hit him in the face.

Many of the players knew May from school. Every year, he'd bring Josh to area classrooms to tell children what it was like to be blind. He loved their questions: Do your kids get away with stuff because you can't see them? **No, because I have secret techniques to stop them. But they always try.** Were you all bloody after your accident? **Super bloody.** When you met Bill Clinton, how did you know it was really him? **I asked him to talk so I could make sure.** He demonstrated his talking gadgets with the robot voices, set up a maze of chairs to show how he could zigzag around with Josh, and printed each kid's name in braille on a card they could take home. Carson and Wyndham thought they had the coolest dad in the world. The couple had never taught the boys to be proud of May. As Jennifer told people, "They just are."

In the time between working and parenting, May squeezed in the remainder of a full-blown life. Much of this was made possible by his exceptional ability to move through the world. Often, sighted people would observe him walking smoothly through a banquet hall or an airport or an unfamiliar house and insist that May could see. Some would even challenge him on it. He was hard-pressed to explain his skill in simple terms.

Part of it stemmed from May's highly refined ability to detect echo. Over the years, he had learned to distinguish tiny differences made by the sounds of voices or footsteps or canes as they bounced off various objects and openings. The information was so subtle that it vanished if May tried to think about it. Many blind people cannot use echolocation—some can't hear the echoes; others refuse to trust them. Echoes were sewn into May's instinct.

Spatial perception and spatial memory were also critically important. As he moved about a place, whether in a friend's dining room or New York's Penn Station, May's brain vacuumed in the relative locations of obstacles, openings, and passageways, then assembled them into mental maps he could recall at will. He attributed this understanding of space—and his ability to memorize and utilize it so fluently—to his lifetime of participation in sports.

And May was flat-out good with his two primary mobility instruments, the cane and the dog. Few blind people use both, but May saw power in each. The cane was simpler to use and didn't need feeding, but it bogged down in crowded situations and never picked up overhead obstructions, the enemy of the fast and free. The dog was difficult to take overseas and had to be fed and walked during business trips, but he was able to detect overhead obstructions, could move quickly through crowds, and was nice company. Of the 1.3 million legally blind people in the United States in 1999, the great majority used canes, while only 7,000 used dog guides.

May's mobility skills lowered the drawbridge to

the world. But it was his approach that took him places. To go where May wanted to go—which was everywhere—one had to be willing to get lost, a terrifying prospect to many blind people. To May, getting lost was the best part. He told people, "I'm very curious. So getting lost doesn't feel like a bad thing. It's part of the process of discovering things." When they asked how he'd gotten so adept at cane travel he told them it was his curiosity, not his cane.

Weeks had passed since May had met Goodman and still he'd given little thought to the doctor's offer. Every so often, Jennifer would ask her husband for his thinking on the subject of new vision, and it was at these times that May appreciated her most. There was no longing in her question, no subtext of urging him along. May confessed to Jennifer that he hadn't thought much about Goodman's offer. He also told her that life already felt good and busy and full. And that's how they left it as winter turned to spring.

As the months passed, however, May did not feel that it was responsible to allow the matter of new vision to linger dormant on his to-do list. He respected the import of Goodman's offer and knew that he should give it the serious consideration it deserved. He began to turn things over in his head.

He tried to imagine a life with vision. But his thoughts always returned to his current life, his real life. He had risked everything on his business, which was now in its most critical phase and demanded his full attention; a single misstep could tear it from its moorings and drown the project. After two recent close calls during similarly stressful periods, his marriage was now thriving and hopeful. He was focused on raising his boys and being present for the moments in their lives—especially the small ones—which already seemed to fly past too quickly.

He tried to imagine what vision could offer. He could already go virtually wherever he chose—and loved the adventure of finding his way. He could already do whatever he desired—sometimes better than the sighted. And he continued to believe that he saw Jennifer and his boys in the real sense of the word—the sense that speaks to what it really means to know a person, what it means to connect to another's soul.

Vision was not calling to May. He knew that the idea of a blind man refusing sight would strike most of the world as unthinkable. But he thought of it this way: What if a sighted person was offered a new sense? What if he was offered, say, the ability to foretell the future? At first, that prospect might seem thrilling. But if the person was already leading a full and rich life, would he really want it? Might it not disrupt an otherwise wonderful life? And what if it turned out to be something wholly different from what the person had bargained for? May wondered how many happy people would proceed if offered a permanent crystal ball or sonar or the ability to read minds. How many of them would say yes to a new sense? And that is how May felt about vision. His life was already complete without it.

And yet, during the breaks in his days, May found himself wondering about what it might be like to see. He might be touching one of Jennifer's fabrics and think, "What would my favorite color be?" Shooting hoops with his sons he might ask, "Would I recognize my boys right away?" At the neighborhood coffee shop where he loved to listen to the lilting conversations and high-heeled clicks of women, he wondered, "Would I still prefer blondes?"

May continued to focus on his work and his family. This was no time to be distracted from what was most important. Still, crossing the Golden Gate Bridge he might ponder, "What would I find beautiful?" Walking in the park he might ask himself, "What would look familiar to me?" Shaving in the bathroom he thought, "Would I look like myself?"

And he wondered about the red hat.

When he was a very young boy, just before his accident, his father had taken him deer hunting, a mystical adventure that had required awakening before dawn, carrying weapons, and wearing a bright red hat for visibility, one that could be seen from distances of forever. This was May's first memory in life. Since losing his vision, he had felt himself just a whisper from being able to see that red hat in his mind; it was always just a hairsbreadth beyond his grasp—there but not there. And he asked himself, "Would I see that red hat if somehow I were made to see?"

One night in August, after the boys had been bathed and tucked in, Jennifer and May sat on lawn chairs under the orange tree in their backyard. She had asked him little about the prospect of new vision. Tonight, she wanted to know.

"So, where are you on this?" Jennifer asked. "Do you think about it?"

"I do think about it," May said. "Every time, I ask myself if vision would really change my life. And every time the answer is the same: I don't think it would. Life is already so full. I don't need it. I don't feel like I'm missing a thing."

For a minute neither of them said anything. Then Jennifer leaned over, kissed her husband's cheek, and said, "Okay."

May's summer got even busier. He amped up his efforts to recruit investors, took his sons to minor league baseball games, kept up with his father, who was not feeling well. He had less time than ever to think about a topic like vision. And yet, something about the subject didn't sit right with May. He couldn't quite put his finger on it. But it felt like it was something that went back a very long way.

CHAPTER**TWO**

On a sunny spring morning in 1957, Ori Jean May sent two of her children, four-year-old Diane and three-year-old Mike, outside to play while she finished washing dishes and feeding three-month-old Therese. The May family had recently moved to Silver City, New Mexico, a mining town, where Bill May had taken a job as an industrial engineer.

Mike and Diane decided to make mud pies. Mike needed a packing container, so he headed to the family's old garage, a place of crooked shelves, cobwebbed containers, and tools that had died of old age. Gloriously, none of it was easy to reach. Mike climbed into the rafters and found a glass quart jar, perfect for mud pies, but filled with a hard, dried powder that would have to be cleaned. He took the jar to a cement horse trough near the garage and plunged it underwater. A plume of gas began to rise. Nearby, a pile of garbage sat burning.

Inside the house, Ori Jean dried the last of her dishes. A moment later she heard an explosion. She ran to the backyard and found Mike lying on the ground, drenched in blood and sharded in glass. He was in shock and whimpering. Diane sat stunned but uninjured. Ori Jean picked up her son and ran inside, where she wrapped him in a blanket and dialed frantically for help. Mike's injuries did not hurt. He just wanted to crawl away and put his head down.

Ori Jean found a neighbor to watch the baby, then grabbed Diane and followed the ambulance fifteen miles to the nearest hospital, drawing a curtain over her fears in order to stay on the road. Emergency room doctors swarmed around Mike. He had lost massive amounts of blood from his face, neck, arms, stomach, everywhere. Critical veins in his wrists had been slashed. A doctor found Ori Jean in the waiting room. He told her that Mike was going to die.

Ori Jean pleaded with God, "Please let him live, please let him live. Do it to me. Do anything to me. Anything is okay if you just let my baby live."

The doctors kept working. Staff scrambled to find a helicopter to rush him to specialists in El Paso, Texas. "We don't think he's going to make it," they told Ori Jean, and she could not believe the words. Mike had just been twirling in the kitchen and walking his tarantula around by a little string leash. **That boy doesn't die, that boy moves and laughs and tells jokes, he does not die.** A helicopter came. Someone drove Ori Jean the 150 miles to

El Paso, a horrible trip, an endless drive silent but for the sound of tires on burning pavement and the murmurs of her prayers. Inside the helicopter, wrapped tightly in blankets, Mike felt the sun streaming through the window warm on his face.

Mike was still in surgery when Ori Jean reached El Paso. She waited for hours. Doctors told her to prepare to say good-bye to her son. More hours passed. Finally, a surgeon delivered different news. It had required five hundred stitches to quilt Mike together. His eyes had been badly damaged. But he was going to survive. The eyes part meant nothing to Ori Jean. Nothing mattered but that Mike was alive.

Mike remained in the hospital for three months, Ori Jean by his side. His face and head and skinny body were bandaged, and his system so stunned that he did not realize he couldn't see. Bill May blamed himself for the accident. The powder in the glass jar had been calcium carbide, a chemical that reacts violently with water to produce the explosive gas acetylene. If only he'd cleaned out the garage when the family had moved in.

Doctors told Ori Jean it could take a year for Mike to recover. And they told her that he was blind. At home, she kept Mike on a cot in her bedroom; she talked to him and stroked him constantly, assuring him that they were all very lucky.

Ori Jean changed his dressings and read to him for hours every day.

A social worker advised Ori Jean to get blindness and mobility training for Mike, and to take lessons herself on how to accommodate a blind child. A doctor told her to start thinking about sending Mike away to a school for the blind. That was what happened to blind children in the 1950s. It was the way.

But it was not Ori Jean's way.

Ori Jean James was born into adventure. Her American parents had eloped in 1922 from Texas to Chile, where her father set out to trade livestock. He knew his cattle. By 1928, when the family welcomed Ori Jean, her father was wealthy. He was also deeply admired by the Chilean locals. It was more his spirit than his money that moved them.

Origen James (for whom Ori Jean had been named) flung himself into Chilean culture. He danced the **cueca** as nimbly as the natives, spoke nuanced Spanish, made the town's customs his family's. He defied legend and warning and rode his horse on the notorious road from Rancagua to Santiago, where he was kidnapped en route by mountain bandits and told to make peace with his God. When one of the bandits freed him under cover of night, Origen promised the man a lifetime job—

and delivered. Weeks later he conquered the same route on the same horse. Ori Jean made him tell the story over and over.

That kind of curiosity was oxygen to Ori Jean's parents. They wanted one thing for their children: a sense of what it meant to explore the world. The family had servants and cooks and maids. But the idea of simply allowing life to happen rather than inhaling it was poison in the James home. A person had to go look.

Ori Jean looked. She joined her father for camping trips across the Andes into Argentina, where they would hunt the llama-like guanaco, chase ostriches, and find their way by the stars. She became lost investigating the giant ice and snow mazes called penitentes. She rode her horse alone into the same kind of bandit-prowled mountains where her father had been kidnapped.

When her father lost his livestock business, he did not seek refuge in the security of America, nor did he go to work for friendly competitors. He built a new business from scratch, bigger and more profitable than before, and the family continued to live where they were meant to live, in the mountains of a country that seemed to stretch forever. That idea—that there was always a way—thrilled Ori Jean. It meant she could do whatever she wanted to do.

When she turned eighteen, Ori Jean returned

to the United States to attend the University of Texas. In a way it felt like she was eloping. During a visit to her sister in Colorado she met a tall and handsome engineering student at the University of Colorado. Bill May had already been accepted into the government's V-2 rocket program, an honor reserved for the highest intellects. He was studying to be an industrial engineer.

Ori Jean and Bill fell in love and married. By 1957 the couple had three children and the world in front of them. In Chile, Ori Jean's father became gravely ill. He'd suffered a heart attack and was told by doctors that it was no longer safe for him to ride his horse. He told them, "If I have to live that way then I'm not alive." He continued to ride, high into the mountains. His wife kissed him before every journey. Ori Jean told him she admired how he lived. A short time later, at age sixty-two, he died. It was the same year that Ori Jean's son, Mike, lost his vision.

Mike's physical recovery lasted nearly a year. When the social worker visited, Ori Jean told her that she wanted Mike to attend public kindergarten and to participate in normal activities. The woman gently reminded her that Mike could not see and asked which activities Ori Jean had in mind. "All of them," she replied.

At home, Mike climbed out of his bed and into

his new world. It did not look black to him—he remembered black. Rather, it looked like nothing,
like the space directly behind one's head. He
climbed kitchen counters, squirmed out windows,
ran down toy-littered hallways—a constant ballet
of tripping and colliding he hardly noticed for his
excitement to get to the next place. Mike felt no
surprise at being unable to see; to his four-year-old
brain he just was who he was.

The kindergarten wanted no part of Mike.
What if he got hurt? What if he couldn't keep up?
What if everything? Ori Jean told them that she
would accept responsibility, even for everything, so
long as they let Mike try.

On the first day of school, she put a pair of dark
glasses on her son and fixed him a brown-bag
lunch. The glasses were the tenth pair Mike had
owned; he had smashed the others by running into
things. Ori Jean tied his shoes, kissed his face, and
sent him and five-year-old Diane to the bus stop.
They held hands and kicked stones along the way.

Mike climbed onto the bus, but when he went
to sit down he faced the wrong way and fell onto
the floor. For a moment he lay stunned. When he
found the seat he thought, "I bet I would have
known how to sit down if I could see." It had been
fifteen months since his accident. It was the first
time he had ever thought about being blind.

At the start of the school day, the teacher asked the children to face the flag for the Pledge of Allegiance. Mike wanted to ask, "Which way is that?" but stayed quiet and tried to face where the voices were pointing. In the bathroom, he could not tell the sink from the trough-style urinal, so he held it in. In the schoolyard, Mike walked in front of a swing set full of flying children. A foot bashed him in the mouth and knocked him over backward. He didn't cry. He just thought, "Where did that person come from?" At home, Ori Jean listened to Mike's account of his first day in kindergarten. She told him that school sounded like fun.

And he ran. Every bit of the world thrilled him—the earthworm's texture, the bumps underneath the cardboard "roller coaster" he used for sledding down hills with Diane, the songs the wind made when he raced to first base during kickball. But in order to know it all, to get it all in before bedtime or classtime or all the other times imposed on a child's life, he had to run; there was no way to know it all unless a kid could run.

There are a million obstacles when a blind person runs. Mike crashed into them all. As his kindergarten year progressed he appeared a walking painter's palette of bruises and scabs. Ori Jean bought more dark glasses. Mike was just the color she wished him to be.

The May family churned along. Ori Jean gave birth to her fourth child, Patrick, an instant roommate for Mike. Bill continued to work as an engineer, designing railroads for the mines. No one had to tell Mike his father was six foot six and weighed 260 pounds. He could feel the bigness when Bill used a single hand to lift him by his shirt and swing him back and forth across the sky, and from the way his father's deep voice bounced off walls. It was around this time that Ori Jean became concerned about her husband's drinking, but Bill insisted he had no problem.

As Mike thrived in kindergarten, Ori Jean was at a crossroads. The Silver City public school, like nearly all public schools in the country, was closed to blind students. Next year, Mike would need to be shipped away to a school for the blind. That prospect was unthinkable to Ori Jean, who believed that immersion in the whole of the world was crucial to leading a full life. She began to ask questions. She began to make phone calls. The landscape of options was thinner than she had imagined.

According to Ori Jean's research, only a very few public schools integrated blind and sighted students. Most were located in big cities like Chicago and Boston, but one was in Walnut Creek, California, which seemed small and close-knit, and was home to one of Bill's friends. Ori Jean put their house up for sale and prepared for the thousand-mile journey west.

The May family arrived in Walnut Creek in the summer of 1959. Ori Jean enrolled Mike at Buena Vista Elementary. Of the school's six hundred students, perhaps fifteen were blind. They were assigned a resource teacher who was to help with logistics. Other than that, they were to be treated like any other student—same classes, same activities, same rules. The first day was a revelation to Mike. He met other blind kids for the first time. And he met Nick Medina.

Medina was the resource teacher for the blind students. He told the class that his vision was impaired and that he considered himself blind, though he walked without a cane and could even drive a car. He was just twenty-three years old and small of stature, but he laid down the law early. He expected the children to do their work and do it well. He would suffer no excuses, self-pity, or whining. He would go to bat for them—do whatever it took—but they would have to earn it. He wasn't going to lay himself on the line for some kid just because that kid couldn't see.

At home, Ori Jean set up the house for her four bustling children, hanging a dinner bell on the back porch and assigning chores. Mike was exempt from none of them. He was required to clean his room, fix his own lunches, help in the yard, and take out the garbage. When the jelly from his sandwich dripped onto the floor, he was expected to find a mop and clean it up. Diane thought he got off too easily—why didn't Mike have to vacuum? Ori Jean told her, in a voice loud enough to carry, "He probably can't do it. You need to be able to see in order to vacuum."

That was enough for Mike. At first his lines were crazy crooked. Ori Jean said nothing—she could see Mike thinking while he vacuumed. Soon he was pushing the vacuum in a back-and-forth pattern and not missing a spot. "All I have to do is remember where I've gone and then I'm good at this," he told his mother.

Mike was not as good at some other chores. His bedmaking appeared expressionist. The clashing clothes he picked for himself made noise. His recipes often contained surprise ingredients, even to him. Ori Jean saw beauty in his effort.

The neighborhood children had no idea what to make of a blind kid. Diane told them, "He's really good at stuff," but they still picked him last for their teams. He swung at baseballs and missed wildly. He ran into trees instead of second base. He fell down all the time. But he could also boot a kickball to the clouds and quickly find kids in games of hide-and-seek. He wasn't afraid of blood.

Before long, the children didn't much notice when Mike crashed his skateboard or jumped into the bushes with his pogo stick. He was playing and they were playing. To them, that made everyone on Kevin Court look just alike.

Soon enough Mike decided to ride a bicycle. Just the idea of it—to be able to move so swiftly and independently—thrilled him. He borrowed Diane's and began to pedal. The bike traced an ampersand on the street and then toppled onto him. Mike tried again. He fell again. He crashed for two more days, seasoning the street with bits of skin as Ori Jean told him, "You're getting there."

At school, things were just the same. Mike took tetherballs to the face and dodgeballs to the groin. He bloodied his nose, cracked toes, and broke fingers. While running to first base in kickball, he stepped on top of the ball, fell backward, and bashed his head on the pavement. He was unconscious for twenty minutes and rushed to the hospital. When he returned to school the next week, he played again.

School would have been a breeze for Mike were it not for resource instructor Medina. Some teachers were willing to excuse the blind students from assignments, but if Medina found out he would step in and force the kids to do the work anyway. He might ask, "Where the hell is your homework?" Some kids would bellyache or ask why he cared about their schoolwork if their own classroom teachers didn't. "Because you should care," Medina told them. "That's what it's all about." Some parents objected to that kind of talk—they did not think a caretaker should confront a child already so challenged. Ori Jean told Mike that she and Medina connected.

Mike liked the other blind students. In ways, they were family, their resource room and teacher a common bond. But he didn't necessarily understand them. Many chose to eat their lunches inside rather than go to the playground with the sighted kids—how could they not want to move? A lot of them walked tentatively, as if bumping into something was the worst thing in the world. Some of them had never even gotten lost.

One of them became Mike's close friend. Mark Pighin was exceptionally bright and witty, and he liked the things Mike liked. Neither broke down when Medina got fed up with their excuses and told them, "Don't give me that bull." Soon Pighin's family was inviting Mike to join them on their two-week summer vacations, a tradition that would last for years.

The match between the boys wasn't obvious. In Mike's view, Pighin was coddled by his parents. They would cut his meat, guide him by the arm even in familiar areas, lay out his clothes.

On a Pighin family vacation, Mike got the idea to explore the shuttered upper floors of the old lodge at which they were staying. He and Pighin made it to the musty attic. Pighin refused to go in—he was afraid there were rats inside, an animal he believed to be three feet long. Mike knew Pighin couldn't leave without him so he went inside, followed by his terrified friend. Pighin kept talking about the rats. Mike, unable to resist, bent down and pinched his friend's ankle. Pighin let out a bloodcurdling scream. The adults came running. When he could speak, Pighin told them he'd been bitten by a rat. Mike couldn't believe his good luck—he was scot-free! But a moment later, he admitted to the pinch and prepared to accept the consequences. It was worth it to Mike. The attic was like an unknown world to him. At least he had gone and looked.

Even as Ori Jean raised Mike to embrace his blindness, she continued to hope that he would see. She had researched eye surgeons since the family had arrived in California and found perhaps the best in the world, Dr. Max Fine, just twenty-five miles away in San Francisco. On three occasions when Mike was in grade school, Fine transplanted corneas into his right eye (his left eye had been too badly damaged to try). It never worked. When Fine told

Ori Jean after the last operation that nothing more could be done—now or ever—she exhaled. No longer would she have to go through that cycle of hope and disappointment.

By 1962, when Mike was nine, things started to strain in the May house. His mother had given birth to a fifth child, a girl named Margie, amplifying the demands on her already hectic days. Bill's drinking, a constant murmur in their lives, began to roar. He lost jobs and was unable to support the family. He fought with Ori Jean. One day, while climbing on the roof of his house, Mike found a bottle of bourbon hidden in a gutter. Bill had sworn that he hadn't been drinking. Mike showed the bottle to his father and said, "You lied to me! Here's your liquor!" then smashed the bottle on the ground. Bill exploded and went after his son. Mike ran into a nearby orchard and scrambled up a tree. Bill demanded that Mike come down, but Mike refused and stayed and stayed until Bill ran out of fuel and walked away.

Mike could feel his father drifting away. This was not the same man who had invented their secret system for walking: a distinct squeeze of Mike's palm one way to indicate an up curb, another to indicate a down curb. The system allowed Mike to walk freely, but the best part was that it came from his father's mighty hand. Even as Bill's drinking worsened and plunged his family into near poverty,

Mike knew he loved his father because he still loved to hold his hand when they walked.

Bill continued to come home drunk, sometimes at seven A.M. and with lipstick on his collar. Fearing that he might hit the kids with his car, Ori Jean called the police and had her husband committed to the Napa State Hospital, a psychiatric facility. It would be the first of several monthlong involuntary commitments. Ori Jean took her children to visit Bill every weekend he was there, bringing sandwiches for picnics on the hospital's manicured grounds. Mike and Diane felt terrible for their father. There were weird people all over the hospital, and their father wasn't weird at all.

The world was too interesting, however, to allow Mike time for such distractions. As he advanced through grade school almost everything fascinated him, and it all had to be investigated. In fourth grade, he signed up for the safety patrol class and showed up for training with the rest of the hopefuls. They were a half hour into the class before the instructor realized what was going on and pulled him aside and told him that a person had to be able to see in order to help children cross the street. The same news was delivered to Medina, Mike's resource teacher.

Medina asked Mike what he thought they should do. Mike told Medina that he knew he could be a good crossing guard. And he said he couldn't stand the idea of not getting a chance. Medina told Mike to go to the principal to make his case, and that he would back him the whole way.

The principal scarcely understood what Mike was asking—he wanted to do what? Mike outlined his plan: he would listen for cars the way he did when he crossed the street himself.

"You're blind," the principal said.

"I can do it," Mike said.

"You have to be looking for cars, not just listening," the principal said. "It won't work. Sorry."

Medina stepped forward. He argued that there were teachers already present during crossing time. And he talked about Mike.

"I know this kid," Medina said. "He can do it."

The principal said he would take the case under advisement.

The school called Ori Jean and informed her of Mike's crazy idea. She told them it didn't sound crazy to her. A few days and many meetings later, the principal gave Mike a vest with a bright triangle shape on the front. The next Monday he was holding up a stop sign and escorting children across the street.

Near the end of grade school, Mike asked his mother to let him ride a bike by himself to downtown Walnut Creek. It was a three-mile trip in traffic. Her stomach twisted with visions of rushing ambulances and bleeding heads. Her mind flashed back to the emergency room in New Mexico. Every maternal instinct she had screamed against the idea.

"It's important to stay on the right-hand side of the road," she found herself saying as tears rolled down her face. "If you hear a car or truck, just stop and pull over. If it gets to be too hard, don't be afraid to turn around and come back. And don't be afraid to be afraid—it's important to know when you're afraid."

Ori Jean knew that Mike wouldn't turn back. Standing at the mailbox, she watched him pedal down the driveway, around the cul-de-sac, and over the top of Kevin Court. And then she couldn't see him anymore.

An hour passed. Two hours. Something had to be wrong. Ori Jean got into her car, but when she went to leave she thought about how it might hurt Mike's feelings if she were to come upon the scene, how it would seem that she hadn't believed in him. She stayed home and vacuumed the living room, then vacuumed it again. After three hours Mike walked in the door. "Hi, Mom," he said, then went to wash up for dinner. She never asked him about the trip—she didn't want it to seem like a big deal.

At home, Bill's drinking worsened. To support the family Ori Jean took a full-time job teaching Spanish at a suburban Oakland school. Her annual salary was less than $5,000. Still, when she brought her children to the grocery store or to the park, she wore earrings and jewelry and made herself as pretty as she'd looked in Chile, when she'd been the daughter of wealth and had servants to brush her hair. She dressed her kids smartly for school and in their Sunday best for Catholic church. In public, there was no sign that the St. Vincent de Paul charity had brought groceries to her house for Christmas that year.

For fifty weeks of every year since Mike had been seven, Ori Jean had immersed him in the sighted world. For the remaining two she sent him to the land of the blind.

Set in the Napa foothills, Enchanted Hills was a summer camp for the visually impaired. It urged independence in its campers. Kids could hike, row, camp out in tents, explore, even get lost, all according to their appetites. Ori Jean had discovered the place in 1961 and enrolled Mike straightaway, sometimes soliciting churches and kind souls for funds. It had felt like home to him ever since.

In the summer before junior high, Mike began to do things at Enchanted Hills that most campers wouldn't consider. He rode horses into areas no one had probed, hiked off the map, negotiated paths paved in poison oak. He described a plan to counselors whereby he would hike away from camp for hours on known trails, then return as the crow flies, up and down through canyons and streams. The counselors drew the line at that one, but none doubted that Mike would have tried. They could not see his eyes behind his drooping eyelids, but when they looked at the way his head tilted upward while conceiving a plan, they could see the pioneer in his heart.

At summer's end, Mike and the other blind students from Buena Vista Elementary matriculated to Park Mead Intermediate. Nick Medina went with them. That meant no whining for another two years. Mike felt lucky. Medina seemed sure and constant, the way Mike tried to feel when the world got too big. It felt good when Medina said, "If I hadn't kicked your butt you wouldn't have gotten that A." It felt great when he said, "I like you, Mike."

Math and science spoke most directly to Mike, though he made A's and B's in all his courses. He remained mostly shy and quiet in class, as he had been since kindergarten. Though he spent much of his day among sighted students, no one teased or bothered him—he wasn't a tattler or dorky, just blind. He continued to take notes and write papers with a braillewriter, a clackety-clacking cousin to the typewriter that used pins to push braille letters into paper. When Mike walked down the halls the ten-pound steel machine swung wildly from his noodly arm. The sighted kids learned to scatter fast when they saw him coming.

The playground remained the epicenter of

Mike's schooltime passion. He continued to crash into poles, fences, and classmates, even losing consciousness in a head-on collision with a football goalpost. Kids wondered how he could charge so fearlessly knowing it was just a matter of time before he bashed into something else, but to Mike that was just the point—he already knew the worst that could happen, and it didn't seem bad at all compared to the feeling he got from running.

By 1965, the five May children were old hat at minding themselves. Ori Jean left early on weekday mornings to teach eighth-grade Spanish, while Bill slept off benders between jobs he couldn't keep. Diane and Mike babysat their younger siblings, cleaned the house, and prepared meals. Mike's specialties included casseroles, spaghetti, and tacos, the messy fruits of the cooking course Ori Jean had insisted he take.

The kids got along well, considering they shared two bedrooms and a single bathroom. Each believed that the others received favored treatment; all watched vigilantly to make sure Mike didn't invoke blindness to do less than his full share. No matter how many times Ori Jean asked, the kids seemed not to remember to keep the floors clean or to put things back where they belonged. Much of Mike's home life was spent sprawled over toys or demanding to know, "Who moved my stuff?" His siblings had a collective response: "Not me."

They also knew the best ways to have fun with a brother who couldn't see. Diane, Theri, and Patrick mixed up Mike's blue and red socks, sending him to school with mismatched feet. They gave him dog food and told him it was breakfast cereal. They mastered the silent arts of pushing their brussels sprouts onto Mike's plate during dinner and stealing bites of his pie at dessert. In hide-and-seek they were not above pointing him in the wrong direction; in Monopoly they paid pennies on the dollar when he passed Go. Soon Mike developed countermeasures, such as taking inventory of his dinner and asking for seconds on dog food.

As he neared the end of junior high in 1967, Mike could feel his home life start to shake. Bill was out of work and drinking more than ever. Sometimes he didn't come home. The family's priest urged Ori Jean to divorce him. She tried four times but was never able to see it through.

Bill's fuse shortened with each of her false starts. The kids tried not to hear the fights, but already they knew the dialogue by heart, especially the part about how shameful it was to give up. One night, Bill threatened to hit Ori Jean. Mike ran into the room, stepped between them, and went into his boxing stance, his fists turned upward in the style of the old bare-knuckles fighters.

"Don't you dare hit my mother!" Mike screamed.

The display shocked Bill. He stood there for a moment, taking in Mike's scrawny body and quivering lip. Mike remained in his stance. Finally, Bill backed off and walked away. Ori Jean threw him out and filed for divorce days later. She was thirty-nine years old and the mother of five children, ages five through fifteen.

In the months after Bill had gone Ori Jean blew up occasionally. Tears streaming down her face, she'd yell at her kids, "You guys, your rooms aren't clean, the kitchen's dirty, you're fighting, I'm trying to go to work and take care of you all, but I'm not going to be able to keep it together unless you do better to help me." Mike thought about his mom a lot during those days, about how she drove the kids to four different schools, how she kept finding ways to send him to camp, how clean she kept the house even when he could hear her crying. And even then, he thought, "She's brave."

After graduating from junior high, Mike announced his intention to attend the local public high school. Las Lomas High, however, did not accept blind students. Administrators said that Mike would be better served by a school fifteen miles away that had resources and staff for the blind. Mike told his mother that he wanted to go to school with his neighborhood friends and that he needed no special resources. He told her he wanted to live in the real world.

Ori Jean petitioned the school. It would be two years before mainstreaming laws hit the books, so administrators were free to refuse her, and they did. She maneuvered, cajoled, charmed, and threatened. She talked to lawyers. Mike could picture his mother taking off her shoe and slamming it on the table if necessary. When September rolled around, he was in. He would be the only blind student in the school.

Not everyone was ready for the invasion. The gym teacher reassigned him to study hall. The woodshop teacher threw him out despite the care Mike took in examining the pickled finger in a jar the teacher had passed around as a warning to the careless.

In class, Mike adjusted to learning without the help of a resource teacher. Courses like geometry and geography proved especially challenging, but he made his usual A's and B's. He hung out with friends from his neighborhood and made new ones from his classes. People on the playground got accustomed in a hurry to his crashing-through style of play. The flurry of Mike's new world, however, was overwhelmed by a storm unlike any he'd experienced so far.

Girls.

He'd had crushes as early as fifth grade, the stuff born of a classmate's giggle or the sound of a cute first name. But this! Overnight, the wonder and mystery and promise of a woman's body suggested itself into every fold of Mike's awareness. It called to him from the hallway breeze of freshly shampooed hair, the distant conversations of senior cheerleaders, the brush of a girl's wrist when she reached to pass back a quiz. During his freshman year, Mike could scarcely conceive a thought that wasn't hourglass-shaped.

He desperately wanted to touch a woman, not just for the pleasure he was certain it would bring but because he so fundamentally depended on touch for his construct of the world. Without touch, objects remained just ideas, and Mike wasn't interested in rubbing up against an idea. Yet he dared not approach a woman for this purpose. He felt too shy to move in directly, too disconnected from the visual clues that signaled consent to know how to advance more discreetly. He considered grabbing a girl's breast outright; no one would blame a blind guy who apologized and said he'd been aiming for a doorknob. He knew people who had done that. But as deeply as he desired the contact, he also considered the tactic beneath him. If something great was going to happen to Mike he didn't want it to happen because he was blind.

If Mike was not yet to know a woman by touch at least he could dedicate the entirety of his mind to the matter. He listened intently to his friends' talk about girls and asked for detailed descriptions of those who intrigued him. His pals went to the heart of the matter: topography, hair, legs, walk, face, topography. They brought around **Playboy** magazines, and though their descriptions lacked detail—"She's naked. She's riding a bike. Her boobs go across two pages"—they overflowed in unabashed admiration, which to blind eyes could be the most vivid description of all.

Still, these were just words—how could a person hope to conceive an idea about these wondrous boobs if he could neither touch nor see them? Mike yearned for the life-sized, anatomically correct dolls he'd heard schools gave to kids in magical lands like Sweden. Instead, he purloined his sister's Barbie doll and went to work, running his fingers over her naked curves, associating all he'd heard about a woman's body with her 39-18-33 measurements. Mike knew that the Barbie lacked the textures and details that caused his friends to howl at the moon. But no matter how much he handled his doll, he could not begin to imagine the nature of those nuances, even as he suspected that they were the best parts of all.

His imagination filled in the gaps. Often, his notions were wildly inaccurate, but it didn't matter—when joined with things he knew directly (silky hair, pretty smells, soft hands, lilting voices) and primed by his friends' worshipful descriptions, it added up to a construct of arousal and beauty every bit as real to him as images were to the sighted. As Mike's life continued he would use those ingredients—imagination, reality, and the power of others' passions—to understand much of visual beauty. Even at fourteen, Mike suspected that imagination might be the most important of them all.

Mike's sophomore and junior years flew past him. He carried a 3.5 grade point average in his classes and excelled at math and science. At home, the kids took care of themselves while Ori Jean completed a master's degree and began a full-time job as a high school counselor.

When a neighborhood friend named Mark Babin encouraged Mike to join the wrestling team at school, he charged in, training and dieting until his five-foot-six, ninety-five-pound body looked like a comb. He made varsity in sophomore year. At one tournament, officials misspelled his name, listing him as "Miko May." His teammates said they were going to circulate a rumor that he was an incredible blind wrestler from Japan. "I like that idea," May told them. "That way there will be two mystiques about me." His coach, Ed Melendez, didn't flinch at keeping Mike on the team, and pushed his blind wrestler physically and emotionally. By the time Mike reached senior year he would be six foot one and 149 pounds, and would win about half his matches, almost all by strategy and stamina.

When Mike wasn't thinking about girls or wrestling he was bouncing himself off the ionosphere. He had fallen in love with the hobby of ham radio when Rob Reis, a friend from an electronics class, had explained how a person could talk to others across the world using just a box of tubes and wires, a microphone, and an outdoor antenna. Mike tried it and was hooked. His conversations with people in Afghanistan and London and Vietnam were fascinating. But the idea of becoming a solo explorer spoke to him. Once he realized he could reach into new worlds otherwise impossibly far away, there was nothing he wouldn't do to make it happen.

One day, Mike and Reis traveled to Santa Cruz to visit a ham radio enthusiast who was rumored to have a 175-foot tower in the mountains. The structure was every bit of it. The man told the boys that they were free to use his radio but that a beam atop the tower needed adjusting. Mike volunteered for the job. He climbed into the wind with no belt or ropes or other support gear, swaying four feet in every direction as he made it through 50 feet, 100 feet, 150 feet—the equivalent of a fifteen-story building. At the top he adjusted a sixty-six-foot beam while the wind moved the tower like a metronome arm. He was terrified—a false step would cost him his life—but he couldn't stop thinking about the places he would reach once he got that antenna pointed right.

At home, Mike announced his intention to build his own eighty-foot antenna. Ori Jean wasn't sure if he was serious. She became convinced when he began mixing cement for the foundation in the backyard. She pushed a million nightmare scenarios out of her mind as she watched Mike put up the first ten-foot section, then the second. By the time he was teetering at forty feet, she could no longer stand it.

"I have to go away from here," she called to Mike. "I can't stand to watch you go up any higher."

"Okay, bye," Mike called down.

Ori Jean got in her car and drove away. Even that night she wouldn't remember where she'd gone. When she returned home there was an eighty-foot tower on her property and a kid in the garage talking into a microphone, saying, "This is WB6ABK. Is there anyone out there? Where have I reached?"

By the time Mike turned seventeen he had mapped out the next four years of his life. He and his friend Reis would study electrical engineering at the University of California–Davis, about an hour's drive from his home in Walnut Creek. Blind electrical engineers were rare, which was one of the reasons he wanted to do it.

Status as a high school senior did little to advance Mike's romantic ambitions. His friends didn't fare much better than he did in love, but they had one incalculable advantage over him—they could drive. It didn't take long for Mike to conceive the myriad ways in which a car conferred freedom. And when freedom was at stake Mike could not stand still.

One day while visiting a blind friend from camp, Mike suggested that they have a look at his parents' motorcycle, a smallish Honda 90. His friend showed Mike how to start it. Then Mike had an epiphany: if they could just drive it to the school grounds they could ride gloriously unimpeded around the track. Mike got on the front, his friend on the back. They turned off the engine, listened for traffic, then started the bike and drove across the street. They repeated the procedure numerous times—engine off, listen, engine on, ride—until they arrived at the school. On the track they began to circle slowly, getting a feel for the arcs of the turns. Soon they had the Honda cruising, opening the throttle on the straightaways. A police siren wailed. Mike managed to stop the bike. His heart was pounding.

"What the hell are you guys doing?" the police

officer asked. "It's illegal to have a motorcycle out here."

He turned to Mike.

"Let me see your driver's license."

"I don't have a driver's license," Mike said.

"Well, then, we have a big problem," the officer said.

"I'm blind," Mike said.

"You were riding a motorcycle."

Mike showed the officer his braille watch. It took a moment for the man to digest what had occurred. Then he told the boys he had to call this one in, that they could have killed someone. He kept lecturing, kept promising to tell their parents, kept mumbling words like "blind" and "unbelievable." The officer finally walked the boys and their cycle home. He didn't tell their parents. He didn't call it in.

Weeks later Mike was in his driveway admiring Diane's brand-new Datsun 510, purchased for $57.59 a month in department store wages, her baby. It pointed toward the street. Warning bells sounded from every logic and reason center in Mike's brain. But he had only a single thought: I need to drive.

He got in the car, lowered the window so he could hear where he was going, and turned the key. The engine, the same one that murmured during rides with Diane, seemed to thunder over all of

Walnut Creek with Mike behind the wheel. He released the parking brake, put the vehicle into gear, and began rolling out of the driveway. He'd negotiated the space a million times before—on bicycle, skateboard, roller skates, in full sprint—but the upcoming ninety-degree left turn suddenly seemed a stranger. Mike kept driving. He wobbled through the turn, his stomach in his throat, and began the climb up Kevin Court, listening to the echoes made by tires against curbs and whatever cars he prayed were not oncoming, adrenaline fighting his hands, no plan for how to return but certain he had to keep going, clutch popping, now the street was narrowing, he could hear it, but he wasn't done driving, he wasn't done going, he stepped on the gas and now the car was cruising, it was in front of him and running away from him, but he wouldn't let go, and then he pushed the pedal or he lost his nerve or the car stalled but halfway up the street the Datsun's engine died and the only sound left was Mike's heaving breath bouncing off the car's sweaty steering wheel. When he found Diane, he apologized for parking her car in the middle of the street and told her it seemed like he'd driven a very long way.

CHAPTER THREE

As August temperatures pushed near 100 degrees, May engaged the afterburners on his business plan. Shuttling between cities, he secured a major investment from a Colorado businessman and recruited a top engineer to refine the GPS software. He registered as a California business, signed distributors, and hired an office manager. When he needed a name for the business, he looked for a word or phrase that got to the heart of what his product offered blind people—the ability to find one's way independently. He chose Sendero, the Spanish word for "pathway."

The business grabbed at him around the clock: liability insurance was too expensive; the unit's $3,500 retail price remained prohibitive; the software had moods. When he found time for leisure thinking he used it to diagram new plays for Wyndham's soccer team or conceive chapters for the serialized stories he told Carson before bedtime. Dr. Goodman's offer of new vision six months ago seemed a million miles away.

May's family was equally occupied. While Carson and Wyndham pinballed between activities, Jennifer piled up paint samples and met at home with her interior design clients. Ordinarily, her business conversations were background din to May, but lately he found himself listening a bit differently. He took note when she described a wallpaper pattern as "restless." He stopped typing when she told a client that a fabric seemed to dance. His curiosity surprised him—he knew that Jennifer spoke this way and he loved it about her. But he'd never stopped to listen so closely before.

And he kept listening. At the dinner table one evening, someone commented on the steam rising from a bowl of spaghetti, saying that they could "see right through it." That idea fascinated May, even as he told himself, "I've known that about steam all my life." He paid attention to a discussion between Carson and Wyndham about the many ways in which a person could write the letter **G**.

August got even busier. So it was interesting to him when he found himself reaching for his telephone one morning and dialing the University of California–Davis Medical Center rather than a potential investor or supplier.

"I'm calling to see if you or the doctors there know anything about a new kind of stem cell transplant surgery that's supposed to give vision to the blind."

A staff member asked May to repeat the question. He ran through it again.

"Stem cell?" the person asked.

"I think so," May said.

"We'll have to call you back."

When they called back, the staffer said that no one at the center had any idea about a stem cell surgery of any kind, let alone one that caused the blind to see.

May called Stanford University. Same answer. He tried renowned East Coast eye institutes. Nothing.

The news made sense to him. May had been told by his lifelong ophthalmologist, Dr. Max Fine, that nothing could be done to restore his vision, now or ever. When Fine died in 1989, the **New York Times** noted his fifty-seven years of experience and called him "a pioneer in corneal transplant." If anyone knew May's prognosis, it was Dr. Fine. He had been especially clear about the "now or ever" part.

In mid-August, May and Jennifer joined members of her family for a weekend getaway at a hotel. May welcomed the respite. On the first evening, everyone gathered for a short boat ride. Onboard, the conversation quickly turned to a group of elegant passengers nearby. Jennifer's family described these people as "bronze, narrow, and Italian-designed," and said that the moonlight "chased the women's jewels." Jennifer noted that the wispy hems of ladies' dresses "lapped at the breeze" and that men "lit cigarettes with flat gold lighters and shaped their arms into triangles so their dates wouldn't slip." A moment later, Jennifer's sister Wendy made a discovery.

"Oh, my God, look at Miss Salmon," Wendy whispered to Jennifer, nodding across the boat toward a woman in her early thirties. "Is she real?"

The woman seemed to have been assembled by a team of male pubescents. Her tiny waist gave way in one direction to a pair of tanned and taut legs that seemed taller than half the men around her, and in the other to a chest so full and eager that no bra could have contained it anyway. Her heels coaxed out unusually perfect calf muscles, while the strip of salmon-colored gauze she used for a dress coaxed out all the rest. Hers was the face of a 1940s movie star. Her long blond hair beckoned men from every era.

"I've got to tell Mike about her," Wendy said. "I've got to tell Mike about Miss Salmon."

"He'll love it," Jennifer said.

Wendy pulled May aside and described the scene. She spared no detail. Jennifer could not discern most of the conversation, but every few seconds she heard her husband say, "Really?" or "Wow!"

or "How do you know that?" And she could hear him ask her sister, "You can see all that just from sitting across the boat?"

The next day, the families gathered in one of the hotel rooms to take a break from the sun. They checked the pay-per-view movie lineup and came across a film called **At First Sight**, starring Val Kilmer and Mira Sorvino, about a blind man whose vision is restored. It seemed a natural, especially as May had mentioned his chance meeting with Dr. Goodman to Jennifer's family. He took a position on the king-sized bed, flanked on one side by his wife and on the other by her sister, as the movie began.

Eyes rolled just a few scenes in. The main character seemed dull and frightened. He became derailed by everyday circumstances. He smiled goofily.

"This guy is a downer," May said.

When the blind man's girlfriend pressured him into pursuing a miracle cure for his blindness, Jennifer fidgeted and mumbled to herself, "Why would someone pressure another person like that? It's so personal."

Halfway through the movie no one was paying attention.

"I'd be back at the pool looking for Miss Salmon if I weren't already sandwiched between two such beautiful women," May said.

The sisters asked if he was still watching the film.

"Not much," May told them. "The main character's not a real person."

When May returned from this trip he asked his office assistant, Kim Burgess, to help him search the Internet; the speech-synthesized screen-reading software he used on his computers worked well for word-processing or spreadsheet tasks, but it bogged down trying to decipher complex Web pages. He told her he wanted to research stem cell transplant surgery for the eyes.

At the same time, he submitted a query to an Internet newsgroup dedicated to issues that concern the blind, asking if anyone knew of such a procedure. He told Jennifer that he still expected to find nothing—if the minds at the universities he'd contacted knew nothing, if Dr. Fine had known nothing, he expected to come up empty on his own.

Soon, information trickled in—a foreign Web site here, an e-mailed answer there. It appeared that there did exist a procedure involving stem cells and vision, one referred to as "corneal epithelial stem cell transplantation." When May used that language on the Web and in queries, the information began to flow. Much of it was bound in the private vernacular of scientists and surgeons;

they spoke of "limbal allograft," "existing symble-
pharon," and "cicatricial keratoconjunctivitis."
May panned the literature for colloquial nuggets
and used a dictionary to machete through the rest.
He determined this much to be certain about the
procedure:

- It was indicated only for very special
  cases—but a chemical burn was among
  them.

- Its evolution was recent and its imple-
  mentation rare—fewer than four hundred had been performed worldwide.

- Very few doctors knew of the surgery,
  and almost none had attempted it.

- If successful, it could restore vision to
  the blind—even to those who had been
  assured they would never see.

May briefed Jennifer on his discoveries. It felt
strange to him to think about vision—he could remember doing it only once before. In his late twen-
ties, he'd heard a man on the radio describe using
hypnosis to help people recover childhood memories, and he'd wondered if a hypnotist might make
him see what he'd seen before his accident. It was a

fascinating proposition and one he'd entertained for a few days before returning to his busy life.

"The stem cell surgery is really interesting," he told Jennifer. "I'd like to know more about it. I still don't think it would change my life, but I have to say, it seems like it's for real."

Vision begins at the cornea. When light enters the eye, it passes first through the cornea, a transparent, circular layer one-fiftieth of an inch thick at the very front of the eye. The cornea has no color, but its job is critical—to allow light in and do the majority of focusing. The cornea must stay clear; otherwise, trying to see would be like trying to look through a frosted shower door or a dirty car windshield.

But how are corneas kept clear? People can't run wiper blades over them as with car windshields. The body, it turns out, has its own ingenious method for keeping the corneas clear. It begins with special cells known as corneal epithelial stem cells. These are not the controversial stem cells taken from embryos or fetuses, but rather cells that exist in every person for a lifetime.

These stem cells reside along the edges of the cornea. If you imagine the cornea as a round window, the stem cells—about a thousand of them—live along the area where the frame would be. The stem cells produce millions of daughter cells. These daughter cells have a single mission: to converge toward the center of the eye, covering the cornea in a transparent protective layer.

This protective layer of daughter cells is the cornea's main defense against dirt, scratches, bacteria, and infection. It also prevents blood vessels and cells from the white part of the eye (known as the conjunctiva) from growing over the cornea. The protective layer itself might get dirty, but every few days the daughter cells that compose it fall off and are replaced by new ones, thereby ensuring perpetual freshness and clarity. The stem cells around the edges of the cornea never tire of making new daughter cells—they do it for as long as the person lives.

But what happens if these stem cells are destroyed—perhaps by disease or burn or trauma to the eye? In that case, they can no longer produce the daughter cells that form the protective layer over the cornea. Soon, blood vessels and conjunctiva cells grow over the cornea, clouding it and then making it opaque. Light is no longer able to pass through the cornea on the way to the pupil, iris, lens, and retina. That means the person is blind. A chemical explosion—like the one that happened to Mike May when he was three—can destroy corneal epithelial stem cells instantly.

Before 1964, scientists had little idea that the edges of the cornea play a role in keeping the cornea clear. And they certainly didn't know of the existence of corneal epithelial stem cells and how they protect the cornea. When surgeons encountered a grown-over cornea, they removed it and transplanted a clear donor cornea in its place. That worked most of the time, because the patient still had stem cells around the edges capable of producing protective daughter cells. It failed, however, in cases when the patient lacked those stem cells. Ophthalmologists believed those failures to be caused by the body rejecting the donor cornea. They never suspected that the patient's lack of stem cells was the cause of the donor cornea going bad.

In 1964, a Colombian ophthalmologist named José Barraquer treated one of his patients—a man who had suffered a chemical injury to one eye—in a new way. He transplanted a section of the edge of that patient's healthy cornea onto the edge of the injured eye. The patient's vision improved. Barraquer didn't realize it, but he had performed a stem cell transplant. Science now knew that, somehow, the edges around the cornea were important to corneal health.

Research along these lines was advanced in the late 1970s in Pittsburgh by Dr. Richard Thoft, who refined Barraquer's techniques and also began transplanting the edges of cadavers' eyes into patients. But it wasn't until 1989, through the work of Drs. Kenneth Kenyon and Scheffer Tseng, that science fully understood the role of corneal epithelial stem cells and how best to transplant them. The process, it turned out, required two surgeries and a good deal of technical skill on the part of the surgeon.

When a donor dies, an eye bank dispatches a volunteer to remove the donor's eyeballs. The eyes are placed in a preservative solution and sent back to the eye bank, where the corneas and surrounding stem cell areas are cut from the eye and placed back in solution. They are then sent to a surgeon for transplantation, preferably within five days of the donor's death. (Surgeons prefer to use corneas and stem cells from donors no older than age fifty.)

The first surgery is to transplant the donor stem cells. After the patient is placed under general anesthesia, the surgeon scrapes away any conjunctiva cells and blood vessels that have grown on top of the patient's cornea. That alone requires an artist's touch, but the hardest parts are yet to come.

The patient is left sleeping while the donor cornea and its surrounding doughnut of stem cells are placed under a nearby microscope. The surgeon uses that microscope—and a midnight-still hand—to cut away the center part of the donor cornea, leaving just the doughnut of stem cells. His job now is to place that doughnut on top of the patient's existing cornea, thereby providing the cornea with a new supply of stem cells.

In its current state, however, the doughnut is too thick to transplant. Still using the microscope, the surgeon thins the doughnut by shaving it from underneath, narrowing it from one millimeter to one-third of a millimeter, all without damaging the stem cells on top. His movements are a tiny ballet of precision and nerves.

After the ring of stem cells has been thinned, the surgeon places it on top of the patient's existing cornea and sutures it into place. The entire process takes between ninety minutes and two hours.

The stem cell transplant by itself produces no vision. That's because the patient's existing cornea has been too badly damaged by overgrowing cells and blood vessels and no longer functions properly. He needs a new cornea, but before he can receive one, he must allow his new stem cells to produce waves of new daughter cells to forge a clear path to the cornea. Without that clear path, future protective daughter cells cannot reach a new cornea.

It takes about four months for the daughter cells to clear that path. Once the surgeon confirms that this has occurred, he removes the patient's damaged cornea and replaces it with a healthy cornea from a second donor. If all functions properly, that new cornea will be protected by the new stem cells and the daughter cells they produce. And that can mean long-term vision.

By 1999, only fifteen or twenty surgeons in the

United States had performed corneal epithelial stem cell transplants. It is likely that the procedure had been attempted fewer than four hundred times worldwide.

May's days stretched from dawn to midnight as August drew to a close. Still, during his free moments, he found himself digging. He called ophthalmologists to ask if they had performed corneal epithelial stem cell transplants—he wanted to know how Goodman's experience ranked among his peers'. He could not find a single doctor who had performed any. He dug into Goodman's reputation and discovered a nationwide respect for the man. When he checked with his insurance carrier, he discovered that Goodman was a preferred provider and that a stem cell transplant might be covered.

In the Caravan one night, with Carson and Wyndham asleep in the back, May told Jennifer that he was thinking of scheduling the B-scan—the ultrasound that would look behind the surface of his eye to determine whether or not he was a good candidate for the surgery.

"It seems like it wouldn't hurt to find out," May said.

"That sounds right," Jennifer said. "It's not like it's a decision to get vision. It's just a step to see what's there."

The next day, May called Goodman's office and

asked to schedule the B-scan. He was referred to a San Francisco specialist in ocular ultrasound, who would perform the scan, after which Goodman would interpret the results. The receptionist scheduled May's follow-up consultation with Goodman for September 23. He thanked her, called the specialist, and made an appointment.

On the afternoon of September 9, 1999, May walked with his Seeing Eye dog, Josh, to the local bus terminal, boarded an express to the Vallejo ferry, took the boat to the Ferry Building in San Francisco, then took a taxi to his appointment. The trip took ninety minutes.

The specialist explained the B-scan to May. He would anesthetize the eye and keep it immersed in a tiny bath of coupling fluid. Then he would place a small electrical probe on the eyelid that would broadcast and receive sound waves. The instrument would image the internal anatomy and structure of the eye in much the way an ob-gyn's machine uses sound waves to image a fetus. The idea was to detect gross pathologies or abnormalities. It would be up to Goodman to explain the results.

The procedure lasted fifteen minutes and was painless. All that was left was to wait for the answers.

May's appointment with Goodman was two weeks away. Sendero didn't care. Its needs were insatiable, its problems always in bloom. Daytime stresses trickled into May's nights. He had never been a sound sleeper—he was often restless, and would sometimes lie awake for hours thinking through business and life. Wrestling Sendero to the starting line did not improve his slumber.

Every so often throughout his adult life, lying awake at three A.M., May would find his thoughts drilling down through the everyday and into the eternal. He would contemplate dying and mortality, try to get his arms around the idea of what it meant to be extinct. He considered what it meant to have no awareness—not even the ability to touch something—and how a person who made jokes and missed his kids by noon every day could disintegrate in the dirt until there was nothing left of him. These thoughts bore no relation to his everyday fears—of flying in bad weather, of sudden explosions—the kind that could be defeated by logic and guts. These were terrifying ideas, the type that lay in wait while he tended to business concerns and bickered with Jennifer about staying organized but that found him before dawn, when his mind had quieted and Davis had gone silent. They were the kind that could shake his core.

He rarely spoke of dying. Recently, however, May had found himself in just such a discussion with his father. Now living in Denver, Bill May had lost another job to alcoholism. Doctors could not promise that he would survive. May flew in to visit his dad. The elder May told his son that he had been thinking about what it meant not to be anymore, that he tried to imagine what it felt like to be gone. "I'm petrified of dying," he said. May told his father, "Me, too, Dad."

A few nights later, May was awake with these ideas. His usual antidote was to think about his accident, about how easily he might have died. Everything after that, he'd tell himself, was icing on the cake. On this night, however, he had a different thought. He wondered if, when he died, he would die bravely. He hoped that he would. Others, many of whom considered him the embodiment of courage, would have bet on it. But there was really no way to know until he got there. And it struck him that this was true about knowing oneself in general. It wasn't who a person believed himself to be or what he predicted he would do in a given situation. It was what he did when he got there that defined him.

On the morning of September 23, 1999, May set out for his appointment with Dr. Goodman. He packed an early working version of his GPS product—complete with laptop and hockey puck–sized satellite receiver—for testing along the route. He was to receive the B-scan results that would determine his suitability for the rare corneal epithelial stem cell transplant surgery. Jennifer kissed him good-bye and wished him luck.

May and Josh took their usual route to the city—by bus, ferry, taxi, and foot. He made business phone calls on the way. He still believed that if vision restoration was possible, Dr. Fine would not have pronounced his case forever hopeless. But as his GPS guidance system delivered him to Goodman's doorstep by tuning in to satellites that orbited the earth, he couldn't help but wonder for a moment if nothing was impossible.

After he signed in, a nurse showed him to a room down the hall and asked him to sit in an examining chair, a request that seemed odd to him given that he was there to discuss test results. Goodman entered a few minutes later and shook May's hand.

"Great to see you again, Mike," he said.

"Great to see you, too. May I call you Dan?"

"Of course," Goodman replied. "I want to take a quick look at that eye."

Goodman dimmed the lights. He opened May's right eyelid with his thumb and forefinger and used the penlight and biomicroscope to look inside. He tested the pressure inside the eye. Then he pushed his stool back and flipped on the lights.

"I've read your B-scan," Goodman said. "The results are excellent. It shows no gross pathology in the back of your eye. Your retina and optic nerve look normal. The back of the eye is anatomically intact and healthy. It's a normal scan."

"What does that mean?" May asked.

"It means we have a good chance to restore your vision," Goodman said. "It means that we can try this."

Goodman understood the magnitude of his words. He watched closely for May's response to the idea of new vision. He paid careful attention to the psyches of all his patients—he considered it part of the gestalt of his practice—and would not move forward with even a routine Lasik procedure unless he believed a patient was emotionally grounded and had realistic expectations. He had a keen gut instinct for such matters, but even so, the analysis was always more art than science.

In one case, he had removed a blinding cataract from the eye of a woman who had been told since losing vision as a teenager that her case was hopeless. It had been a highly complex surgery but it worked—a day later she could see almost perfectly. Her reaction startled Goodman. She had been happy and content as a blind person. Now sighted, she became anxious and depressed. She told him that she had spent her adult life on welfare and had never worked, married, or ventured far from home—a small existence to which she had become comfortably accustomed. Now, however, government officials told her that she no longer qualified for disability, and they expected her to get a job. Society wanted her to function normally. It was, she told Goodman, too much to handle.

In another case, Goodman performed Lasik surgery on a working mother. In all respects she seemed a happy and normal person. The procedure corrected her mild nearsightedness to perfect vision. During a checkup three months later, she flew into a rage, lunged to within inches of Goodman's face, and screamed, "You've ruined my life! My marriage has failed, my husband has left me, my kids won't talk to me, and I just lost my job! And it's all because of you!" After Goodman calmed her, she explained that she had been depressed before the surgery and believed that if she got rid of her glasses her husband would find her beautiful, her children would believe her a better mother, and her boss would think her a good worker. Goodman told her, "You have a problem I can't help you with. I'm sorry I didn't realize it earlier." The woman ran out, yelling at everyone in the waiting room.

Such cases were rare; Goodman had done thousands of procedures, from routine to complex, and in virtually every case the patient had been grateful for his efforts and the results. But they reminded him to watch carefully, especially in the kind of rare situation in which he now found himself with May—a discussion about giving vision to a man who had been blind nearly for life. So far, May looked as calm and centered as he had in February when the men had met.

"How does it work?" May asked.

Goodman explained the process directly and in layman's terms. He would perform two surgeries. In the first he would transplant donor stem cells onto the surface of May's eye. He would wait perhaps four months while the stem cells replicated and produced healthy surface cells. Then he would transplant a donor cornea. The first surgery would produce no vision. The second surgery could.

May asked how many stem cell transplants Goodman had performed. Goodman told him that this would be his seventh. He said that all of them had been successful to one extent or another.

"How many of those patients had been blind for life?" May asked.

"None," Goodman replied.

The doctor looked for May's reaction. May seemed to smile at the sound of the word "none."

"There are risks associated with doing this," Goodman said. "It's important that you understand them very clearly."

"Okay," May said. "Let's hear them."

Goodman leaned forward and began to list these risks.

The chances of success are just fifty-fifty.
There was only a 50 percent chance that the new cornea would stay clear and not reject during the first year.

The stem cells and the cornea could reject at any time in May's life.
Even if the transplant worked, May could lose his vision with no warning and at any time, and this would be true for the rest of his life. He might see for a month, a year, or forever—no one could predict how long, and he could never presume that his sight would be permanent.

The extent of sight restoration is unknown.
Cases of vision restoration after a lifetime of blindness were so rare—Goodman knew of none—that it was impossible to estimate how well May would see.

A failed surgery could cost May his light perception.
Trauma to the eye from surgery, infection, or even a temporary pressure spike were among the myriad potential causes that could snuff out the slight but valuable light perception May used daily.

The potential side effects of cyclosporine are serious—and include cancer.

To prevent his body from rejecting the stem cells and cornea, May would need to ingest cyclosporine, a highly potent immunosuppressive drug. The list of potential side effects included liver failure, kidney failure, heightened blood pressure, raised cholesterol, tremors, vomiting, hair loss, appetite loss, and a decreased ability to fight infections. But the most serious among them was the increased risk of cancer. One of Goodman's own patients had died recently from an immunosuppressive-related cancer. May might have to take the drugs for six months, a year, or maybe for life, depending on the extent to which his body might try to reject the new tissue. Even a six-month program could invoke the side effects. And it was possible to be stricken years after ending the cyclosporine treatment.

Goodman studied May's response. He had remained calm during the discussion and had even made small jokes between risks. His follow-up questions were brief but on point. He seemed to Goodman well-grounded and realistic.

May asked the doctor about the required hospital stay and the anesthetics. He still had painful boyhood memories of forced hospital confinements during his failed corneal transplants, and lingering sicknesses from the ether that had been used to put him to sleep. Goodman assured him that anesthesia had come a long way since the early 1960s, and that he probably wouldn't require overnight hospitalization. He would, however, need to travel frequently to San Francisco for follow-up care.

"I know that this is a very personal decision," Goodman said. "You should take all the time you need."

"What's the next step?" May asked.

"The next step is to book a spot on the calendar for the stem cell transplant. It usually takes about six weeks to get in."

May's mind was awash in the risks Goodman had described. But it seemed a good idea to get on the list. If he decided to pursue the surgery he would have the spot; if he decided against it he could simply cancel. Booking a slot obligated him to nothing.

"When do you have time?" May asked.

"Let's check with the front desk," Goodman said.

The calendar opened up around mid-November. May looked for a time that would require the least intrusion into his workdays. He settled on November 22, 1999, the Monday before Thanksgiving, a quiet work week.

"Thanks, Dan," May said, extending his hand. "This has really been interesting. A lot to think about."

May gathered his things, took hold of Josh's

harness, and walked back into the San Francisco day. Soon he was on the ferry and making his way home. An hour ago he had gone for a simple test result. Now the world had shifted. He wanted to give himself time to digest what he'd heard, but the doctor's phrases—**50 percent chance; without warning; extent unknown; risk of cancer**—leapt in and out of his thinking. He had much to consider. He had much to sort out. He had to ask himself whether he could face the risk of dying in exchange for the chance to see.

CHAPTER**FOUR**

No guitar player was ever more thankful for his ability to pick and strum than was May in the summer of 1971. The state of California had invited him, along with several other blind college-bound students, to the oceanside campus of the University of California–Santa Cruz for a seven-week college training program. The idea was to prepare them for the realities of university life. One of those realities, May figured, was women. He made sure his guitar had fresh strings.

The program was as laid-back and hippie-vibed as Santa Cruz itself. The students took literature and psych courses, then hung out at the beach and talked about peace. When instructors advised them to hire sighted students to read their classroom assignments aloud, May found one who wore patchouli oil and liked to recite psychology texts on the grass outside his dorm. He drifted off in her scent in a way Freud would have understood.

In high school, women had been rumors to May. At Santa Cruz, they were as near as his guitar case. One of the program's students, a quiet woman named Nancy, swooned to his phrasing of Crosby, Stills and Nash songs. He knew she was attractive— he could tell by the shift in direction of men's voices when she entered a room, and by the easy way she seemed unsurprised when sighted men paid attention to her. He knew she was wonderfully built when he touched the back of her upper arm, a sure indicator of fitness to the attuned blind man. He aimed to sit beside her on the beach in the hope that her long, silky hair would brush against his hand.

One evening, a few students gathered in May's dorm room to sing and play guitar. One by one the others left, until only he and Nancy remained. He knew it was the time to make his move, but did he have any moves? At the movies once during high school, he'd clumsily reached for a girl's hand and had been rebuffed—how was he supposed to start reaching beyond that now? May sensed that Nancy was equally inexperienced. He put his arm around her and onto her hair, and pulled close to kiss her. She moved into his touch. The feeling of connection and softness was overwhelming, and there was no turning back. But how was he supposed to proceed? The Barbie dolls that had been his teachers were smoothed over in the places he needed to go. He had never enjoyed the gift of learning that stag films conferred upon his friends. He had believed things would be obvious when this moment came, but as he and Nancy fumbled with each other's clothes and made noises that seemed to sound right, the helping arms of the gods remained folded. May searched for important parts he'd learned about from **Playboy** and pals, asking himself, "Is this it? Is that it? How will I know when I get there?" After the night wound down and May had gotten there, he told himself, "This is a new and wonderful world."

The couple dated through the summer and promised to keep in touch even as they attended colleges hours apart. May registered at UC-Davis— the only blind student in a body of sixteen thousand. The school, however, did not offer Santa Cruz–style courses in stories and feelings. Its administrators wanted their engineering majors learning calculus and physics and chemistry.

May struggled from the start. The technical nature of his curriculum—including its heavy reliance on graphics—began to drown him. It did not help that he spent five hours a day training as a member of the collegiate wrestling team. He barely squeaked by. After a time he found new tutors and discovered calculus texts written in braille. He hung on.

Though May learned to get by in classes, he still stumbled in his quest for romance. Traveling in engineering circles did not situate him among the university's coed elite, and when he did speak to women his patter was patchwork. At dorm-sponsored dances, he forced himself to approach females, but the blaring music and wall-to-wall crowds frequently sent him off course. Often, when aiming for a beautiful woman his friends had located, he found himself asking a football player or even a wall to dance. One guy asked him, "Are you stoned?" because his eyes looked different. "He wouldn't dance with me," May joked to his friends.

School got tougher sophomore year. May's classes were more advanced, and the wrestling team swallowed more of his time. At Christmas, nearly gaunt from training, he announced to his brother Patrick that he was going to wrestle one of the Donaldson twins at an AAU tournament.

"Not the Donaldson twins!" Patrick exclaimed. "They're famous! They're animals! They pin their opponents in, like, five seconds. Whichever one it is, he'll kill you!"

May wrestled anyway. He refused to be pinned—that was everything to him. But the twin beat him up badly. After the match, May knew he was done wrestling. He hadn't enjoyed a Thanksgiving meal in years because of his dieting regimen, and he had no time to study. The decision came as a great relief. By the new year he'd put some meat on his bones and stood a fighting chance in the classroom.

Liberated, May bounced through campus, guiltlessly hitting favorite haunts like A. J. Bump's, Vic's Ice Cream, and especially the Giant Hamburger, where he ordered burgers with everything and bought entire fruit pies when they were on sale. His appetite to go places sometimes delivered him into the no-man's-lands of Davis. All it took was a bad shortcut across a field or the wrong tong in a forked pathway and he could be lost for hours. Sometimes he would arrive at places he hadn't expected, cross paths with interesting people, stumble upon some feature of the landscape or trinket shop or ball field that he'd never dreamed was there. It was this stumbling that gave May a sense of the world's potential—it was all so big and fascinating if one was willing to get lost. When friends asked if he wasn't scared to lose his way, he confessed that sometimes he was, but he felt it was worth it, that some of the best things seemed to happen when you didn't know for sure where you'd end up. When they asked how it felt to finally find his way, he told them that getting unlost felt like a kind of seeing.

By junior year May was carrying a B-plus average, but something still didn't feel right about electrical engineering. When he dipped his toe into an international relations seminar he was hooked. Engineering was formulaic and defined—circuits go together in a certain order—but there was mystery in cultures. He went to the registrar's office and changed his major to political science. He was going somewhere else.

In the summer of 1974, between his junior and senior years in college, May applied for a job as a counselor at Enchanted Hills, the camp he had adored as a boy. For years, the place had employed only sighted field staff after a blind counselor had lost track of a camper. May petitioned the director and made his case. The camp remembered his spirit and made an exception.

He connected with his campers. He told them that years before, he hadn't been allowed to pursue his camp dream—to hike by trail miles away from Enchanted Hills, then return as the crow flies, through water and rugged terrain and who knows what strange creatures.

"Let's do that first," he said.

They skirted poison oak and rattlesnakes and walked into branches. They fell. It was tough going but they made it. May loved the breathiness in the campers' voices when they threw off their backpacks and said, "That was cool."

Near the end of the summer, May had a discussion with some older campers. They admired him and asked how he managed to seem so confident when so much of a blind person's life could be scary. He wanted to give a pithy answer, one worthy of these teenagers about to go out in the world, but he struggled—he had never analyzed the parts that defined him. So he told the campers about his life, his mom, how he never felt right unless he tried, and as he spoke he realized that all his stories said the same things:

- Have adventures

- Speak to your curiosity

- Be willing to fall down or to get lost

- There's always a way

"I think if you can do those things you will find your way in the world," May told them. "I think if you can remember to do those things you will always be okay."

In his senior year, May made the move of college men's dreams—into a coed dorm. Women streamed in and out of the five-story building at all hours. He could hardly sleep for the thought of Coco, the junior redhead who slept next door. One of the residents, a freshman named Marcy, became his girlfriend. He still cared for Nancy, his first love from Santa Cruz, but distance had faded their relationship.

Like Nancy and some women he'd known in between, Marcy was a looker. That was important to May, partly because the idea of beautiful women thrilled him, partly because he didn't want anyone to think he didn't know better. Many women found May handsome. He was six foot two and 160 pounds, square-jawed and with a lively smile, and in top physical condition. He conceived of his own looks modestly—he knew he wasn't the football player type, but no one seemed to run in the other direction, either.

Around Christmas, May starting dating a woman named Cathy. That should have ended his relationship with Marcy, but by now he had noticed in himself a reluctance to be without a backup girl-friend. He tried never to lie to these women, prefer-ring secrecy instead, but he knew it was dishonest all the same, and he did not like that part of himself.

As graduation drew near May turned his thoughts to the future. Law school seemed the log-ical choice. There was honor and prestige in the profession, it allowed creative thinking, and it paid well. In 1975, the blind were lucky to have jobs, and those who did often ran vending stands or op-erated telephone switchboards. Law sounded right to him.

Law school, however, would have to wait. When May discovered that a student could earn academic credit by studying abroad, his only ques-tion was, "Which country do I pick?" Many students chose places like England or France, but that seemed too easy to him. Ghana, in West Africa, did not. A professor had primed his interest in the area, and he'd had brushes with the country, as when he'd admired a friend's Ashanti stool and when he met a Ghanaian gray parrot who could sing songs from television commercials. The sponsoring agency just needed to find a family for his six-month stay.

No family wanted him. And they certainly did not want his new dog guide, a German shepherd named Totie. The Ghanaian military used dogs as attack animals; villagers did not know them as pets. The agency told May his trip would probably be canceled because of their inability to find him a family. But the group leader urged him to go anyway, saying they would figure it out when they got there.

May and Totie became instant aliens in Ghana. Taxis refused to stop for them. Restaurants demanded that May sit outside. The staging dormitory for visiting students wouldn't allow him in. May developed a system for hiding his dog from taxi drivers. When they stopped the car, he and Totie jumped in and refused to get out. The drivers would leap from their taxis and yell and protest, sometimes for fifteen minutes, but ultimately they had no choice but to get back in and drive.

The agency continued to search for a host family as May tried to survive in Ghana's capital, Accra.

The streets were a gauntlet of broken sidewalks, open sewers, and maniac drivers. The blind in Ghana were well cared for but rarely seen in public. Locals followed May around town, shoving closer for a look at his strange animal and gathering in the hundreds to take in the spectacle.

After three weeks in Accra, May still had no family. The agency put him on a van bound for a spartan coastal village called Kumbuli, near the Ivory Coast, where villagers had agreed that he could work and live. Kumbuli stretched just three hundred yards end to end and had no electricity or running water. Its cash crop, coconut palm oil, sustained the village chief, his four wives and thirty-six children, a population of four hundred, and a medicine man known as Mr. Natural. None of them knew what to make of May or Totie. On the day he arrived, May struggled to explain to excited villagers that his dog was not a gift of food to be butchered. They settled on a goat instead. May was expected to help slit its throat and bleed it, and he did so. He felt a very long way from Vic's Ice Cream in Davis.

The villagers put May to a decision: he could observe while they broke ground on a school or he could join them; they would be comfortable either way. He signaled that he was ready to work. They tried him at everything, and all of it was grueling— digging dirt, piling dirt, moving dirt, dumping dirt.

He was fastest while carrying hundred-pound buckets on his head to a spot one hundred yards off-site, so that became his job, and May decided that he would drop from exhaustion before he let these people down, these people who didn't understand him but who never questioned that he could do what they could, who had entrusted a man with ruined eyes to build a place to help their children know the world.

Soon, May was a villager. He ate with the natives and played his guitar for them. They knew little English and he even less Nzema, but the villagers could sing along with a few of his songs, like "Jamaica Farewell" ("But I'm sad to say, I'm on my way . . .") and harmonize to them all. He gorged on perfect pineapples, letting the juice run down his arms before he ran into the ocean to rinse off. He learned to digest **fúfu,** an unchewable, starchy paste dipped in hot sauce and swallowed whole, and to appreciate the taste of plantains, peanut sauce, and yams.

May's work was backbreaking. Dressed only in shorts, he carried the heavy buckets of dirt in blistering heat, often under attack from sparrow-sized beetles and an array of other dive-bombing and power-crawling creatures. During work hours, Mr. Natural minded Totie, proudly parading her around the village and basking in the mystical powers she conferred. No one walked Totie but Mr. Natural.

It was during the off-hours, and especially at night, that May's life approached unbearable. He was hungry all the time and food dominated his thinking. He desperately missed his family and his girlfriend. He lusted to sleep but could not—the nights sweated with the echoes of crickets and animals that cried like human babies. Even when he was exhausted, the profound loneliness of his life in Ghana forbade rest; instead he lay on his straw mat in his thatched hut in a constant purgatory, his dreams indistinguishable from his thoughts in their perpetual search for companionship. He came through nights more drained than he had entered them. He had no radio or books. He received no letters. Months passed like that. He felt himself to be on the end of the earth.

One morning, May awakened in a tuberculosis hospital run by German nuns about twenty miles from Kumbuli. He heard screaming and crying in the ward, someone dying from TB, a nurse said, and he struggled to figure out where he was. Someone told him he had malaria and had been sick and in and out of consciousness for a week. He would have died, they said, but for the care of Mr. Natural, who had applied special herbs and compresses and used magical forces to keep him alive.

May tried to leave the hospital, but he had lost too much weight and was too weak to stand. An agency representative arrived with good news: a family had volunteered to take him in and help him recover. And he was welcome to go back to work whenever he felt able. May could not imagine continuing. He had nothing left. He said that he needed to go home.

Once he could walk, May boarded a plane and headed back to California. He could not imagine a situation more difficult and challenging than that he'd faced in Africa. He could not imagine a more profound loneliness than the kind he'd slept with every night in Kumbuli. But nothing rivaled the pain he felt from quitting on his journey before he'd seen it through, and as the flight attendant offered him a hot meal and a refill on his drink he told himself he'd do anything to never feel that way again.

After Ghana, there was no going to law school; there could be no adventure in learning contracts. May wanted to work for the State Department, maybe live in a foreign country. The fastest track was a master's in international relations. He was admitted to Johns Hopkins' School of Advanced International Studies, one of the nation's premier programs. He would start the two-year course of study in the fall of 1977.

May recharged his batteries before graduate school by working at Enchanted Hills and doing odd jobs at the San Francisco Lighthouse for the Blind and Visually Impaired. It was in the Lighthouse hallway that he met a thirty-five-year-old blind man named Jerry Kuns, a force in the Bay Area blindness community. They discovered a mutual fascination with how a blind person might use the subtle visual communication skills—a slightly raised eyebrow, a vague nod, a smile with the eyes—that seemed the exclusive province of the sighted. They agreed that much more could be taught to the blind than the standard "look up and toward the person you're talking to." They believed the blind could learn to flirt and gesture. They promised to pursue those lines further—hopefully together—sometime down the road.

In the fall of 1977, doctors removed May's left eye, which had become infected during his illness in Ghana, and replaced it with a prosthetic. After that, May loaded up his sister Theri's Volkswagen van and made the sixty-five-hour drive with her to Washington, D.C., to study the world.

Johns Hopkins was a revelation. The professors and the course work were riveting, the students (all of whom had international experience) interesting, the city electric. Early during the first year, the CIA came to Johns Hopkins for on-campus interviews. The students joked and jeered.

"I'm going to sign up," May said.

"Would you really work for them?" his friends asked.

"I don't know," May said. "It's not politically correct. They're mysterious. People think they create unrest. I kind of have to check it out."

It took just two interviews before the agency offered him a position as a political risk analyst—thirty hours a week while in school, full-time afterward if it worked out. His job, in the Africa division, would be to analyze information about assigned countries from both covert and overt sources, then make a report should anyone, including the president, desire to know. The security clearance took two months. When he accepted the job he became the CIA's first blind employee.

He loved the work, his boss, and the agency's aura. He began to think about becoming a secret agent. Near graduation, after his second year at Johns Hopkins, May looked into working full-time for the CIA. He inquired about becoming a spy. A higher-up in the agency leveled with him.

"A prerequisite for being a spy is being inconspicuous," the man said.

"So?" May asked.

"So, you're anything but. There's no way you can ride a bus into a village and mingle with people as though you're an aid worker or newspaper reporter."

"But a blind guy with a dog might be the last person they'd suspect as a secret agent," May argued.

"Maybe in a city. But there are times you have

to go out to the hinterlands, gathering information from locals who aren't supposed to be talking, and if these people feel at all uncomfortable about this strange person in their environment they won't get close to you."

And that was the end of May's career in the CIA. He had worked there for nearly two years. They agreed to leave the door open.

After graduation May returned to California, where he began applying for jobs at banks, one of the primary routes for a holder of a prestigious international relations degree. He knew the job wouldn't speak to his soul, but he needed an income and was willing to give it a chance. The banks were less inclined to experiment. They seemed impressed by him in interviews but didn't call back—he never received so much as a rejection letter. When he called to follow up, they'd say they were still thinking about it, code for "We can't take a chance on a blind guy." He interviewed for a year and received no offers. He took a job selling Time-Life books by phone and played guitar on San Francisco's streets. He thought, "This is not what I should be doing with this degree."

In 1980, he auditioned for and won the lead role in an Oakland community theater's production of **Butterflies Are Free,** about a blind man moving away from home and his overprotective mother. He had no acting experience but figured it would be interesting. He had no idea.

On the first day of rehearsal the director stopped him mid-dialogue.

"Mike, you have to look perplexed when you say that," she said.

"How do I do that?"

"Feel perplexed."

He tried to feel perplexed, but the director said his face wasn't changing. This was the essence of the subtle visual communication he and his friend Kuns had been so interested in learning.

"I want to really learn to do this," he said.

The director told him to feel the expression on her face. He moved his hands over her features and tried to bend his own to match. She pushed and tugged on his face, crinkling his forehead and lifting an eyebrow.

"That's it!" she said. "Now you're perplexed! Remember that!"

Soon May was practicing his visual communication skills and expressions on attractive women he encountered.

"It works," he told Kuns.

The play ran for six weeks. A reviewer from KCBS radio in San Francisco said that May's rush to the end of the stage during his temper-tantrum scene made him fear that the actor would plunge into the crowd, much like Marlene Dietrich had during her famous fall from the stage in 1975.

After the play closed May finally found a bank job. A college friend, Rich Boulger, connected him with the Bank of California, where the boss promised to do what it took to support him. The regular paycheck broadened his world, but the work, in the end, did not. He had begun to think of himself as a kind of pioneer, someone who wanted to lead into the wilderness rather than follow by rote. The bank was fine for the moment, but when he sifted through his papers and made his phone calls, there were no wildernesses in sight.

As the winter of 1980 approached, May's friend Rob Reis called and proposed an absurdity.

"Let's go skiing."

"You mean cross-country skiing, right?"

"Nope."

Reis knew of a downhill skiing program for the blind at California's Kirkwood Mountain Resort, near Lake Tahoe. It had been launched by Ron Salviolo, a man May had met a few years earlier at Enchanted Hills, where Salviolo had worked as an expert in deaf-blind counseling and had amazed May with his ability to find just the thing that made a kid great.

At the resort, Salviolo, a long-haired hippie type from New York, got May going by towing him down the bunny hill with a bamboo pole. By the end of the day May was on his own and guided only by Salviolo's voice commands: "Turn left . . . easy right . . . go, go, go . . . slow down aaannnndddd . . . stop!" The freedom was a revelation to May—he was winging through open space faster than he could run, faster than he'd dreamed of running, whooshing through without a cane or a dog, free to turn and fly without the undertone of obstacles that had forever been bound to his awareness.

Soon he was tackling Kirkwood's toughest runs and skiing at speeds that spooked some pros. In 1981, he and Salviolo entered the national downhill competition for disabled skiers. May's category was B1, totally blind male. The winner would qualify for the World Winter Games (later to be known as the Paralympics). Most competitors had been skiing for years, not months. May and Salviolo smoked the competition. They were going to Switzerland.

The United States team landed in Geneva in March, where they boarded a bus for the various resorts that would host the 1982 World Winter Games. The team was assigned a twenty-seven-year-old Swiss translator named Fiona, whose smiling accent—a heady mix of Swiss, French, Scottish,

and American—transfixed May from "**Bonjour.**"
The amputees whispered about her beauty. May
was captivated by her descriptions of the passing
countryside. She did not say, for example, that railroad tracks went up a hillside; she said that the
tracks were like two black snakes playing tag on
their way to a mountaintop school. Flowers were
not orange but "sunburst." The world outside the
bus excited her and she couldn't wait to describe it
all. Fiona painted pictures in May's mind, and he
knew he had to know her.

The skiing competition began the next day.
May and Salviolo stood in wonder as team after
team skied with the guide safely stationed yards behind the blind skier.

"Let's do it our way," May said.

They began their run, Salviolo in front, the tips
of May's skis just eighteen inches behind, a strategy
that made for unprecedented speeds but wildly increased the risk of catastrophic entanglement. They
registered fifty-four miles per hour on course radar
guns—unthinkable in the sport.

"He can kill himself!" cried the competitors.
"He will crash! It is crazy!"

They won three gold medals. On the hill, Salviolo told people that May had been crashing through
his entire life.

The team was scheduled to return to the States
a few days later. May used the time to put himself

near Fiona whenever possible. In a souvenir store, he bought a small model of a Swiss chalet; he often learned about great sites like the Eiffel Tower and Statue of Liberty by touching their gift-shop replicas. Fiona described the ski village to him as he ran his fingers along the model. She made it move for him.

Many men clamored for Fiona's attention, but she was drawn to May. She was intrigued by his capabilities and impressed by his intensity, but it was his kindness that touched her. She saw him mentor younger blind teammates without lecturing, encourage them in even tones but with an unwavering faith in their hearts. She saw him put his arm around a twelve-year-old girl near tears from a tyrannical father and say, "You ski beautifully. We believe in you." When he played his guitar people looked like they believed in things, and she found herself believing in him.

Near the end of the trip, May and Fiona went for an evening walk, up icy stairs and over cobbled pathways around the village. They walked long past midnight, until they seemed the only two moving things around. Earlier that day, she had pushed his hand from her knee, but now when he reached to hold her hand she took it and held it against her cheek. She began to describe her love for the antiquity of old Europe and again May was transported. When she took him to an ancient house and described how it sat on the street like an elderly widower in the park, he believed he knew what that house looked like, and he marveled at the things a person could know visually so long as his heart was right.

On their final night in Switzerland, the American athletes gathered at a hotel to celebrate. Spirits flowed and everyone danced—in wheelchairs, on prosthetics, holding dog guides. May snuck away to the lobby and booked a room. He and Fiona finished their celebration in private.

The next morning, the American team bus was loaded and running, but a head count showed one person missing. A taxi screeched to a halt behind the bus, and May and Fiona got out. The athletes erupted into cheers. Fiona turned red. May kissed her good-bye and boarded the bus, and in a moment the Americans were gone. He could hear the countryside pass by his window, but now there was no one there to describe it. In half a day he would be home, where his girlfriend Cathy awaited. As the bus approached the Geneva airport, May leaned over to Salviolo.

"Ron," he said, "I'm staying."

May caught the next bus back to the hills. Fiona and her parents invited him to stay at their home. The couple spent a week in Switzerland, then toured France and England before May had to return to the States to begin interviewing for work.

They promised to keep seeing each other, but worried about how it could proceed. Fiona said she could never leave her beloved Europe. May, who needed to establish a career and who had family in California, wondered if he could permanently live abroad. They took a final walk and he listened to her watch the world, and within hours he was on his way home.

May returned to much fanfare in California, where the media had caught wind of his Swiss heroics. He gave radio and television interviews in which he described the downhill style he and Salviolo had pioneered. He took a job at ESL Incorporated, a high-tech firm, where he and his friend Reis planned to start a division that would sell satellite imagery to the government and to multinational corporations. And he ended his relationship with Cathy; he could think of no other woman now that he'd known Fiona. He thought constantly of her, but she continued to say she never could move to the States. He began the terrible process of considering the idea that he and Fiona might never be together.

At a party in May's honor, a close friend from Johns Hopkins named Joost introduced him to a woman named Roxanne, a university student and former model. He was struck by her intellect and independence, as well as her passion for helping the poor. His friend said, "Mike, she's gorgeous." He still longed for Fiona but got Roxanne's phone number and said he'd be in touch.

Soon, they were dating. Roxanne had an appetite for adventure and travel beyond any woman May had met, and she struck him as afraid of nothing. They spent nearly every day together for a month, windsurfing, biking, and staying overnight at Enchanted Hills, the ultimate romantic getaway. Roxanne did not need to live in Europe. May fell in love with her.

Six months after they started dating, May and Roxanne became engaged. Their future looked bright, if a bit uncertain. In 1983, Roxanne announced her intention to find a job teaching school in Peru. May loved the spirit of the adventure even if he didn't quite understand its timing. He and Roxanne's mother planned wedding details while she was away. Weeks later, she called and told May that she was having an affair and that she no longer thought they should marry.

May could not remember a pain so profound. He flew to the Galápagos Islands to meet Roxanne and try to rescue the relationship, to no avail. He couldn't concentrate at work. His second Seeing Eye dog had just died from a hemorrhage at age three. He turned in his resignation at ESL, packed his belongings, and headed to Kirkwood, where Salviolo had built a house that he said was right for broken hearts.

Salviolo's place, the highest in Kirkwood, was snowed in often, a perfect opportunity to open a bottle of wine, fire up the woodstove, and talk about lost love. At night, the men trekked to a lakeside resort, where May played guitar and Salviolo tended bar, and May passed on the chance to meet women he would have charmed before. By day, they began a foundation for teaching skiing to the blind, and trained for the upcoming World Winter Games in Innsbruck, Austria, where they would defend their gold medals. By the time the Games arrived, May and Salviolo were the heavy favorites.

It took just moments in Innsbruck to realize that the world had caught up to them. Just two years before, they had introduced the daring guide-in-front technique, which had trounced the competition. Now every team was using it. May stumbled in one of the runs, and he and Salviolo settled for three bronze medals. But it was sweeter in ways for the trail they'd blazed for the winners.

At an American team meeting, officials made an exciting announcement: the amputees had been invited to ski in a demonstration run at the Winter Olympics in Sarajevo, Yugoslavia, now just days away. The room erupted in cheers. When things quieted, Salviolo stood.

"What does that mean for the blind skiers?" he asked.

"There's no room for the blind," an official said. "You guys take up two beds and there's just no space. Be happy. We were lucky to get the amputees invited."

May turned toward Salviolo.

"We're going," he said.

"I'm already there," Salviolo replied.

May made no secret of their plan. When asked how they intended to get to Sarajevo, May's answer was "Somehow." When asked what they intended to do there, he said, "We don't know." Their attitude irked team officials, who assured them that such acting out would change nothing. "That's fine," May said. "We're just going as tourists to cheer on our buddies."

The amputees, a rough and rowdy crowd that included Vietnam vets and ex–standout athletes, counted May and Salviolo among their friends. The two skiers had witnessed one amputee sawing off his prosthetic leg after a bitter loss, had stood guard while another shimmied up a flagpole to steal a flag, and had drunk beer from another's hollowed-out leg. The amputees had no problem with the idea of the duo following them to the Olympics.

May and Salviolo rented a car and headed to Sarajevo, where they found a tiny hotel room, a miracle. As the Games began, May put in a call to a KCBS radio news director he knew and proposed using his tape recorder to get interviews and file reports for affiliates. The man arranged press credentials for him and Salviolo. They were in.

The men went to work, clutching their microphones, rushing to interview gold medalists, and filing their stories from the press room; some of their reports were broadcast across America. On the day the amputees were to race in their demonstration, May and Salviolo strapped on their skis and went to the top of Mount Jahorina to do interviews. After the last amputee had made his run, Salviolo took May's arm.

"Mike," he said, "I think we can take our shot. Let's get in the starting gate."

The idea was crazy: this was a foreign country, armed guards stood everywhere, and their own organization had forbidden their participation. May turned on his tape recorder and stuffed it in Salviolo's backpack.

"Let's do it," he said.

The men wedged into the starting gate. A moment later they were flying down Mount Jahorina, the tips of their skis trademark close, the wind and sun streaking past faster than May had ever known, Salviolo's calls of "hard left . . . easy right . . . go-go-

go!" a music he heard without hearing as the world emptied of obstacles to give free rein to those whose hearts told them to go. Near the bottom, a Yugoslavian guard stepped onto the finish line and drew his gun. Salviolo yelled, "Get out of the way!" People screamed in foreign languages. May knew there was trouble. He had no idea what lay ahead. He could veer off now and still say he'd skied in the Olympics. He tucked in for maximum speed, braced himself for everything, and streaked across the finish line.

The throngs who had gathered mobbed the skiers. Reporters and photographers pushed close for interviews. May had become the first blind Olympic skier. Inside him, the kid who had signed up to be a crossing guard held on to the victory ski poles and wouldn't let go.

CHAPTER FIVE

Carson and Wyndham rushed their dad when he returned from his San Francisco appointment with Dr. Goodman. They knew nothing of the B-scan results he'd received or that he had the chance, in three months, to see them. They just plowed into his hips like defensive linemen and began diagramming their day's adventures, each pleading, "No, no, Dad, listen to this!" when the other made headway in his story. In May's office, a stack of "While you were out" messages awaited.

Late that evening, after the kids had been tucked in and May had returned his business calls, he finally made his way to bed. Jennifer had waited hours for news of his B-scan results.

He brushed his teeth.

He went back to his office to charge his cell phone.

He searched for the audiobook he had misplaced.

Finally, he climbed into bed.

"So?" Jennifer asked.

"So, the B-scan was normal," May said. "It turns out I'm an excellent candidate for the surgery."

For a moment, the ceiling fan's murmur was the only sound in the room.

"Oh, my," Jennifer said. "Oh, wow. That's really, you know, kind of amazing."

"It is," May said.

"It never crossed my mind that it was real."

"Mine, either."

May and Jennifer continued to lie still on their backs.

"There are risks," May said.

"Okay."

"A lot of risks."

"Okay. Tell me about them."

"Well, to start with, there's just a fifty-fifty chance this thing will even work. I could go in for both surgeries, go through all the anesthetic and hospital stuff—you know how I feel about that—take all the time to recover and heal, and still it's just a coin flip.

"And even if it does work—even if I get vision—it could fail at any time, I could lose it without any warning, and it's not like I'd be out of the woods after a year or two. It could happen anytime for the rest of my life.

"Then there's the vision itself. Dr. Goodman can't say how much I'll get. It could be a little, it could be a lot. It's possible I could drive. He's had good results with other patients, but they all had significant vision at some point in their lives. He says it's just too hard to tell on a guy like me who's been blind nearly forever. So that's three risks. And that's not all. Are you ready for more?"

Jennifer said she was ready.

"If the surgery fails, it could cost my light perception. I don't know exactly why or how it happens, but it sounded like there were a bunch of ways it could. And once it's gone, it's gone."

Jennifer's heart began to pound when she heard about the light perception. At least light perception allowed him to sense whether it was day or night outside, and to detect a brightly lit doorway in an unfamiliar dark room. She believed light perception to be fundamental to her husband's feeling for the world.

"And then there's this, Jen: in order to make the surgeries work I would have to take some pretty serious drugs. Dr. Goodman gave me a list of potential side effects that went on and on, and believe me, they aren't pretty. One of them is cancer."

Jennifer's head still was spinning from the previous risks. She could barely process the word "cancer."

"It sounds so much different now that it's real," she said. "The words sound different."

"They do."

The couple lay for a moment in silence.

"How do you feel about it?" Jennifer asked.

"I'm not sure," May replied. "I've got to let it simmer. I still don't think I need it, Jen. I still don't think it would change my life. But I did sign up for the surgery."

"Oh! Okay. Well . . . okay . . . that's kind of amazing . . . ," she said.

"I wanted to book a time. It takes several weeks to get on the list. But I can back out anytime. It doesn't commit me to anything. It just means I'm on the schedule."

"Do you have a date?"

"November twenty-second for the first surgery, about eight weeks from today."

"Eight weeks until you drive to Kirkwood and I finally get to be the one to sit back and watch the mountains and the sunsets roll past? I can't wait that long," she joked.

"Eight weeks seems like nothing," May said.

"It's like it will be here tomorrow," Jennifer said.

After that, only the ceiling fan made noise in the Mays' bedroom.

The silence lasted another six hours. May awoke to a business that clung to his breast like an infant and spit problems nonstop. All the while, he could hear the clock ticking toward surgery. Before he knew it he was just four weeks away.

Jennifer remained careful to give her husband room to roam the idea of new vision, but he was not the kind to take meditative walks or to ruminate endlessly. Often when he desired perspectives on important issues, he found them best in conversation with the important people in his life, a select group of family and friends he referred to as his "personal board of directors." These nine or ten people were his sounding boards. They did not feel compelled to proffer opinions, nor did he require them—it was usually enough that they were smart and loved him and gave him whatever chance he needed to hear how his ideas echoed when voiced aloud.

As October wound down, May found time to talk to every member of his board. As always, they discussed family, business, vacations, movies, football, everything. This time, at the end of the conversations, he also mentioned new vision. He reported the results of the B-scan, told them he had signed up for the surgery, and explained the risks. He was always careful to say that he could cancel at any time.

The board's reaction was nearly uniform. They acknowledged the gravity of the risks and downplayed none of them. They added "amen" to his reminder that his life was already full and rich without vision. They assured him that no matter what he decided they would support him. And then they told him—every one of them—that they believed in him.

During quiet moments at home, May briefed Jennifer about these conversations. She had been careful to give him space for his thinking, so these reports became headlines in her curiosity. He told her that talking to his board gave shape to the risks associated with pursuing new vision, and that the conversations sometimes raised questions that seemed drawn from a philosophy class.

"What kinds of questions?" she asked.

"Well, for example, it's one thing to say clinically that the extent of vision restoration is unknown. It's another to ask just how much vision makes it worth the risk. Is it two percent? Fifty percent? Ninety percent? That's an interesting question."

"Very interesting."

"Here's another: Is it better to have vision and then lose it, or is it better never to have tasted it at all?"

"You can probably ask that about a lot of things," Jennifer said.

"And, of course, is it worth . . . all the medical risks, those nasty drug risks, just for the chance to see?"

Jennifer didn't rush to answer any of the questions.

"Is there a general consensus among the board?" she asked.

"They're like you," May said. "They don't give me answers or try to convince me. Mostly they listen. They say they believe in me."

"Thanksgiving's coming soon," Jennifer said.

"I know," May said. "And I'm so busy it feels like it will be here tomorrow. These risks are serious, Jennifer. There are a lot of reasons not to do this."

As Thanksgiving week drew nearer, May had a different kind of conversation with the newest member of his personal board of directors, forty-four-year-old Bryan Bashin, the director of the Society for the Blind in Sacramento. Bashin had lost his vision to Stevens-Johnson syndrome, a rare disease in which the body, often following an allergic reaction, mounts a massive immune response by wallpapering itself in blisters. If the blisters go to the surface of the eye, as in Bashin's case, the patient can go blind. But here was the kicker for Bashin: Stevens-Johnson syndrome was one of the very few causes of blindness—along with chemical burn—that could be treated by stem cell transplant surgery. In effect, he and May were in the same boat.

The men had met a few years before, when word drifted into Bashin's office about a blind entrepreneur named May who was involved in cutting-edge technology and who seemed as much explorer as businessman. The idea of such a person called to Bashin—to him, the pool of cool blind guys seemed perpetually shallow. When he later read that May intended to demonstrate a prototype of his company's portable GPS system in Anaheim, he proposed to May a one-mile race to Disneyland between cane and GPS users. In Anaheim, the sun melted May's unit's wires; he used dry ice and hot glue to Frankenstein the gizmo back to life. Bashin recognized parts of himself in May's instinct. "The guy is gonzo," he told himself. "I've gotta get to know him."

After May moved to nearby Davis, Bashin invited him to join his agency's official board of directors. The friendship grew fast from there. The men shared many interests, from science to Indian food to the outdoors to wine, women, and song. But more than that, they were kindred thinkers. They shared a perspective on how the blind seemed groomed by the custodial establishment to lower their expectations, to become objects instead of actors, nouns instead of verbs. Neither could abide the deferring, postponing, waiting, dreaming, and sitting apart that seemed endemic to the lives of so many who had lost their vision. They agreed that the highest good for a person, blind or sighted, was in pushing forward in one's chosen realm, not just because it led to a fuller life but because it seemed the way to know oneself. These instincts underlined Bashin's life as clearly as they did May's, though he had arrived at himself in a much different way than had May.

Bashin had grown up in a San Fernando Valley that was shedding its wilderness for a new suburban skin. The smells of newly sawed lumber and hot tar became the flavors of his youth. It was the perfect place for the curious to explore, and Bashin was always curious.

He had inherited his interest in things, and especially in science, from his father, an agile intellect and self-taught engineer who worked for Space Technology Labs (now TRW) designing solar-powered systems for satellites. Often, his dad brought home space-age materials like honeycomb aluminum substrates—"some of the lightest stuff in the world," he told Bryan—and magical formulas like dry ice for kitchen-table experiments. The boy's playthings were surplus castoffs from the Los Angeles space industry: meters and transformers and motors that seemed capable of miracles if assembled in the right way. To Bashin, science seemed mystical for its invitation to find that right way.

One day, after a bike ride with friends when he was twelve, Bashin asked his father to scratch his back—it felt like he had mosquito bites. The next day he woke up with welts and a fever. This was the beginning of Stevens-Johnson syndrome. By Saturday morning he had lapsed into a coma. Blisters covered more than 90 percent of his body. Doctors fought for his life. He went home a month later. As his skin problems resolved it became obvious that he had some vision issues, though no one knew at the time that this was the boy's entrée into blindness.

While his friends entered their teen years trying to understand their new bodies and urges, Bashin set out to deny his failing eyes. He felt conspicuous just for being thirteen, but now that he struggled to see it felt like everyone in the world could see him. He still had some useful vision, however, a godsend to a kid determined to pass for sighted.

His vision slowly worsened. In eighth grade, he was assigned to a special support homeroom along with twenty-five other visually impaired students. Eighth graders possess magnificently tuned geek detectors, and Bashin's began flashing code red. His classmates wore Coke-bottle glasses and moved like they were trying to pin the tail on the donkey. He cataloged the ways he was different from them, then set out to underscore these differences by refusing to learn braille or use a white cane. What he needed was to find the really cool blind guys, the paradigms for a better way. He sensed they were out there but had no idea where to locate them.

Through high school, Bashin continued to deny

the loss of his vision. He thought constantly about vision restoration and researched the latest advances. The idea that there might be scientific hope set him on a road of research that would last for years.

When Bashin enrolled at the University of California–Berkeley, he took up photography, the most visual endeavor he could find, and used the field's powerful lenses to reach back to a world that continued to slip away from him. On campus, he met a blind grad student who had toured Europe solo over the summer, a feat Bashin couldn't fathom. The guy was accomplished, but more than that he had "it," and in 1973 "it" meant finding girls, scoring pot, and hanging with the general culture. Bashin didn't come close to thinking of himself as blind, but he promised not to forget this person.

After graduating college, Bashin moved to Sacramento and began syndicating science stories he wrote for newspapers and magazines. One of his pieces became a finalist for a National Magazine Award, the industry's highest honor. He continued to research the latest techniques for vision restoration, always hopeful for breakthroughs, always disappointed that nothing could resuscitate his trashed corneas. His heart broke one day when he took a kill fee for a major magazine piece he'd been assigned but could not complete because he could no longer read his own notes.

His vision continued to worsen into his thirties. Once in a great while, however, the central spot in his corneas would clear and a great whoosh of world would flood in. When that happened he would drink in the cascading images, whatever they were. He didn't need sunsets; he could lose himself in the saturated green of a traffic light or swoon to the grooves cut into escalator steps or marvel at the latest women's hairstyles. These moments of visual clarity were like opening a backward photo album: his mother had wrinkles, his house needed paint, a new grocery stood in the lot where he'd once played ball. In the mirror, he could see that his sideburns had grayed. All of it was happy consolation because all of it meant he could see.

By 1993, when he was thirty-eight, Bashin had lost the remaining trickles of his vision. Still, he wouldn't mourn. He just considered himself a sighted man who couldn't see, and as long as one was sighted there was hope.

One of the few concessions Bashin had made to his decaying vision was subscribing to the **Braille Monitor,** the monthly audiotape magazine of the National Federation for the Blind (NFB). He had allowed two years' worth of issues to pile up in a shoe box, too ashamed to listen. One day he felt a twinge of curiosity and popped a cassette into his recorder. He heard about blind archaeologists doing groundbreaking fieldwork, blind architects setting new trends, and all other manner of blind people doing whatever moved them. It seemed to occur to none of them to defer or postpone or fantasize. They acted. Bashin devoured twenty-four issues in a weekend.

He knew now that he had to address his blindness. But before he was going to go out and learn to use a cane, he needed to know absolutely that science couldn't help him. He scheduled appointments with prominent ophthalmologists across America to learn firsthand if any of them could restore his vision. None of them could help him.

Bashin finally made his way to Detroit, where the NFB was holding its annual convention. All around him the blind moved freely and with seeming impunity, yet he couldn't figure out how to go from his hotel room to the coffee shop downstairs. When he finally made it, he met several blind men who told him they'd just returned from Greektown, a mile away. Bashin couldn't comprehend that— how could a blind person actually walk somewhere, find something, and then have a good time on top of it? Like the blind guy from Berkeley who'd toured Europe solo, these men had something special, and Bashin wanted what they had.

After he returned from Detroit, Bashin took a walk near his home and got lost. It was twilight and there was no one on the street, and he didn't know which way to go. He was terrified. It occurred to him to just walk, but he also knew that he might walk the wrong way and get farther and farther from home, so he stood on the corner and waited, though he did not know what he was waiting for; he just remained, hoping someone would come along, and seconds or minutes or hours passed until he finally heard a footfall and pressed down his humiliation and asked for directions. He began his cane-training days later, on August 1, 1994, at age thirty-nine. The instructors told him he would always remember the day he'd first held a white cane, and they were right.

Soon Bashin was seeking out confident and cool blind people. He met many through NFB and in his new job as director of the Sacramento Society for the Blind, and he began to develop a feeling for what they meant when they spoke of being actualized. The Holy Grail of blindness wasn't in becoming a superman. Instead, it was in making blindness just another of one's many characteristics, in being ordinary for doing what one wanted to be doing, in being a guy who wakes up in the morning and says, "Damn, I'm late" rather than "Damn, I'm blind." When he met Mike May, Bashin was impressed with his accomplishments. But it was May's ease at being a regular guy that compelled him.

By late 1999, May's friendship with Bashin had deepened. They might speak for hours by phone late at night or meet for an extended dinner at a Sacramento ethnic restaurant. Carving out that kind of time took work, but it was worth it to both of them.

Bashin listened in early November when May laid out the prospects for his stem cell surgery. He asked questions about the B-scan results and probed May's knowledge of Dr. Goodman's biography. He inquired about recent advances in the surgical technique. May recalled that Bashin had told him about his own probes into vision restoration, and asked if they contributed to Bashin's curiosity.

"They do," Bashin told him. "Over the years I've made investigations and done a lot of research. I didn't want to impose that on you now because this is your time and your deliberation. I had decided that vision restoration wasn't right for me at this point in my life. But I have to confess, Mike, that talking about your case has me thinking again about my own situation. Stevens-Johnson syndrome is one of those rare indications for the stem cell surgery. Theoretically, it can help me, too."

"Well, I'd love to know your thinking on it," May said. "It would be great if the conversation could benefit us both."

May sounded out the risks for Bashin, a checklist that tolled more ominously with every recital. He didn't have to tell Bashin that he couldn't dream of vision adding anything to the depth of love and feeling he had for his kids; Bashin could hear it in the everyday stories May related about his family.

Bashin took it all in. He laughed and nodded when May listed beautiful women as among his top motivations to see. He made May promise to warn him before driving to Sacramento so he could have plenty of time to flee from the streets. Like Jennifer, he didn't rush into counterarguments or solutions or advice. He considered his friend an explorer and heard his words as the sounds of a map unfolding. But as he listened, Bashin also found himself reflecting on a set of stories he had uncovered in the course of his own research into vision restoration. He did not speak of them now to May, nor was he certain he ever would. They were stories known to just a handful of people worldwide. They were stories unlike any he could have imagined.

Between the dawn of time and the year 1999, history had recorded no more than sixty cases of vision restoration after long-term blindness. The first dated to Arabia in the year 1020; the next was not chronicled for another seven centuries. Fewer than twenty of the subjects had been blind since age three or younger—like May.

Though the cases spanned a thousand years and were spread across the globe, the subjects seemed to share two primary characteristics. First, their new vision was strange and unfathomable. Second, they suffered a deep emotional crisis for daring to see.

None of the cases was better observed than that of fifty-two-year-old Sidney Bradford, a married cobbler from the working-class Midlands region of Britain. Bradford had lost his vision, likely to infection, at the age of ten months. He lived an active life, building things in the woodshop he had constructed, painting his house while on his ladder, and riding his bicycle through the countryside by holding the shoulder of an adjacent cyclist. He moved through the world confidently, even brazenly, rarely bothering with a cane, wielding his circular saw with impunity, and rushing into busy intersections as if daring cars to strike him. When a surgeon told him in 1958 that a series of two corneal grafts might restore his vision, Bradford signed up and got ready to see.

News of the planned surgeries made the local newspaper. A copy found its way one hundred miles to the desk of thirty-five-year-old Cambridge University psychologist Richard L. Gregory, a renowned expert on perception. Gregory knew the extraordinary rarity of such cases and immediately obtained permission from the hospital to visit. He barely had time to plan—the first surgery already had been completed—so he and his assistant, Jean Wallace, stuffed his car with every apparatus, test, illusion, Rorschach inkblot, camera, and measuring device they could fit, then sped west to the Wolverhampton and Midland Counties Eye Infirmary, near Birmingham. They arrived the day after the second surgery.

Gregory could scarcely believe that the man he met had been blind. Bradford guided himself about the hospital room and through corridors without feeling around or bumping into obstacles, and was able to tell the time immediately from the nurse's clock no matter how many times Gregory moved its hands. He not only spotted a magazine that Gregory had brought along but read its title aloud. He could name virtually every object in his room, and his ability to perceive colors was excellent. Bradford thrilled to his new vision, and Gregory thrilled to have found him. When Gregory began to run tests and make observations, he found Bradford to be eager and willing, cheerful and outgoing. What he discovered, however, was more complicated.

Faces meant nothing to Bradford. He could not recognize a person by face, detect a person's gender by his face, or make anything of facial expressions, and this was true no matter how hard he tried or how familiar the person. It wasn't that faces were invisible or blurry to him—it was that they conveyed no meaning at all. When his wife smiled, Bradford knew neither that she was happy nor even that it was she.

His hospital window, some forty feet above the ground, afforded him his first opportunity to look out onto the world. At once, he believed the ground close enough to reach by foot if only he dangled himself from the ledge. He seemed to recognize objects only if he knew them by touch and expected them to be there, such as a parked car or the pocketwatch on his table. But when he came across things that hadn't been called to his attention or that he didn't anticipate, such as a building or an extra chair in the room or even a quiet person in the hallway, he seemed not to see them at all.

Bradford was keen to view Gregory's color slides of familiar English scenes. But when the images were projected on-screen, he could say nothing about the objects depicted, and in fact seemed to see only splotches of color. When asked whether an object shown on the slide was positioned in front of or behind another object, he could not fathom a guess. To Gregory, it was clear that Bradford saw no depth in pictures. And yet, when moving about the hospital, he reached for and handled things quite readily.

Gregory wasted little time unpacking the classic optical illusions he had brought along. Among others, he showed Bradford the following:

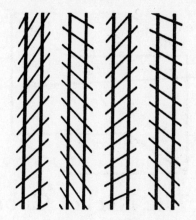

The Zollner Illusion

Normal observers judge the vertical lines to be non-parallel, and many see "jazzing" in them. Bradford correctly judged them to be parallel and "all calm"—in other words, he was not susceptible to the illusion.

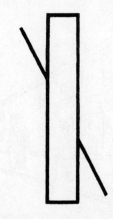

The Poggendorf Illusion

Normal observers see the slanted lines to be on separate planes. Bradford correctly perceived it as "all one line."

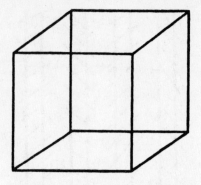

The Necker Cube

Normal observers not only see the cube in depth, but see its front side shift positions back and forth with their continued gaze. Bradford perceived neither the depth nor a shift, asking, "What is depth?" when questioned on the matter.

Perspective Size Illusion

Normal observers perceive the men to be of increasing size from left to right, though in fact they are equally tall. Bradford, to begin with, did not know the figures to be people. After being told, he was asked for their relative size, and said, "The first man looks smaller, but the last three look the same."

Bradford remained a cheerful, if easily fatigued, subject. He proved able to recognize capital but not lowercase letters, likely due to the fact that he'd had access to block versions of the former but not the latter at school. Using the ballpoint pen his wife had given him as a gift—his first-ever writing instrument—he managed to scratch a barely legible version of his name, along with rudimentary drawings of things he knew by touch, such as trucks and tools. Nothing, however, was reflected in his drawings that he had not already known by touch. He could clearly discern the quarter moon—evidence of good visual acuity, or sharpness—but was surprised to learn that a quarter moon was not shaped like a quarter piece of cake. Gregory and Wallace conducted more tests and made more observations, then arranged to meet with Bradford after his discharge to see the rest of the world.

Bradford burst forth from the hospital and onto the Birmingham streets. Marvelous was everywhere to him, thrilling a foregone conclusion. Everywhere he turned he discovered another color or movement or object worthy of his gaze.

Days after his discharge, Gregory and Wallace

went to meet Bradford in London. But when they gathered on the first night, Bradford did not seem his usual cheerful and curious self. Instead, he appeared fatigued, and his companion reported that he hadn't been much interested in the passing visual scenes during the ride into London. When questioned on the matter, Bradford told Gregory that the world seemed a drab place.

The next morning, Gregory and Wallace set out with Bradford for a walking tour of London. He came to life in Trafalgar Square, where he marveled at the blankets of pigeons that flew all around him, laughing as he used his new vision to follow their swoops and dives, stroking their bodies to know what they were like. But when Gregory led him to other city landmarks, Bradford again seemed tired and apathetic—buildings bored him, streets looked dull, the parade of faces meant nothing. Unexpected nearby noises did little to attract his gaze; he just kept looking straight ahead but seemed not to see much at all.

Bradford even moved differently than he had before. While blind, he had marched into intersections. Now, however, the cars attacked his eyes from every direction, and he could not move for a deathly fear of being struck. If Gregory hadn't dragged him by the arm they might not have budged all day. Even when they reached the safe side of intersections, Bradford struggled to step up, often mistaking a shadow for a curb. This was not the world he had spent a lifetime traversing so confidently.

Gregory proposed a trip to the Science Museum in South Kensington, where he hoped its collection of machines and tools—the long-standing stuff of Bradford's passions—might spark the man's interest. Bradford struggled, however, to understand the exhibits, these meaningless shapes behind ropes that remained maddeningly beyond his touch. He could say virtually nothing about the simple lathe that Gregory showed him, though he knew the tool's function and had long dreamed of using one. Gregory persuaded an employee to open the glass case, allowing Bradford a chance to touch. He closed his eyes and fervently ran his hands over the lathe. Then he stepped back, opened his eyes, and declared, "Now that I've felt it I can see." After that, using only his eyes, Bradford could describe how it looked. Gregory knew he would never forget this moment. It was as if touch had switched on Bradford's vision.

The group next visited the zoo at Regent's Park. Gregory was friendly with the zoo's head of mammals, the famed zoologist Desmond Morris, and had arranged for Bradford to be allowed into some of the cages. Before they began, Bradford was asked to draw a picture of an elephant, which he managed in rudimentary form. A half hour later, when Gregory took him into the elephant's cage, he walked around the animal three times without noticing that it was there. He laughed at the sight of two giraffes peering at him from above, the only occasion on which Gregory would see Bradford laugh at something he saw.

Gregory and Wallace stayed another day with Bradford. They were careful not to press him, as vision seemed heavy labor that tired him greatly. He continued to struggle with curbs and, on more than one occasion, nearly plummeted off a staircase for failing to perceive that there were steps below. He remained baffled by faces even when he studied them closely, and knew that he could spend days with someone and still not recognize that person's face when it came time to say good-bye.

And he noticed chipped paint.

He might pass a lamppost or a park bench and stare intently at sections where the paint had peeled, and when he understood what he was seeing he would go listless and turn away. When Gregory asked of his distress, Bradford said that he had expected to see a more perfect place when his bandages came off, that he had always imagined the sighted world as a kind of heaven. Now he knew it was less than that. He could see it in the frayed wood and stained fabrics and smudged windows he encountered daily, that no matter which way he turned things fell short of what he'd hoped they would be. He could see the truth in chipped paint and it disappointed him.

Six months later, Gregory and Wallace made a trip to Bradford's home. He continued to describe the world as drab, and though he had used his vision to help build things and tend to his garden, he still lived much as he had while blind, keeping the lights off at night, shaving in the dark, and showing little interest in films or television. He could do more than he could before, yet this seemed its own burden, as few were inclined to continue admiring a man who wasn't supposed to be blind anymore.

Though he could make no sense of faces, Bradford somehow found his own to be repulsive and his wife's to be ugly. He was greatly let down, he told Wallace, to discover that his wife wasn't as beautiful as he'd expected. He continued to note the imperfections in the things he saw, and to express his disappointment that the world was not as he'd wished when he was happier, in times when he was a different man. "We formed a strong impression that his sight was to him almost entirely disappointing," Gregory would later write. "He was not a man to talk freely, but was obviously depressed, and we felt that he had lost more than he had gained by recovery of sight."

Bradford's depression deepened. In a letter to Gregory, his wife wrote, "He is very disappointed about everything. But when he feels better he says he will do more drawings for you." Six months later she wrote, "He is not any better. I wish you could help him. . . . It seems to me our world is not grand as we thought."

On August 2, 1960, just nineteen months after his second surgery, Bradford died. He was fifty-four years old and had been perfectly fit. To Gregory's mind—and he was certain of it—Bradford had simply given up and let go.

One might wonder, after learning of Bradford's case, if it mustn't be an anomaly. The answer lies in three obscure sources: a German book lost for years, a virtually unknown pamphlet printed in the early 1970s, and the single case study of a famed neurologist. Together, they describe the few dozen cases known to history of vision restoration after long-term blindness. Together, they tell a story remarkably similar to Bradford's.

None of these subjects saw normally after their surgeries, no matter how good their visual acuity. Parts of their vision worked beautifully, others not at all, and still others in unusual and enigmatic ways. Nearly all of the subjects perceived motion and color immediately and accurately, as if they'd seen all their lives. But it got more complicated after that.

Like Bradford, these patients could make nothing of human faces. They struggled to accurately perceive depth, distance, and space—essential components for understanding the visual world. And they strained to identify objects by vision alone, even those they knew intimately by touch. In case after case, the subjects yearned to "switch on" their vision by touching what they saw; without touch, one after another seemed lost.

Often, their vision was confusing, frustrating, and tiring, an avalanche of rapid but uninterpretable impressions. None seemed to see automatically and effortlessly, as the normally sighted do. Patient after patient struggled with scale, perspective, and shadows, seeing colorful but meaningless mosaics where others saw the world. Some closed their eyes to stem the flow; others could not remember one impression before the next flew in to replace it. Few made anything of pictures or photographs. Expectations and other senses drove many of their visual perceptions, yet those expectations and other senses might be wildly wrong.

And that was just the vision. In their hearts, things were magnitudes worse.

Patients became depressed, a fate few seemed to escape. Marius von Senden, who collected the bulk of the case histories in his hard-to-find book **Space and Sight,** wrote:

It also emerges from the reports as a whole, that the process of learning to see in these cases is an enterprise fraught with innumerable difficulties, and that the common idea that the patient must necessarily be delighted with the gifts of light and colour bequeathed to him by the operation is wholly remote from the facts.

Alberto Valvo, in his pamphlet **Sight Restoration After Long-Term Blindness,** observed:

One of the most striking overall findings is that patients recovering sight often suffer from depression, and tend to regress to behavior characteristics of their blind period.

But it was the words of the subjects themselves that conveyed the texture of their crises. "How comes it that I now find myself less happy than before?" one fourteen-year-old girl asked her father. "Everything that I see causes me a disagreeable emotion. Oh, I was much more at ease in my blindness!"

"I still often have fits of crying," wrote a thirty-eight-year-old man. "I don't know why, unless perhaps because I have seen too much during the day. In the evening, I prefer to stay in a darkened room, like a crying baby. . . . This is too long and unhappy a road, leading one into a strange world." The man dreamed of "significant aggressiveness" toward the surgeons who had given him vision.

One twenty-five-year-old man wrote, "I still have the painful feeling that I am not up to the task of returning completely to seeing, and I do not know whether I shall be able to manage it."

The despair was not lost on those who studied these patients. The case histories are rife with phrases like "lost all her good-humour as soon as she was compelled to see," "ever more disillusioned in his hopes," and "would sooner not see at all." Of his fifty-year-old subject, renowned neurologist Oliver Sacks wrote, "He found himself between two worlds, at home in neither—a torment from which no escape seemed possible."

It was a landscape Bradford would have understood, one that stretched in every direction for innocents who did not know better than to ask the gods for the terrible gift of new vision.

May knew nothing of these cases. But Bashin did. As their conversation wound down one night, Bashin told May that his own research had shown that cases of vision restoration after a lifetime of blindness were astonishingly rare. He provided May with the names of the authors whose studies he'd read—Gregory, Sacks, and a few others—and told him he could find them in the library or on the Internet. He did not describe the strange details and dire outcomes, nor did he insist that May read the cases. Instead, he told his friend, "You might want to check them out. I think you'd find them interesting."

Late that night, May told Jennifer about his talk with Bashin.

"It turns out he's also a candidate for the stem cell surgery," May said. "The two main indications for the procedure are chemical burns and Stevens-Johnson syndrome—me and Bryan."

"Is he going to do it?" Jennifer asked.

"I don't know," May said. "But it seemed to spark him to consider his own situation more closely. It'll be interesting to see how he thinks about it for himself. Bryan's a good, good thinker."

"What else did you guys talk about?"

"Business, camping, gadgets. Oh, and he referred me to a few case histories of people who got their vision restored after being blind forever. He said they were interesting."

"Are you going to read them?"

"I might."

May and Jennifer sorted out the next day's schedule and compared notes on upcoming appointments. They talked about building an addition to their house, which was growing smaller in direct proportion to their sons growing bigger. Then, before they turned off the lights, May asked a final question.

"Do you think it's worth it, Jen?"

"The vision?"

"Yes."

"I think you should do what your heart tells you to do," she said.

A few nights later, May and Bashin spoke by phone. Less than three weeks remained before the scheduled surgery.

May told Bashin that he still hadn't decided whether to go forward. Then he asked if Bashin had thought more about his own prospects for the operation.

"I don't think the time is right for me," Bashin said. "I don't want to deal with the risks of cyclosporine. Also, I don't have normal tear function, which is an additional complication for me—every time you have an operation it weakens the eye and you might just have one shot, so the timing might not be right on that count. I'm in a new job and can't afford to take off a month to see how this goes. And I don't know that I want to risk my light perception. For me, it probably makes more sense to wait for the science to advance."

"That all makes a lot of sense, Bryan," May said.

"But I think there's a more important bottom line for me," Bashin added. "I already know what vision is. I have vivid visual memories, I can still see all kinds of marvelous and subtle things in my mind's eye. I can remember standing on my rooftop as a ten-year-old looking at mountaintops thirty miles away. What I need is something I can depend on, a tool that I can use reliably and long-term. But I don't think I need the experience of seeing, Mike. I've already been on that journey."

May told Jennifer about his phone call, and that Bashin had decided to wait on vision restoration. When she asked if he'd read the case histories Bashin had mentioned, he told her that he had not.

"But I have been thinking about a couple other issues."

"What are they?" Jennifer asked.

"They're some other reasons why it might not be the right time for me to go forward."

"Like what?"

"Well, this is a critical stage for Sendero. I can't afford to be distracted now. I can't afford to get laid up. Either of those things could endanger the business. If I'm not right, even for a month, it could jeopardize the business."

"Okay. What else have you been thinking about?"

"I've been thinking about us. We've come through some tough times. Marriages are such finely balanced equations. Maybe throwing something major into the mix, even if it's great, upsets the formula. Maybe getting vision requires so much time, with all the doctor visits and the adjustments, that it takes away from our lives. I mean, we're already incredibly busy. We already have lives that don't allow much time for our marriage."

Jennifer took May's hand.

"I believe in you," she said.

CHAPTER SIX

May returned from the 1984 Sarajevo Olympics triumphant but jobless. That's when his high school buddy Rob Reis called and pitched him on the impossible. He and some engineers were going to start a company that would make the world's first laser turntable.

"The world's first what?" May asked.

Reis explained it this way: standard phonographs and turntables used a needle, or "stylus," to play the vinyl record albums of the day. That method had worked for years, but not without its problems: the stylus picked up noises, pops, and hisses, and also wore down the record. If someone could figure out how to play an album without ever touching it, the result would be pristine audio fidelity and records that could last a lifetime.

"That someone is us," Reis told May. "We'll do it with lasers. The lasers can read the record grooves."

May saw promise in the idea even before Reis finished talking. He signed on to raise capital and run marketing for the company. They called the business Finial Technology, after the architectural ornament used to adorn the tops of gables and other like structures. It would be a four-man concern: Reis, two other engineers, and May.

"I can't promise we'll be around long-term," Reis said. "This is a true start-up. It'll be day-to-day."

"That's what I'm about," May said. "Let's do it."

Finial was beautiful from the start. Working from a tiny two-room shop, the engineers perfected and shrank the lasers, while May proselytized and ignited buzz and raised capital, all in the name of a new way to hear music. Soon the engineers moved the laser to its launchpad—a hand-cranked turntable—for its first test. The four men held their breath as May laid a Cat Stevens record on the platter and began to turn the handle. For a moment there was only silence. Then, with nothing touching the album but a beam of light, the thump and slap of a bongo began to fill the room with sound.

Engineers do not make great dancers. Blind guys can be worse.

The four men in the room boogied as if James Brown had jumped into their bones.

When they finally caught their breath, they felt as if the sky had sung to them.

"From light," they said. "It's all from a beam of light."

Finial was soon the talk of the audiophile community. May wrote the instruction manual for the system and demoed a prototype for the **New York Times** and others in a $700 top-floor suite at the big consumer electronics show in Chicago. People fought to get in. It was revolutionary stuff— something Sony and Philips and the other titans of sound hadn't pulled off. By 1986, Finial had raised $7 million in seed money and employed forty people. It seemed just a matter of time before the principals became millionaires.

It was around this time that May made a major discovery on the slopes at Kirkwood. A curvy and athletic twenty-nine-year-old blonde named Jennifer Smith, one of the instructors in the ski program for the blind he and Salviolo ran, had recently parted ways with her boyfriend. May and Smith had spoken briefly in the past. If anything, Salviolo confirmed, she was more beautiful than ever.

"She'll probably be at the bar tonight," Salviolo said. "A bunch of people are getting drinks and then going to dinner."

"I'm there," May said.

He arrived at the bar freshly showered and groomed, and wearing one of his best shirts. Smith, however, was surrounded on all sides.

"Tap me the moment a chair opens up," May told Salviolo.

The tap came a half hour later. May bolted from

his seat and flopped into one next to Jennifer. The landing was so big and familiar that she believed he had mistaken her for someone else.

"Mike, it's Jennifer Smith here," she said.

"Yeah, I know," May said.

Their conversation was easy from the start. She had been to Chile; his mother had been raised in Chile. She was at Kirkwood teaching two girls who had been campers at Enchanted Hills; he had read those two girls the bedtime story "The Blueberry Pie Elf" every night when he'd been their counselor there. She didn't believe in coddling blind kids; he told her about driving his sister's car when he was in high school. Her voice ran and jumped and smiled. His tanned face and wavy hair and the lines around his eyes grinned to the twists and turns in her good stories.

At dinner, they knew only each other. While new acquaintances of May's often were careful to avoid using phrases like "did you see that movie . . ." Jennifer let it rip, unworried about words when so many stories needed telling. Her appetite for new experience—and her willingness to find it alone— called to him. His focus on her, as if the world had narrowed to a point across the table from him, made her feel heard in ways she hadn't known.

Soon enough, the subject turned to dating. Jennifer had heard whispers that May might be a bit of a rogue, but she wasn't sure whether to believe it.

"I'm a monogamous person," she said.

"Oh, I'm not," May said. "There's a whole world out there."

"I think it's too complicated going out with more than one person," she said. "It seems to me it never ends nicely."

The conversation moved to other subjects. May and Jennifer kept connecting.

"Would you like to go out sometime?" he asked.

"You call me when you're monogamous," Jennifer said. "That's a good time to call."

They wished each other good night, and Jennifer went to her room.

"All my senses are firing," May told Salviolo. "This one's special."

May phoned Jennifer the next day.

"Okay, I'm monogamous," he said.

They agreed to meet that Friday night at a restaurant in Napa. She had no idea it was eighty-five miles from May's home in Sunnyvale, California.

A guitarist warmed the candlelit room while they got to know each other. As before, May locked into Jennifer. She told him about her current stint as a student at Rudolf Steiner College, where she was studying the spiritual aspects of art and therapy—the "granola and woo-woo" stuff, as she called it. That was where some men checked out in conversation with Jennifer. May confessed that granola wasn't his thing, but he kept asking questions and was moved by her passion.

"I'm a color person," she told him. "I don't connect with math and science. I live in a world of colors and impressions."

May told her that he saw numbers in colors—that sevens were green, fives were blue, and so on—and that he could add numbers with ferocious speed because they separated into colors in his mind. No one had talked to her like that before.

After dinner, Jennifer offered to drive May home. Instead, he suggested that they detour to Enchanted Hills Camp, which was nearby and not yet in session. He gave her precise directions—"Okay, turn left here and then go 2.8 miles until you see a white hand-painted sign"—which she found astounding, and before long they were inside the director's house, which was fine since May's mother, Ori Jean, had recently taken that job.

Inside, May went to his trusty Plan A. He built a fire, unpacked his guitar, spread a blanket, and played Jennifer's favorite songs. They were the only two people on the 311-acre grounds. Jennifer found some sheets and made the bed, then pulled the blanket over them. She did not want to make love yet, but they traced around those edges. "You look beautiful," he told her, and she believed he saw her.

In the morning, May asked if Jennifer might like to ride horses. She told him that she'd been riding since girlhood. She chose English saddle and he would go bareback. They set out on the trails, riding fast. Jennifer watched as May ducked under trees, leaped off his horse to move barbed-wire gates, and traversed tricky hills and ravines, but she never second-guessed him, never asked if he was sure he should be riding like that; she just kept riding alongside him and believing he'd be okay, and May could hear that belief in the thundering hoofs of her own horse that she never slowed for a moment to make them safer, and that sound meant everything to him, that sound of a person who lived in a world of impressions having the impression that he could do anything.

When they slowed they talked some more. Out here, feeling like this, Jennifer wanted May to know everything about her, even the weaknesses and flaws, because if he could love her then, she could imagine loving him for a long, long time.

Jennifer Smith was eight years old before she could pronounce the word **otolaryngologist,** but she always knew what her father did for a living. As one of the country's preeminent inner-ear surgeons, he developed and performed procedures for giving hearing to the deaf.

Mansfield and Charlotte Smith welcomed Jennifer in 1957, then two more children by the time they settled in Saratoga, California, a few years later. Though the family was well-to-do and lived in a beautiful home, the Smiths were not out to raise softies. Every year, Mansfield took the family backpacking in the Sierras, requiring the kids to read topographic maps and learn the other skills of orienteering, even if it meant that they got lost along the way, which they did every time. The trips were rough and the outcomes in question; more than once Jennifer heard word of hikers just a mile away who had died for not raising their tents ahead of the punishing snows. By campfire, Mansfield told ghost and adventure stories, tales that could lead anywhere, which was the place Jennifer adored most.

Jennifer and her sister Wendy weren't girly-girls. They climbed trees, pedaled bikes until the chains fell off, and ran miles a day in their Keds. Jennifer never believed she was pretty. By sixth grade she had conclusively determined that she wasn't cute. The other girls had bras and eyeliner and boyfriends. Jennifer hadn't developed, didn't own a single lipstick, and spent boy time riding (and shoveling up after) the horse her father had leased for her. In photos of the time she is five foot four, 105 pounds, tanned, and with long blond hair—a flat-out looker, and California style to boot—but it would be years before she could glance in the mirror and see anyone there but plain.

But for her grades, Jennifer would have gone to the family's chosen elite private high school. Everyone knew she was smart, and everyone knew she tried, but schoolwork scraped against her brain; it was as if she knew the answers but somehow couldn't get them onto the page. Her grade-point struggle continued at Saratoga's public high school, where she fought to make B's in classes where less capable students breezed to A's. If it weren't for art courses—her deepest passion—or the other few that didn't require writing, she might have fallen off the academic map entirely.

Things went better for Jennifer socially. She traveled seamlessly between cliques but belonged to none, making friends with cheerleaders, actors, druggies, toughs, and jocks. She had a first boyfriend in sophomore year, and even dated some football players, though they never stayed with her once they realized she wasn't willing to give them what they wanted. She couldn't understand why the jocks kept calling—if they opened their eyes and looked closer, they could have easily seen what she saw in the mirror every morning.

While her friends were admitted to the best universities, Jennifer enrolled at a local junior college, where she vowed to reapply herself. But it was the same story—whenever she was asked to write, she could not push the thoughts from her head to the page. She dropped out and tried another junior college. There, a roommate with a laundry aversion proposed a deal: she would type Jennifer's papers if Jennifer would wash her clothes. Jennifer agreed and began dictating her homework while the woman typed. Immediately, her grades improved. She transferred to Lewis and Clark College in Oregon, where she signed up to major in history and joined the ski team.

Her grades dropped the moment she stepped on campus, causing her to sink into a depression, one she had felt coming on for years from this constant scholastic struggle. She trudged to the student counseling center, but what was the point? They would tell her to try harder, as everyone had, though she couldn't imagine working any harder. In the office, counselors ran a battery of tests and discovered that despite her high intellect she had the spelling skills of a second grader. This suggested a learning disability related specifically to writing. They advised her to take her exams orally and see what happened. She got A's. She liked the good grades. But she loved knowing that she had been trying all these years, after all.

After graduating, Jennifer was tested further and diagnosed with dysgraphia, an impairment of the ability to write. She knew she would struggle with office work, so she made forays into more intuitive areas such as occupational therapy and teaching elementary school art. Along the way, she fell in love with a handsome man from a wealthy family. He had big ambitions, loved the things she loved, and wanted to marry. From a distance he appeared her perfect match, but something was missing. The man had dreams and endless potential, but he never stepped out in the world to risk making them happen, he never seemed willing to crash through even though the things he wanted went to crashers. She apologized and let him down gently, but what she wished to say was that she needed a person who understood why she jostled in her chair and waved her hands when telling stories of going lost in the Sierras, why it wasn't crazy to say that the best part of those hiking trips was having maps that never quite guaranteed where you were.

Jennifer continued to hang with the sandals-and-incense crowd, investigating different areas of spirituality in search of a career she could love. In 1985, when she and a boyfriend took a trip to Kirkwood, he convinced her to join him and volunteer for the resort's program for blind skiers. That's when she met the program's cofounders, a long-haired hippie type named Ron Salviolo and a ruggedly handsome blind guy named Mike May.

"We'll see you out here for training tomorrow morning," Salviolo told Jennifer.

"Sounds great. We'll be there," she replied, then flipped a hip and skied away.

As they continued to talk while riding horses at Kirkwood, Jennifer told May about her learning disability, about being depressed in college, about doing "sweats" and going on "quests" and the other spiritual things she continued to explore but that some wrote off as quackery.

"I don't write it off," May said.

"What part of it?"

"Any part of it."

"What about my learning disability? That's a major flaw. I still can't write."

"I still can't see. So what?"

The couple rode for several more hours. By day's end they were exhausted and packed up to go home. Jennifer asked how May had gotten to the restaurant where they'd met the night before. He told her he had taken a train, then a bus, then a taxi.

"Oh, my gosh!" Jennifer said. "How far did you travel?"

"About eighty-five miles," May said. "Piece of cake."

"I'm driving you home."

"You don't need to do that."

"Let's go," Jennifer said. "You lead the way."

When they arrived at May's home, neither wanted to say good-bye. He invited her in for dinner, and the meal lasted well into the evening. By the time May dried the last of the dishes, he asked Jennifer to stay the night, and she agreed. It was clear that the night would end intimately, but neither had any birth control, so they decided to make a quick trip to the drugstore. Once inside, however, each seemed frozen to the ground.

"You know where to look, don't you?" May asked.

"Not really," Jennifer replied. "I've never bought condoms before."

"I haven't either," May said.

For a moment, the couple stood speechless. Then each began to laugh and insist that the other be the one to look.

"We'll both look," May said finally. "Let's go!"

He and Jennifer began to walk down the aisles—first calmly, then briskly, then in a flat-out run, teasing and tickling and poking each other along the way, grabbing for boxes that might be cookies or condoms, wondering aloud whether two such randy people had ever before spent so much time lost in a drugstore's nail polish section.

On Monday morning, May and Jennifer finally said good-bye. Their planned Friday night dinner date had lasted two and a half days.

The couple couldn't get enough of each other after that. She did her best to describe the world to May—she was good at things that didn't move, such as nature and art; she was less capable at sporting events or other unfolding scenes. Movies were her Mount Everest. Excited by the on-screen action, she'd race for words: "Uh-oh! . . . Oh, my! . . . Did you see that? . . . The guy in the black just shoved the guy in the purple! . . . Oh, no, what's she doing here?" May joked that he could have followed the movie better if she were blind, too.

Dating May was a sudden education for Jennifer. Many blind people she met depended on the sighted to guide them, to find them chairs and fill their glasses, to fix their dinner plates at buffets.

"I'm obviously not jumping up to get you appetizers," she remarked to May at a party. "I don't seem to be a hoverer. I hope you don't think I'm a callous person."

"I like that," May said. "I don't want someone hanging on to me. That doesn't mean you shouldn't grab an appetizer for me. I'm always grateful for a good Swedish meatball."

"Of course," Jennifer told him. Then she would go in search of that meatball, get diverted by a good conversation, and forget all about May, which he also liked.

May and Jennifer continued to fall more deeply in love. It rarely occurred to her that the man she was dating was blind. Still, every now and again, she found herself longing for little things she tried to tell herself were unimportant. On a dinner date, it was she who opened the door, chose the table, read the menu, and hailed a taxi, and if she happened to be dressed in her best outfit and shoes and coat that evening she might have wished for a moment that her date was doing those things for her. She knew that May saw her inner beauty, and she adored how he constantly told her she looked beautiful. Yet, every once in a while, when her hair and mascara and dress came together just right, she might wish for her boyfriend to swoon at the sight of her. Instead, she settled for standing before the mirror and describing it for May as he shaved.

"Man, I really look good in this," she'd say.

In 1986, it seemed like the men who'd put together Finial Technology would make millions from their laser turntable. In late 1987, their dreams began to crumble under the weight of two letters: CD.

The compact disc had once seemed a minor threat to Finial. It cost the record companies ten dollars to press a CD but just one dollar to press a record. And while it also used laser technology, the CD sounded vaguely artificial—it didn't have the tonal warmth that vinyl records produced.

But the CD took off. Players cost just a few hundred dollars, not the $3,000 it took to buy a Finial turntable. As CDs got more popular, the cost of mass-producing them plummeted. And that's how fast it ended for Finial. Investors issued severance checks to the principals, including May, and showed them the door. The men took their Cat Stevens record with them on the way out.

Jennifer had never seen May so disheartened. He looked drained, and she wondered whether he might return to the bank or even the CIA, where a regular paycheck and the certainty of tomorrow were assured. "This one really hurts," he told her.

In March 1988, May prepared to shut down his remaining senses in order to conquer the world.

He and Salviolo had been training in the up-and-coming sport of speed skiing, where the goal was to go as fast as possible through a one-hundred-meter stretch of hill: no gates, no twists and turns, just speed. Sighted competitors had been timed in excess of one hundred miles per hour. There were no blind competitors. When May tried it he understood why.

Participants wore snug, flared helmets that covered their ears and muted the world. The skis, wider and thicker than those used in downhill, absorbed the ground's vibration, leaving little sense of connection to the earth. The skiers' tight crouch reduced not just wind resistance but the very feeling of movement. In effect, the sighted speed skier knew he was moving only because he could see that he was moving. The blind speed skier—deprived of almost all sensory input—could feel like he was floating, even while he traveled at speeds that could kill him.

May's first few runs were unlike anything he'd experienced.

"Not being able to hear is an incredibly vulnerable feeling for me. It's a huge mental block," he told Salviolo. "It feels like my legs and head are disconnected from each other. I've gotta say, Ron, being cut off from my other senses is terrifying."

May had good reason to worry. If he fell, the best he could hope for were burns generated through the acrylic suit. Worse was going into an "eggbeater," in which a limb and ski pole get tangled, causing a violent tumbling that can catapult a skier twenty feet into the air. May didn't want to think about the next category of injury.

He and Salviolo did what they always did: invent a system to get better. They rigged two-way radios to their helmets, placing a "talk" button in Salviolo's ski pole so that he could direct May through the one-hundred-meter timing area. This time, Salviolo would ski behind May for aerodynamic purposes. When May exited the timing area, Salviolo would yell, "Break out!," whereupon May would stand up into a violent boom of a collision between skier and air.

"You're a human guided missile this way," Salviolo said. "You have to trust me one hundred percent to steer you, even if you can't hear or feel a thing. But if we do this right, I think we can compete with the big boys."

"Big boys" meant sighted skiers, the Holy Grail to a competitor like May.

The partners trained for two years, refining their technique and attracting the attention of the legendary speed skiing champion and world record holder Franz Weber, who agreed to be their coach. In early 1988, they heard word of a weeklong competition at the Les Arcs ski resort in Savoie, France, a place that was said to have the best speed skiing course in the world. As a blind skier, May would not be allowed to enter the competition. But he and Salviolo decided to go anyway, and for a single purpose—to set their own world record.

Heavy snows prevented the duo from starting high on the mountain, the key to attaining maximum speeds. On the last day of the event, during a training run, they were timed at sixty-five miles per hour, the fastest speed ever recorded by a blind skier. May believed he could break one hundred miles per hour, but snow closed down the runs. Still, he had his world record, one he would own for decades to come. When he returned to California, Jennifer told him she believed he could do anything.

Now that Finial had ended, May could live anywhere. He and Jennifer decided to make the leap to

San Francisco, where they took an apartment at Second Avenue and Hugo, near Golden Gate Park, and began living together as a couple. Jennifer was attending graduate school and studying art therapy, while May continued to look for his next business opportunity. Late one night, after Jennifer had returned from the last of her final exams, May poured her a glass of wine and sat her by the apartment's grand fireplace.

"Will you marry me?" he asked.

"Yes, I'll marry you," she said.

They hadn't discussed marriage, but they'd been making check marks in the boxes all along. They had their annoyances, to be sure: Jennifer seemed chronically disorganized, a minor disaster for a dynamic blind guy who didn't want to trip over yet another tossed-and-forgotten shoe. May seemed perpetually on the go, often exhaustingly so, and sometimes made plans for both of them without consulting her. But they accepted these things as irritants, what every couple swallows in order to be together. The reasons they said yes to each other ran much deeper.

May spent the first six months of his marriage brainstorming for new business ideas. One of them, the most unlikely for a California native, blazed to the front of the pack.

Bun warmers.

Countless sports fans were freezing their behinds off in arctic football stadiums across America. If May could make a fanny-sized version of the instant, disposable hand warmers popular with hunters and outdoorsmen, he could warm a football-crazed nation.

He invested his own money and raised more from investors. He would call the business Maytek Sports.

In early 1989, May's friend Sheri asked if he and Jennifer might like to move into her house in Ashland, Oregon. She was leaving the country for a year and needed someone to mind the dogs. The rent would be cheap and the views, atop a hill on 160 acres, glorious. They said good-bye to their families, packed their bags, and headed to Oregon.

Ashland was no San Francisco. Having left open a gate on their first night of residence, they awoke the next morning to find their neighbor's cows grazing on their lawn. Jennifer knew from her experience with horses that animals could be shooed away vocally, so she sent May out to do the same with the cows.

"I can't, I'm naked!" May told her.

"Quick, you've got to do it!" she said.

And so May went outside wearing nothing but slippers, and began mooing and waving his arms at the cows. None budged. They simply looked at him inquisitively while Jennifer doubled over in laughter from the safety of the kitchen.

Not long after, while dressed in their bathrobes and drinking their morning coffee on the back porch, the couple heard the unmistakable sound of a rattlesnake beside them. Without a moment's hesitation, Jennifer sprang from her chair, ran around the house, picked up a shovel, came back around, and, while still on the run, beheaded the snake with a single blow. May scarcely had time to process what had happened. Jennifer waited for the snake to stop wiggling, then scooped it up and dropped it in the garbage can.

"You chopped off its head?" May asked.

"Cleanly, I might add," Jennifer replied.

She took a moment to catch her breath, then looked down at the shovel blade.

"Wow," she said. "I can't believe I did that."

These were the Mays' adventures during their first weeks in Oregon. They freed goats stuck in gates, toppled down deceptively muddy hills, and put a deer out of its misery after it had broken its neck jumping into their garden.

All the while, May focused on warming the bun. In order to build prototypes of his product, he purchased a secondhand ten-foot anaerobic chamber, the kind with holes in the sides and rubber sleeves attached to allow a worker to assemble parts inside it without exposing the chemical ingredients to oxygen. That worker was Jennifer. It fell to her to stick her arms into those sleeves and put together the bun warmers. As May made his phone calls and scheduled demonstrations, he could hear the squeaks of Jennifer's arms moving inside the chamber, a sound he loved for its constant announcement that she believed in him.

After Jennifer had assembled a sufficient supply of bun warmers, she and May took to the road to sell them. They scheduled appointments with pro and college teams, then drove from stadium to stadium across the country, changing into their business attire at nearby gas stations before demonstrating the product for skeptical executives in the bowels of empty stadiums. The pitch lasted fifteen minutes, with May explaining the product and Jennifer, playing the part of Carol Merrill from **Let's Make a Deal,** looking pretty and assisting. The bun warmers heated perfectly, but none of the decision makers seemed overwhelmed, a change from the show-stopping effect of the laser turntable. They returned to Oregon with nibbles from the Buffalo Bills and the Green Bay Packers but little else. May said he'd have to work harder to convince these people how much they really needed his product.

Jennifer didn't think twice about making babies with a blind man. She knew that May was meticulous and would never leave a baby gate open or lose track of a crawling infant. Twice a week they babysat their friends' two children—their "trainer kids," as they called them—and Mike took them to the park, made pizzas for lunch, and even taught them to windsurf. When a friend asked Jennifer if she'd considered the hurt children might feel knowing their father couldn't see them, she'd say, "Oh, he'll see them. He'll spend more time with them than any father I know."

The Mays loved Ashland so much they bought a house there. A year later, Maytek went on life support. Jennifer went to work as a teacher's aide to provide for the family. Money grew tight. May burned hotter at Jennifer's disorganization—he could not abide knocking over another wineglass left haphazardly in the middle of a business desk, or waiting forty-five minutes while Jennifer again searched in vain for her car keys. She found it increasingly difficult to work for her husband, who too often seemed to believe that his method was the only method, and who could get testy or even downright angry when she continued to do things her way. The couple argued, a departure for them, and sometimes they said things they didn't mean. But it always seemed to dissipate with a walk down the hill or a dinner at a neighbor's house.

In 1991, May and a blind friend from Oregon, Bill Belew, started a business called Custom Eyes.

The idea was to build personal computers for the blind. Using May's business acumen and contacts and his partner's technical skills, they believed they could produce and sell computers that could talk, emboss braille, and convert text into speech— everything a blind person might need. It was do-or-die time for May. He needed this one to work.

Custom Eyes bolted from the starting gate and didn't look back. Blind people nationwide ordered computers faster than the company could build them, but the part customers liked best was the personal service May and his partner provided, a folksy level of unlimited technical support that was the antithesis of the two-hour telephone hold times endemic to mainstream manufacturers. The noose began to loosen in the May household.

In 1992, May and Jennifer welcomed their first child, a son named Carson. In the hospital, May took lessons from nurses on changing diapers and making bottles, and when they returned home he held Carson, bathed him, burped him, and comforted him at night. During the days, even while he worked, he carried the baby in the front-facing pack he wore, telling him fairy tales and plans for his new business. When Carson began walking, May called on a lifetime of focus and mobility skills just to keep track of him.

"There's no pattern to where he's going!" he told Jennifer.

She didn't panic. She just kept allowing May to take Carson to parks and grocery stores, kept watching as he trained his Seeing Eye dog to help him follow the baby's zigs and zags. Jennifer loved the view from her kitchen window when May towed Carson to the street on the garbage can dolly, then held hands with him as they walked back home together.

Money grew even tighter in the May household. Custom Eyes was doing well, but May had to use the proceeds to grow the business and pay the employees. Jennifer sometimes found the ATM empty and had to use credit cards to pay for groceries and electricity. She spent increasing portions of her day feeling bulldozed by May, who constantly wanted to go, go, go—on business trips, on drives, on another hike, on an eight-hour ride to Kirkwood—and seemed angry and exasperated when she finally said no. She told him that she didn't like the methods he used to get his way, pushing until he wore her down.

For May, going was elemental. And what was he supposed to do? He couldn't jump in the car and drive himself to Kirkwood, though increasingly he wished he could. As these lean months wore on it seemed to May that his marriage was becoming less the open-ended road to experience he'd loved and more an interference in his natural way. On business trips he basked in the attention of attractive women who didn't complain about grocery shopping and nursing. He stayed faithful to Jennifer, but all of it made him wonder whether his marriage was built for the long term.

He and Jennifer agreed to try to do better, and for weeks at a time they did, but inevitably the same notes sounded and the same songs played and neither seemed to be who they had been anymore.

"This isn't working," May finally said. "I think we need to move on."

Jennifer was stunned. "Do you mean divorce?" she asked.

"I think so," May said.

Divorce meant that one person didn't want to deal with the other person anymore. Jennifer couldn't process the word. How could he not want to deal with her?

"We're not happy. Why stick with it if we're unhappy?" May asked. "Don't you think it's the right thing?"

"No, I don't think it's the right thing," Jennifer said.

"How do you know?" May asked.

"I just know. It's not time to give up."

Jennifer's voice was suddenly calm and certain in a way May hadn't heard it before. She didn't sound panicked or even worried. She just sounded like she believed, more deeply than she had about anything in her life, that they weren't done knowing each other.

"We still have things to learn, Mike," she said. "We picked each other for a reason. If we throw in the towel now we won't get there. So, no, I don't think it's the right thing."

"But it's not good the way it is."

"Then we need to work on it. We need to go to counseling. It might be ugly and uncomfortable, but it'll be worth it. We've been heading somewhere since we met seven years ago. I want to keep going there, wherever it is. I still want to go there."

May agreed to attend counseling. Little came from the sessions themselves—Jennifer believed her husband charmed and outsmarted the therapist, and May didn't buy into the counselor's earthy approach. But it was enough to force the couple to examine and address their issues. And it was enough to cause May to rethink some things.

He saw that he had lumped together financial and Jennifer frustrations. He recognized a tilting back toward his instinct to cut and run in romance—a trait he disliked and had worked to overcome. He knew he had piled immense complexity onto the life of a woman who would have chosen a less harried existence but for the fact that she adored him. And he understood that the fresh and uncomplicated ladies he met on the road also lost their keys and got sick of driving sometimes. How many of those women, he wondered as he listened to Jennifer sleeping beside him in their bedroom, would have stuck their arms into vinyl sleeves and assembled bun warmers in the basement? How many would have been his Carol Merrill?

So they tried. The storm passed in a month or two, helped along by the increasing success of Custom Eyes. Sales doubled in each of its first three years, providing May with an annual income of about $30,000, which went a long way in Ashland. As he saw it, the business had excellent growth potential but could not expand further unless it was relocated to Portland or California. His business partner, however, loved Ashland and wouldn't move. May knew he would have to make a decision.

In 1994, Jennifer gave birth to the couple's second child, a son named Wyndham. Wherever the family went, Jennifer carried one of the boys, May the other. He summoned every bit of concentration and ingenuity to keep track of the boys when he took them to the park, and he trained his Seeing Eye dog, Josh, to do the same.

Not long after Wyndham's birth, May flew to Chicago to attend a convention. On the airplane, he happened to meet Jim Fruchterman, the CEO of Arkenstone, a California company that made reading systems for the blind. When Fruchterman mentioned that his company was considering building a product that utilized global positioning system technology to help blind people get around, the words hot-wired May's instincts. He had never heard a business idea that sounded so promising or that seemed capable of doing such good for people. Near the end of the flight, Fruchterman told May that he was looking for a vice president of sales and asked him to call if he ever decided to leave Custom Eyes.

A few weeks later, May flew to California to learn more. Fruchterman made him a startling offer. May would be given a staff of seven, a network of forty dealers, and an unlimited budget with which to travel the world. Best of all, Arkenstone had committed to moving forward with the GPS. May thanked Fruchterman and told him he would discuss it with his wife.

Jennifer couldn't argue with the offer's appeal. But the idea of leaving Ashland, where the family had its own farm animals, canyon-top views, and the closest of lifetime friends, shocked her system. This was the place she and May had promised would be forever. He told her the GPS was a new frontier. She told him, "Let's go." May sobbed when Jennifer packed the last of their possessions and closed the door to their van.

May's job with Arkenstone put him all over the world and put him there often. But the solitary life in San Jose, where the family had moved, took its toll on Jennifer. It wasn't just that May was gone so often, it was that she felt he didn't hear her concerns when he was at home. Jennifer needed his attention and help, but it never seemed to her to work out that way—he was just too tired and busy, and then he was gone again. She could feel the resentment and anger building inside her.

For his part, May was trying to build a career and make better lives for his family. He too was exhausted and needed to exhale rather than run errands or go shopping—things Jennifer had a knack for asking for the minute he stepped in the door.

As it had before, the road beckoned May. Every port seemed to offer admiring women who didn't complain. There were close calls, times when he phoned his closest women friends to talk him off the ledge. Sheri from Oregon was particularly good. She would remind him that no matter how clean a fling looked, it was always more complicated, not just with the mistress but with how he'd feel about himself and his life when it was over. She told him to remember what he had at home. And he would climb down from the ledge and go home.

Again, May broached the topic of divorce. Again, Jennifer told him that she didn't believe they were finished, that the road for them was still open. They agreed to keep going.

After a time, May's travel schedule lightened,

and the marriage lightened with it. But things were getting heavy at Arkenstone. The company, which had done much to develop a GPS system for the blind, had in the end decided not to pursue it. May argued passionately that they reconsider, but the board voted him down. The GPS still seemed a beautiful product to May. He approached Fruchterman with a different plan. He would quit Arkenstone and start his own GPS company, one that licensed Arkenstone's software as its foundation. He would work with Charles LaPierre, one of the inventors of the technology and a brilliant thinker. Fruchterman liked the idea but wanted to see a business plan. May went to work.

As she always had, Jennifer signed on to the plan. Now free to live in a quieter setting, the family found a home in Davis, California, a university town that was familiar to May from his undergraduate days, and that felt friendly and earthy in ways reminiscent of Ashland. It was April 1998. For four years, May had enjoyed an unlimited travel budget, the backing of an established company, and the security of a regular paycheck. Now he was leaping into unknown waters with a product no one had ever made before.

"That's me," May thought. "I'm back."

CHAPTER SEVEN

Just three weeks remained until May's scheduled surgery in San Francisco, but all his thoughts pointed east. A Colorado businessman was ready to make a major investment in Sendero, a deal that would add layers of muscle to the start-up's ninety-eight-pound frame. May worked the phones, refined his prospectus, and grabbed sleep when he could.

He always, however, found time for his sons, seven-year-old Carson and five-year-old Wyndham. The men of the May household continued to wrestle after school, scour the Internet for pictures of weird animals, walk to the doughnut shop on Sundays, and tell stories with pretzel-shaped plots before bed. Ordinarily, May lost himself in these moments, but lately they had him thinking about a world in which he could see. He might be throwing the Frisbee and wonder, "Would I know Wyndham had made a spectacular catch before he announced it himself?" Or he might run his fingers over one of Carson's art projects and think, "Would I know right away why this collage won a school prize?"

He and Jennifer had mentioned the prospect of new vision to their sons. They'd told them that a doctor in San Francisco might be able to help Daddy to see, but that the doctor needed to do a new kind of operation that might not work, and even if it did work, Daddy wasn't sure he wanted to do it.

"But what if I did want to do it?" May would ask them. "What would you guys think if I could see?"

They wanted to know what was in it for them: the new amusement parks he could take them to, the new sports he could play with them, the new bike paths he could show them. He loved their answers. Then May would warn, "You're not going to be able to sneak around as much, right?" and the worried sound they made was sweet to him because it wasn't the sound of them worrying for him.

May considered himself lucky to be so closely aligned with Jennifer in his child-rearing instincts. More than anything, they wanted their sons to grow up curious about the world, to be interested enough that they couldn't help but explore it. It wasn't always easy for him to point his children toward curiosity. Better than most people, he knew what could happen in a split second to a kid left on his own to explore. Sometimes, when Carson and Wyndham sought to leap from the cliffs in their lives, his reaction was to jump in between and forbid it. When that happened, he tried to listen back in time for the echoes of his sneakers as they flew across playgrounds and threw him into goalposts, and when he heard those echoes he would come back to the present, take a deep breath, and tell his sons, "Go try it."

November blew into Davis through the back door. Just twenty days remained to decide about new vision. If time didn't seem tight already, May was scheduled to leave in two days for a weeklong business trip to Switzerland. In their bedroom, he and Jennifer packed a suitcase and reviewed the landscape.

May went over the list of risks of pursuing new vision. Jennifer couldn't argue with any of them. She agreed that Sendero was at a critical juncture and could not afford distraction. She conceded that marriages were indeed finely balanced equations vulnerable to sudden change. She even joked about the list of stressors published periodically by psychiatrists.

"They say that if you're experiencing any two of them you're in dangerous territory," she said. "I'm looking at our lives and counting, 'six . . . seven . . . eight.' "

May laughed, but he knew there was truth in her joking. If anything, his reservations about new vision had become even more serious in recent days as he came to contemplate a new kind of risk, one that had roared into his life unexpectedly and had shaken him with its power. It was a risk that made him question who he really was.

For decades, May had believed that blindness was cool, that life was every bit as good without vision, that there was always a way. These ideas were more to him than guideposts for living—they were how he understood himself, they were what made him Mike May. What would it say about him now if he chased vision the moment a doctor told him it was possible, and especially at such risk? What would that show about how he truly felt about being blind? He shuddered to think that he'd been deceiving himself about the importance of vision, and about who he was as a person. Yet he couldn't help but reflect on his long-standing thought—that a person could believe himself to be anything, but it was what he did when he got there that defined him.

May began to think a lot about who he was. Faced with the loss of his blindness, he could imagine a world in which the special things he did became routine, where catching buses in Europe was expected, where skiing moguls was ho-hum. Vision, for all its reported wonders, also made men ordinary, and it hit May that he didn't necessarily want to be ordinary, that maybe he enjoyed or even thrived on the accolades and attention that came to him for being blind, and he wondered why someone might choose to see if that meant no one would see him anymore.

And what of his blind world? For years, May had been part of a community of blind friends, agencies, and colleagues. The notion of seeking vision felt like a divorce to him, and he found himself wondering if he would still have visitation rights and who might take custody of his relationships. He had asked Bashin and Kuns, two of his closest blind friends, about how the community would receive him if he became sighted. They could only say, "We'll still be your friends. But the community overall? We just don't know." And no one seemed able to tell him. There were agencies set up for people who went from sighted to blind, but nothing for people who went in the other direction—it just didn't happen.

Even if the blind world stuck by him, May wondered if he would still be himself. By all accounts, vision was among the most dramatic and fundamental aspects of a sighted person's life, basic to one's self-conception. He had no doubt that being able to see would change him, yet he couldn't begin to fathom the nature of that change. People routinely changed jobs, even spouses, but very few changed themselves, and May could only wonder where that kind of change would take him.

These were new risks to May, existential risks, and they swooped into his November with ferocity.

"These are big ones," he told Jennifer as they closed his suitcase. "Add them to the list of risks we already made, and you really have to wonder."

The next morning, May's sister Diane called.

"Dad died," she said. "I found him in his apartment."

May had been expecting this call for years, and yet as he pressed the receiver to his ear, he couldn't quite believe it had happened. Alcohol had nearly killed his father a dozen times, yet the man had always pulled through, always hung on to say that this time would be different, that he was tired of missing life. May's relationship with his father had been cordial but not close, but as he hung up the phone he felt that he still had things to tell his dad, that this was not the right time for his father to die.

"My dad died but I wasn't done talking to him," May told Jennifer.

"What is it that you still wanted to say to him?"

"It sounds strange. But I wanted to tell him what I decided about the surgery. And if I went through with it, I wanted to tell him what it was like to see."

Jennifer asked about his trip to Switzerland, scheduled for the next day. He said he would still go, then conduct a ceremony for his father when he returned. The next morning, she drove him to the airport and told him again how sorry she was about his father.

May unfolded his travel cane at the passenger drop-off area.

"He missed a lot of life," he said, then kissed his wife good-bye.

May collected his luggage in Geneva and caught a train to familiar mountains. He had arranged a three-day visit with Fiona, his onetime love. She was married now, and to a man May admired, but she and May had never stopped caring for each other, nor had he stopped loving the way she saw the world, even if it happened now in airmailed letters.

At her chalet, Fiona and May toasted the visit and caught up on each other's lives. Before long, they were walking the town's streets and visiting its gardens, touching old wooden doors and kneeling beside strange flowers. Fiona saw movement in statues, life in water, wisdom in bridges, and she described it all to May in a streaming narrative of picture sentences that twirled a step ahead of wherever they went.

Fiona knew that May remained undecided about new vision, but out here his dilemma was void.

"Look at all this stuff!" she exclaimed. "Why

wouldn't you want to see it? You'll be able to see the burgundy in these plants. You'll be able to see those church bells wander when they ring. Why wouldn't you want to see?"

Standing in the shadow of Mont Blanc, a beautiful woman by his side, a world breathing all around him, May could not think of a good answer why not.

At the chalet, Fiona and her husband sat with May and discussed the possible surgery, now just fifteen days away. As the daughter of a scientist, she was keen to know the details.

"How is it done exactly?" she asked.

"I don't really know," May answered.

"How many people have had it before you?"

"I'm not sure. Not many. I know it's very rare."

"Have the results been good?"

"I don't know."

"Is there a way to find out?"

"Well, there are a few case histories."

"Have you read them?"

"No."

"Why not?"

"I haven't gotten to it yet."

"Do you think you will read them?"

"Well, the surgery is scheduled in two weeks. I'm not going to be home for another five days. And I still haven't decided to go forward."

Before he left, May went on a final walk with Fiona.

"There's Mont Blanc," she said, gently turning May's shoulders. "I'm going to describe it to you now. I want you to come back when you can see and I'll show it to you again."

May returned from Switzerland on November 11, 1999. The next day, he brought his guitar to a wooded area of a park in Chico, a town some one hundred miles from Davis, to conduct the memorial ceremony he had arranged for his father. Guests sat on folding chairs amid a grove of trees. Ori Jean, now living in Florida, did not attend. She hadn't communicated with her ex-husband for years.

May had no idea what he might say or how the ceremony might unfold. He only knew that a torrent of emotion had been building since Europe—about life, about vision, about generations, about time—and that it felt right to give way to those feelings in lieu of a prepared eulogy, whatever those feelings might say.

He began by singing Kate Wolf's "Give Yourself to Love" and Harry Chapin's "Circle," songs he loved for their family themes. Then he spoke about his father. It wouldn't honor Bill May, he said, to pretend that he hadn't led a painful and difficult life; nor would it help to remember him by forgetting that he'd sometimes hurt them. But what he asked the guests to consider was how, in the throes of this tragic existence, Bill May had remained a

wonderful thinker, an interested person, a loving father, and a likable man. He asked family members
to share their favorite memories, and as they came
forward he could feel his emotions charging harder,
they still needed expression, something still needed
to be said, and when the last stories had been
shared, May stepped forward and spoke, never
stopping to shape what he'd say, just letting his
words go while he let his father go, and what he said
was that this lost life was a wake-up call, a reminder
to anyone who might be waiting for a better time to
do their living that none of us has forever, to grab
now, and all the thinking and wondering and risk
assessment he'd done in Europe and for the last year
came pouring out, and for a moment he didn't
know exactly what he was saying, but he remembered what he said near the end, he remembered
saying to the guests, "Let's not wait around," and
then he took his guitar and played a Kathy Mattea
song called "Seeds," one he loved because it talked
about the difference between dreamers and those
who do.

Two days after his father's memorial service, May
asked Jennifer to sit with him at home. The surgery
was eight days away. He still had not read the case
histories, still had made no decision.

"It's time to commit one way or the other. I've
taken all the factors and separated them into two

columns, pros and cons. It's amazing. The con column is overflowing: there are the health risks, the fifty percent chance the surgery won't work, the risk the vision won't last, the chance it'll be snatched from me without warning, the uncertain quality of the vision itself, the risk to my light perception, the fact that I don't know anyone who's been through this, the strain on Sendero, the potential pressure on our marriage, the questions about who I am and who I've conceived myself to be all these years, not to mention the fact that life is already great without it—all of these factors are piled up and spilling over in the con column."

Jennifer kept listening.

"And then I look at the pro column and there's only one thing there, it's all by itself. And that one thing is my curiosity. That one thing is the chance to know what vision is all about. And no matter how I look at it, that single factor seems to outweigh the entire mountain of reasons not to do it."

For months, Jennifer had stayed neutral, careful to allow her husband the space to make such a highly personal decision. Now he sounded different. Now he was talking about who he was.

"I think you should do it," she said. "I think you should go for it."

The next afternoon, May gathered his sons at the kitchen table.

"I want to talk to you guys," he said.

"Okay!"

"You know I've been considering having some surgery that might help me see, right?"

"Right!"

"Well, I've been thinking about it for a long time now. It turns out it's complicated. There's lots of stuff to consider."

"Like what?"

"Well, for starters, I could go through all the surgery and it might not even work. Or the vision might not last very long. Anyway, it's just a week until I'm supposed to go into the hospital. So I want to tell you what I've been thinking."

The boys kept smiling and looking at him.

"All my life, whenever something seemed interesting to me, I went out and tried it. Sometimes I got bloody, as you guys know from my stories, and sometimes I ended up on big adventures. But no matter what happened, I was always happy I tried. Trying meant that I knew what things were like. Like when I crashed Aunt Diane's bike. I didn't want to sit around my whole life wondering what it was like to ride. That would have been worse than crashing, don't you think?"

"Yeah!"

"So, I've been thinking about this surgery for a while now. And I keep wondering what it would be like to see. It's not that I need to see or that my life will get better if I can see—I mean, my life is pretty great already with you guys and Mommy and all the things we do. What seems great is getting the chance to know what this vision stuff is all about. Can you imagine anything more interesting than getting a chance to see what it's like to see?"

"Yeah, that would be cool," Carson said.

"Yeah, you could drive us!" Wyndham said.

"So what I'm telling you guys is that I'm going to do it. I'm going to do the surgery next week because I wouldn't really be me if I didn't. I don't know what's going to happen, but that's a big part of the fun, too. And the best part will be figuring it out with you guys. You two will help me figure it out no matter what it is, right?"

Carson and Wyndham looked at their dad. It was light outside. Dinner was still an hour away.

"Come on, Dad," they said. "Let's shoot some baskets."

CHAPTER**EIGHT**

Mike May had traveled the world but he'd never been nervous to pack a pair of socks. Now, in his bedroom on the night before the first of two surgeries designed to give him vision, he fiddled with his footwear as worries flew through his brain: Will the anesthetic sicken me as it did during my childhood eye surgeries? Will there be stem cells available when I get to the hospital? Why am I putting knives in my eye when my life is fine already?

Jennifer put her arm around her husband and helped him fill his suitcase. Then they walked to the kitchen to talk to their kids.

"We'll be staying at Manpa's house tonight; it's very close to the hospital," she said of her father's home in Menlo Park. "Tomorrow morning, Daddy's going to have his first surgery. It won't make him see, but it gets him ready for the next operation a few months later, and that's the one that might give him vision."

"You guys behave for Grammy OJ," May said, referring to his mother, who had arrived to babysit.

"We'll be back tomorrow night. I'll probably look like a mummy with all the bandages on my face, so beware."

May and Jennifer arrived early that evening at her father's home. They were due at St. Mary's Hospital in San Francisco at six A.M. the next day. They climbed into bed early, but May couldn't sleep. He still tasted the ether of his childhood operations, still wondered if some poor soul who'd checked "Donor" on his driver's license had died that night, still poked at memories of being trapped in hospitals by people who hadn't asked if he wanted to see.

They made it to the hospital the next morning with time to spare. On checking in, they learned that stem cells had indeed become available. The staff dressed and prepped May, even using a marker to highlight the eye to be operated on, a curious move given that his other eye was plastic.

A few minutes later Dr. Goodman entered the room, greeted the couple, and reviewed the surgery. First, he would scrape away the conjunctiva cells that had grown on top of May's existing cornea—the ones that had accumulated because May's stem cells had been destroyed and therefore could not produce daughter cells to keep the area clear. Then he would remove a ring of tissue from around the donor's cornea—a ring that contained the stem cells—and place it around May's own cornea, securing it with sutures. The trickiest part would be shaving the ring under the microscope from a thickness of about one millimeter to one-third of a millimeter, all while May waited unconscious on the table, the truest test of Goodman's tremorless hands. If all went well the surgery might last ninety minutes.

Goodman wished the couple good luck and departed. At the same time, the donor stem cells were being delivered to the operating room in a red-and-white Igloo cooler, the gift of a young man killed the day before in a motorcycle accident.

The surgery went smoothly from beginning to end. May awakened in the recovery room bandaged, in pain, and nauseous. Goodman entered a few minutes later and squeezed May's shoulder.

"It went great, Mike," he said. "Things are looking good."

He explained that it would take three or four months for the transplanted stem cells to make enough new daughter cells to cover the corneal surface and to forge clear pathways for future daughter cells. If that happened, Goodman could transplant a new cornea into May's eye, one that would stay protected and be kept clear. He instructed Jennifer in applying postoperative medicines and reminded them to visit the nephrologist he had recommended.

"We're halfway there," Goodman said. "Let's keep our fingers crossed."

Shortly after the surgery, Jennifer drove May to Sacramento for his appointment with the nephrologist, a medical doctor who specializes in kidney function and diseases. Nephrologists are more expert than ophthalmologists in using immunosuppressive drugs to prevent transplant rejections, which is why Goodman had made the referral.

The doctor skipped the small talk. May would need to take cyclosporine in order to prevent his body from rejecting his new stem cells, as well as the new cornea he was to receive in the coming few months.

"There are risks of side effects with a drug as powerful as cyclosporine," he said. "You need to consider them. They're serious and they're real."

The doctor listed the risks from bad to worse: appetite loss, diarrhea, tremors, nausea, vomiting, hair loss, increased susceptibility to colds and flu, high blood pressure, elevated cholesterol, heightened vulnerability to infection, decreased ability to fight infection, ulcers, kidney failure, liver failure.

And then he dropped the bomb: cancer.

May and Jennifer sat dumbfounded. They'd been briefed by Goodman about these risks—he'd even told them of a patient who'd died from such a cancer. But his warnings had never anchored with them; somehow they'd both pushed his words to a hiding place. They'd barely discussed it. May wanted to tell the nephrologist, "Wait, this is something I hadn't bargained for." Instead, he managed to ask, "What are the chances that I'll get . . . the serious side effects?"

"It's hard to say. I don't deal with healthy patients like you. The people I treat are usually very sick—they need major organ transplants, their lives are on the line. If they do get sick, it's tough to figure how much was due to the medicine and how much to their existing illness. But they're in a different boat than you are. The risks are worth it to them because their lives are in grave danger. You're the picture of health."

The doctor wrote a prescription and gave May a schedule for checking his blood work. Driving home, May and Jennifer wondered aloud about how the gravity of these risks had not really registered with them. On that ride, and in the subsequent days, they would talk about whether new vision was still worth it, whether it was worth it to risk dying in order to see. The conversations always ended the same way: May told Jennifer that he'd chosen to go forward for important reasons and that those reasons hadn't changed. And then he told her this: I never back out.

Four months remained until May's second surgery. He used the time to throw himself into Sendero, preparing the company and its product for a spring launch at one of the nation's premier technology conferences for people with disabilities. He pushed away thoughts of new vision—and just about everything else—in a headlong rush to turn his GPS prototype into the real deal.

A week before the second surgery, while skiing in Telluride with Salviolo, May began to shake and turn nauseous from the cyclosporine. He lay in his rented condo and wondered if this was what it felt like to die. He pulled himself together and, on the last day of vacation before the surgery, made it to the top of a mountain. He stood there for several minutes, inhaling the open air and the surrounding peaks, knowing that he might never again experience this sport he loved, this world he loved, in this way that had been his character, his life, since age three, the blind way, a beautiful way, the only way he knew.

"This might be it," he thought as he turned his head across the panorama. "God, it's been fun."

May reported to St. Mary's at dawn on the morning of his scheduled second surgery. He didn't bother to say good-bye to his blindness or otherwise reflect on what might be a big change—he knew it would be weeks before the results were known, just as it had been weeks before his bandages had come off after the stem cell transplant. The date was Monday, March 6, 2000. His big technology conference was just two weeks away.

Goodman transplanted the donor cornea—from another young motorcycle victim—without incident. When May awoke, his eye was bandaged but he felt none of the nausea he'd experienced the first time around.

"I know you're busy, Mike, but I need to see you in my office for ten minutes tomorrow, just a quick checkup to make sure things are healthy," Goodman said.

The next morning, May and Jennifer arrived at Goodman's satellite office in San Mateo. A nurse showed him to an examining chair in a small room. Jennifer found a stool a few feet away.

"I just called your mom," Jennifer told May. "The boys are off to school. Carson forgot his jacket. And a package came for you."

"That must be the replacement antenna I ordered," May said.

Goodman, dressed in a white lab coat and bow tie, opened the door and went for the sink.

"Good morning," he said, washing his hands. "How did things go last night? Any bad reactions to the painkillers?"

"No, this time it went really well," May said. "I ate a good dinner and slept all night."

"Excellent. Let's have a look at those stitches."

Goodman coaxed the tape along in quarter-inch increments, careful not to cause May to flinch, then lifted away the mounds of gauze he'd used to cover the eyelid. May's eye remained closed, the area around it not inflamed, a good sign. May expected to hear Goodman's instructions for changing the dressings and keeping the wound clean. There were always a lot of steps for cleaning an eye, and it was a hassle, too, with medicines and drops and such, but suddenly Goodman wasn't talking about dressings, he was doing something strange and asking something strange, too, he was pulling open the eyelid with his thumb and forefinger and he was asking, "Can you see a little bit?" he was asking . . .

BOOM! WHOOSH! OOHHHHHHHH-HHH . . .

A cataclysm of white light exploded into May's eye and his skin and his blood and his nerves and his cells, it was everywhere, it was around him and inside him, inside his hair, on top of his breath, in the next room, in the next building, in the next state, glued to Goodman's voice, on his hands, it was fantastically bright—such intensity had to be bright, so, yes, bright—but not painful, not even uncomfortable, and it rushed toward him and around him, yet it didn't move, it was always moving, it was always still, it came from nowhere—how could something come from nowhere?—it was all white, and now Goodman asked again, "Can you see anything?" and May's face erupted into a smile and someone inside him made him laugh and then talk, and he said, "Holy smoke! I sure can!" and those words made Jennifer's heart pound and her throat clench and she whispered to herself, "Oh, my God."

Now, a second into light, the brightness began to take on a texture—could he touch it?—and a second after that it stopped rushing from every-where and now seemed to come from a place, it was **out there,** it was coming from the buzzing sound overhead, and May's mind went away from the light for the briefest moment so that he could re-member that the buzzing in a doctor's office came from fluorescent lights, and as soon as he remem-bered that he flung back to the light, which now came from somewhere definite, it came from the fluorescent light above for sure, and a second after that it wasn't just light anymore, there was a bright shape in front of his face he knew must be the office door, he remembered where it had shut, and there were walls around him, he knew it because the light to his sides was different from the light above and he didn't have to think about why it was different, he just knew it was a different color—color!—his old friend color, color was right there and it was turned on, he didn't have to back into his brain to think about it, color was just there and he knew it and he could call to it if he wanted to, and now to his left there was a blob of black and to his right a new kind of white moving alongside his arm, Goodman's coat, it had to be Goodman's coat, doctors wear white coats, that's really white and—whoa!—the black blob on the left was sharpening, it was getting lines and edges, it was becoming something more than color and something more than light, it was an object, objects have lines, it had to be a piece of equipment because objects in doctors' offices are equipment and—boom!—now it looked like equipment, and now that he knew it was equipment he could see a shiny silver line underneath the black object and that made sense, he'd felt that thing before and it was where it was supposed to be and now he knew what it was, it was the metal arm that held the piece of equipment that Goodman used to look into his eye during exams, now he could see it was the arm, now he could see.

Now Goodman was moving, he was somewhere else every moment, his white coat streaking against dark walls and shining on the room, and then darkness came out of Goodman, on top of him and to the sides of him—his head and hands!—head and hands right where they were supposed to be, his hands another new color, not white but friendly to white, and as Jennifer moved toward her husband

May could feel his adrenaline asking to be allowed in, begging to do its job and tell him that something overwhelming was occurring, something sublime and colossal, but his instincts wouldn't turn him over to such emotion, to allow him to say what was in his throat—"Oh, my gosh, it's happening!"—because he sensed that he could not pay attention to feelings and to this new world at the same time, that if he were to think, the images would disappear, that the images required more than just his eye for their existence, they required all of him, and he knew that he didn't want those images to go away, even if it meant postponing the explosions of joy he could feel bubbling underneath.

Tears began to flow down Jennifer's cheeks. She rose from her stool and walked to her husband. Goodman was still there and examining but she couldn't help it, she needed to be near her husband, and when she reached his chair she bent forward, rested her hands on his knees, and leaned in close to look into his eyes.

"Hi, sweetie," she said.

At those words, May saw a brilliant and rich and saturated color coming from just below his wife's voice, a million-candlepower blast of light different from any other in the room, and his heart raced because somehow he knew the name for that light coming from Jennifer, he knew automatically why it looked so beautiful connected to her.

"That's blue," he told himself. "Oh, my gosh, that's blue."

A second later other shapes began to fill in around the blue patch, shapes that he knew must be Jennifer's torso, arms, legs, hands, neck, and head. This was his wife. This was his beautiful wife. She must have worn a blue sweater today.

He looked for her face above the blue and there it was, just where it was supposed to be, pink and different from the blue and a perfect shape, his wife's face, his wife's shape, her face, and he needed to see more, he didn't want to cry for fear of losing the image, so he concentrated on the fact that hair came above the face, and he tilted his head back and there was another new color, a soft white, not like the fluorescent lights above it, a white with some yellow in it, and a thousand teenage fascinations and California dreams flooded through his biology as he looked at that soft white above Jennifer's face and thought, "So that's blond."

May pulled his gaze back down to Jennifer's face. The parts were all where they were supposed to be, her eyes, ears, nose, mouth, everything. He found her eyes and she found his, and Jennifer knew now that he could see her, she knew because his eye didn't waver or drift or do anything but look to her, and another tear rolled down her cheek as she realized for the first time that his eye, free of the bluish-white scar tissue that had blinded him, was a deep and lovely brown, its natural color, a color she'd never considered, the color it was before the accident, his color, it was him.

Goodman rubbed May's shoulder and choked back tears. He didn't want to cry during their moment.

May wanted more of Jennifer. He leaned closer and squinted for a better look.

"Uh-oh," Jennifer said with a nervous laugh. "You're making a funny face!"

May's face lit up in a smile. He reached for her shoulders and found them perfectly, and pulled Jennifer's lips toward his.

"Oh, yeah!" he exclaimed. "Come, baby!"

He kissed his wife. They laughed during the embrace.

When they pulled away, May looked again to his wife's face and then her hair, and now he seemed to see more than blond in her hair, he seemed to see many blonds, some lighter, some darker, and he wasn't sure he was really seeing this until he remembered that Jennifer had said she streaked her hair, and then he saw it for sure.

May directed his gaze to Jennifer's chenille blazer, a paisley print of green, chestnut, and rusty red.

"What do you see?" she asked.

"I can see the design on your sweater," he said, tracing the paisley swirls with his right index finger.

"On my jacket? Oh, my goodness," Jennifer said. The word "design" overwhelmed her. More tears streamed down her face.

"Can you see my face?" she asked.

May looked toward her mouth. He could see her cheeks bunch together and raise up. He knew that bunched-up cheeks meant a smile.

"I can see you smiling," he said.

"Oh, good!" Jennifer exclaimed softly. "Oh, that's incredible!"

May needed to see more of this smile. His instinct, however, was to touch it as much as to look at it. He raised his hands and pushed them toward Jennifer's face. She remained still for him. He ran his fingers along her bunched-up cheeks. Instantly, as if someone had touched two wires together in his brain, Jennifer's smile leaped into his understanding in a way it hadn't just moments before when he'd seen it by vision alone. He took his hands away but he still saw the smile, still understood the smile, it was still there.

May broke into his own big smile.

"Wow!" he said.

Jennifer moved to the side to allow Goodman a better look. When she did, May spotted something shiny over her shoulder.

"What's across the room over here?" he asked.

"That's a mirror," Goodman replied. "Want to take a look?"

"I can't see that much from here," he said.

"That's because the mirror is angled down-ward," Goodman said.

May stood up from his chair and walked, flu-idly and without his cane or assistance, toward the shiny object. He hadn't seen himself since age three.

Once in front of the mirror, he squatted down and leaned forward until he was perhaps a foot away. For a moment he saw only a dark mass, but that mass quickly coalesced into the image of a man, com-plete with a pink blob where the face should be and dark patches where the hair and beard should be.

"That guy looks tall," he thought.

He continued looking.

"That's me," he thought. "But I'm too close to him. I'm invading his space. I'm right up in his face. This is too personal. I shouldn't do this in public."

"Oh, what an ugly cuss!" he joked aloud, still gazing at his reflection. Goodman and Jennifer laughed.

"What do you see?" Jennifer asked. "Do you see your beard?"

"I can see my cheeks raising up," May said, pointing to his face. "My beard. Dark shirt . . ."

"That's navy blue," Jennifer said.

"Navy blue," he repeated.

May continued to look. He wanted to touch the mirror, yet he still felt he was invading the man's personal space.

"That's me," he told himself. "Go ahead. It's okay."

He reached forward and touched the reflection. Though he understood the concept of mirrors, it was startling, almost otherworldly, to reach for a real human being and instead touch glass, stunning that someone could look so real—as real as Jennifer had looked moments before—and somehow be absolutely flat.

"Is that really me?" he wondered to himself, and he knew he would need to spend more time looking in a mirror when he got home in order to know more.

May turned and walked back to his chair, where Goodman commenced an exam that lasted perhaps ten minutes. He inspected May's eye, which looked healthy. Goodman then stepped in front of May, held up a number of fingers on his right hand, and asked May to count them. The fingers, like everything May saw in the room, looked sharp, not blurry or out of focus. May understood the concept of blurry, of messy, because things could feel blurry and messy to the touch.

"I see three fingers," he said.

"That's correct," Goodman said. "That's excellent."

Goodman gave instructions for caring for the eye, and warned May against getting bumped or poked. Jennifer, still dazed and astonished, absorbed maybe half of his directions. May watched the doctor's face, a pink blob in which he saw little detail, and knew that he wasn't seeing perfectly, that this couldn't be 20/20. And yet the vision was so thrilling, so unexpected, so everywhere and vibrant, so much evolving already, that the future of his eyesight didn't occur to him except that there was a future and that, as had always been true for his life, that future was a place where anything could happen, where there was always a way.

Goodman told them they were free to go. May wanted to thank him properly, to make a moment of his gratitude, but he couldn't stop smiling, couldn't stop wanting to run out the office door and sprint down the hallway and charge onto the street and look at everything. So instead he used his sight to find Goodman's white coat and stepped forward and hugged the doctor and he said, "Thanks, Dan"; but he didn't let go, and for a moment time disappeared, the way it had when May sat down backward on schoolbuses and crashed into swing sets and climbed ham radio towers, the way time had always disappeared when he was about to find out what was there.

Jennifer was next to hug and thank Goodman. In turn, he thanked her and May for trusting in him, and with that he bid the couple good-bye. May reached for his cane and took Jennifer's shoulder, and he led her toward the office door, which he was able to locate with his new vision.

May took a single step into the reception area before he slammed to a halt. What was this glorious place? What were these magnificent things? Colors and shapes shone on him from everywhere, busy people moved in random ways, things seemed as big as they wanted to be. He moved his head around, gulping the splendor of the waiting room into his eye. He pointed to the ground.

"Look at those shapes! Look at those colors! Are they on the carpet?"

"They're part of the carpet," Jennifer said. "It's the carpet's design."

May could see people waiting for their appointments. None of them moved or seemed the least bit excited. He could not believe they were just sitting there ignoring this carpet—how could a person just sit there when such a carpet was happening?

Jennifer directed May's attention to the hallway door. Again, he located it perfectly by vision, though he found himself relying on auditory cues like echo to figure its distance. Once in the hallway, another carpet—this one equally industrial and ugly by Jennifer's judgment—leaped into May's fascination.

"It's kind of a blond carpet," May said. "What's the name of that color?"

"That's beige," Jennifer said. "It has speckles . . ."

May didn't hear the part about the speckles—
his attention had already shifted to a colorful square
blob on the wall.

"What's that?" he asked.

"That's a painting," Jennifer said.

May walked to the wall and leaned forward,
putting his eye perhaps a foot from the picture. He
took the green in the painting to be grass or trees,
and the blue to be sky. But he couldn't figure the
meaning of the other colors or shapes, nor could he
tell if he was looking at glass or canvas. Overwhelmingly, his urge was to touch the painting—
touch always told him what something was—so he
ran his hands over its surface. Instantly, he knew
that he was seeing canvas, and it now looked like
canvas to his eye. But his touch revealed nothing
about the identity of the objects shown in the painting; it didn't tell him if the red blob in the middle
was a coffee cup or a fox or a barn, which made
May feel momentarily foolish—of course a person
couldn't identify an object by touch if that object
wasn't really there, if it was just a glob of spread-out
paint on a canvas.

"What's in this painting?" he asked.

"It's a nature print," Jennifer answered. "There's
grass, trees, a little flowing brook, a small red bridge,

and a sunflower. See the sunflower? It's brown and yellow."

The brown and yellow suddenly made more sense to May. Yet he still had the feeling that he needed to touch it to really see it. Again he reached out and ran his hands over the painting. Again it startled him to feel just a flat surface.

None of this struggle diminished his excitement. Everywhere May turned he found new wonders, and he asked Jennifer about them all.

"Is that blue space a doorway?"

"Yes."

"What's that red-and-white shape that's so bright?"

"That's an exit sign."

"Are those more paintings on the wall?"

"Yes."

"Is that a person . . . on that door?"

"That's the 'female' symbol for the bathroom. That's the ladies' bathroom door."

"Are those numbers on the door?"

"Oh, my gosh. Yes."

The elevator was perhaps a hundred feet from Goodman's office. Five minutes had passed and they weren't halfway there. May wanted to see everything, know everything, touch everything. Jennifer raced to keep up with his questions, even as a dozen new ones rushed in during each of her answers, and as she watched her husband travel from wall to carpet to doorknob to fire alarm, she was struck by how much there was to see in the world, in a hallway, that sighted people never even noticed.

May made his way slowly down the hall. Jennifer watched him press up close to see things, and noticed that the objects he saw best seemed to have high contrast against their backgrounds, but she thought nothing of it; he was just learning to see. It was all fantastic and new, and she had to stay focused herself, not just to help her husband but to be present for this time, to remember it as it was when she told her children about it years from now.

Every time May saw something new he faced a wonderful crisis: whether to keep looking or to move on to the next thrilling sight. Despite his excitement, he still didn't quite have a handle on what he was feeling. As in Goodman's office, he knew that if he diverted his attention to the joy and pleasure he sensed were underneath he would lose his awareness of the visual, and more than anything he did not want to lose his awareness of that.

Finally, May arrived at the end of the hallway. There he saw a big silver rectangle and two round shapes beside it. Grinning widely, he reached forward and pressed the bottom circle—a bull's-eye—which lit his finger with its bright white light and confirmed his suspicion—this was the elevator. The gears moved to answer his call, a sound of music to May.

He and Jennifer rode the elevator down, then walked toward the building's exit. He readied his cane, she pushed open the door, and . . .

WHOOSH!

Sheets of brilliant blues and greens and reds and yellows wallpapered the fresh outside air that swirled around his body, an entirely different bright than he'd seen inside the building, a lustrous coating he could see no matter how he cocked his head, he wanted to tell Jennifer about it and . . .

BAM!

Puzzle piece–shaped objects, ablaze in light and color, kaleidoscoped onto his eye, at arm's length and miles away simultaneously, each stamped onto ground and sky and everywhere, they seemed to . . .

HUSH . . .

Darkness appeared beneath his feet, a gray he followed forward with his eye until the ground turned suddenly bright, yet still gray—two grays that were the same but different. He thought about that for a moment, how the same ground could be two such different grays, and he realized that he was standing—of course!—in the building's shadow.

"We're in the shadow," May announced. "It's dark here but sunny there."

"That's exactly right," Jennifer said. "That's great, Mike."

"There's color everywhere," May said, turning his head upward. "This is a blast! I can't wait to share this with the kids."

Jennifer rummaged through her purse, thinking she might have left something behind in Goodman's office. May used the time to take in the shapes and colors around him. Some made sense to him: cars of every color with their wonderful engine and tire sounds; the curb painted red, signifying "no parking" that his friends complained about; the dark bushes that lined the street; the green of a traffic light. He waited for that light to turn to yellow and then to red, and it felt wonderful, mighty, to expect something visually and then to see it happen before his eyes.

A woman called to May and Jennifer from down the street. It was Antonia, a childhood friend of Jennifer's whom she hadn't seen for years. They embraced, and Jennifer struggled to explain why she couldn't stand there and chat. May did it for her.

"Guess what?" he said. "I couldn't see yesterday. But I can today."

Antonia cocked a suspicious eyebrow. She knew May was blind.

"It's true!" Jennifer said. "Mike just got his vision about ten minutes ago, so I can't talk now, I gotta go—I'm really sorry, Antonia, but I'll call you soon, I promise!"

With that, May took his wife's shoulder, put his

cane in front of him, and began walking. He moved automatically, his gait confident and balanced. Though he could process the image of objects only one at a time—as if watching a slide show—things that moved seemed to do so smoothly and naturally, whether it was a bird flying or trees swaying or cars turning left at the light, and these moving things were easy to perceive, like colors; they were just there to see.

At the intersection, he and Jennifer stepped off the curb and into the street. Jennifer confirmed that the white lines under his feet showed a crosswalk. When they came to the other side May's cane indicated a curb, yet when he looked down at the curb he didn't perceive a change in the height of the pavement, just a shadow of a slightly different color than the street.

"I'll get better at that," he told himself.

They kept walking. Every step or so, May asked another question.

"There's blue stuff all over the ground," he said. "What is it?"

"That blue shows there's a gas line under the ground," she said.

"Why is it dark on the ground over there? Is that a shadow?"

"No. That's a manhole cover."

May could scarcely believe his luck. These markings on the ground were a fantastic discovery.

"They're everywhere!" he said. "Why don't sighted people ever talk about them?"

He'd begun to ask Jennifer another question—this one about cracks in the sidewalk—when she realized she hadn't had a chance to ask him a question yet. They were nearing their minivan.

"Can you see the sky?" she asked.

May looked up. He breathed in a blue so rich and so everywhere that he could think of nothing to say other than "I see it."

"You're smiling," she said.

A moment later May looked ahead and saw a bright red object that appeared, with the exception of being bigger, much like the cars he'd seen passing by. He knew right away that it had to be their van. He walked toward it, reached for the door handle, and let himself in.

While Jennifer searched her bag for sunglasses, May craned his head around to the left, so that his working eye pointed toward her.

"You look beautiful," he said, taking her hand.

So much had happened in the last half hour that it hadn't occurred to Jennifer that her husband could see her.

"Thank you," she said. "So do you."

The van's interior didn't beckon May—he knew about all that stuff already—so he concentrated his focus outside, on the world-sized dashboard of amazements out his window.

Jennifer drove down the series of residential streets that led to the highway. Everywhere he looked May could see traffic signs—bright shapes atop skinny poles that somehow didn't fall over—but he was far more drawn to their color than to their messages. He delighted when cars applied their brake lights, and he worried for pedestrians who stepped too closely in front of their van at cross-walks. The human stride made sense to his eye.

Again, May yearned to touch what he saw, but he was helpless behind the shield of windows that surrounded him. How strange it felt to see so much from this van and yet be cocooned in glass and unable to touch any of it.

Jennifer took the on-ramp, hit the accelerator, and merged into highway traffic. May's heart leaped into his throat—cars of all shapes and sizes darted, weaved, shimmied, and juked around the van, moving at speeds magnitudes faster than those he'd mused over in town, invading the van's personal space, nearly clipping its bumpers and doors during lane changes that seemed profoundly unnecessary—why wasn't Jennifer panicking? WHY WASN'T JENNIFER PANICKING?

"Can you believe we ran into Antonia?" Jennifer asked.

The question jarred and then reassured May. If Jennifer wasn't thinking about traffic, this must be how highway traffic always looked, sighted people must be used to this storm, they probably . . .

"Whoa, Jen! Why did you just change lanes?" May asked. "There wasn't even a car in front of us!"

"The traffic always slows down a few miles ahead," she said. "I wanted to get in the carpool lane ahead of time."

To May, that sounded like a lot to think about.

Motion looked beautiful outside his window. Lane markers flew past the van while an assembly line of roadside signs ticked away to his right. Nearby cars looked close enough to touch, and more than once May found himself beginning to reach for them before his brain telegrammed his hand with the message "Impossible."

"Jen, watch it, that was close!" he exclaimed when a small car darted in front of the van.

"I might be the first woman ever to say this," Jennifer noted. "But it's wonderful to have my husband critique my driving."

Crossing the Bay Bridge, May could see the water below; he knew it was water by how it moved and shimmered. He asked Jennifer a million questions—about white shapes in the bay, a floating construction crane, the town across the way—and except for a voice about an octave lower, he was seven years old again, asking Ori Jean to describe everything she saw from this very bridge, never knowing that she had faked answers on foggy days because his heart had needed to know.

On another bridge, May asked Jennifer if the shapes in the middle of the road were bushes.

"No, those are pillars," she said. "They're too regular and square to be bushes. Bushes have more random shapes."

May filed the information: **bushes are more random.** And he stared in wonder at the shards of sunlight that staccatoed like Morse code through the gray metal spires that supported the bridge. No one had ever told him about broken pieces of light.

He could not get enough of the sight of other cars. Effortlessly, he could estimate their acceleration and deceleration. Yet when one car moved away from his field of vision and he shifted his attention to another, it took five or ten seconds before he began to visually understand that new car, to feel like he really had a grasp on what it was. And he had the vague notion that if someone were to put a car somewhere he didn't expect to see it—say, on top of a tree—he might not figure out that it was a car for a very, very long time.

He began to practice identifying the different types of vehicles, asking Jennifer to stay even with various cars, pickups, vans, and trucks so that he could study their traits. He looked for clues— pickups had long and flat rear areas that cars did not; vans were more square than pickups—and soon he was impressing his wife with his ability to call out the kinds of vehicles heading east with them under the California sun.

Soon enough, May wanted to read signs. There was no hope for the pole-supported signs on the side of the road—they were too small and flew by too quickly. But the huge green highway signs that hung overhead and stretched across the road looked more inviting. In forty years, no one had mentioned that there were signs over the highway; he'd assumed all signs stood on the side of the road. May watched the green signs approaching. He knew that objects were supposed to look bigger as they got closer, but to him the signs just seemed to grow clearer and more detailed as they drew closer, not bigger.

Before May could try to read them, however, he had to convince himself that the van would fit under the signs rather than slam into them—until the last moments, each sign looked to be resting on the road itself. When he assured himself there would be no collisions, he turned his attention to reading. From a distance, he could see only the green of the sign. As the van drew nearer, he could discern its white lettering. But the van always passed under the sign before he could identify its letters.

Seeing trucks proved easier. With Jennifer's

help (she was masterful at pulling alongside semi-trailers and holding her position, even while holding his hand), he could recognize that the giant shapes painted on their sides were letters, even if he couldn't, at the moment, identify the particular letters themselves. He was better at remembering the visual impression left by a truck. The big yellow one with black letters on the side, Jennifer told him, was a Ryder rental truck. The massive red one with giant swirly white designs on the side carried Coca-Cola. That kind of information nested easily in his memory.

"This is phenomenal," he told Jennifer. "It's a constant flow, it's thrilling. I'm having so much fun."

She reminded him that he was due for the every-half-hour teardrops Goodman had prescribed. May found the bottle, tilted back his head, and squeezed. Glistening blobs streaked toward his eye, they moved faster than cars, and splashed wet and cold, and everything looked fuzzy for a moment before things returned to normal. It was another sign to May that his new vision was sharp, not blurry.

Soon Jennifer had reached a wide-open stretch of Interstate 80, a natural place for conversation. They marveled at what had happened this day, that an hour ago they had expected a simple bandage change and now he could see. They reviewed what they would have done differently had they known today was the day. May said he would have brought his sons along to share the experience, gone to the Golden Gate Bridge, had a party for friends and family, and prepared something articulate to say like Neil Armstrong had when he'd landed on the moon.

"Well, forget about the Neil Armstrong part," he said. "Things always seem better when they're spontaneous."

"Yeah," said Jennifer. " 'Holy smoke!' wasn't bad."

For her part, Jennifer said she would have worn different clothes. "Something bright, colorful, and sexy. Maybe a really tight yellow tank top, something like that."

May grinned like a little boy. And he was touched—he could hear a wisp of nervousness in her voice as she imagined a more momentous outfit, the kind she didn't wear every day.

May still hadn't examined Jennifer closely. His working eye was on the wrong side of the car, and it didn't feel appropriate to twist around and stare. At the same time, he wasn't particularly inclined to check himself out, other than an occasional glance at the patterns on his pants and shirt. He could do more of this personal looking later and in private.

Near Napa, May tried to find the beautiful rolling hills he'd heard people admire. Right away, he could see the hills, dark masses rising into the blue skyline, and the trees, green bunches balanced on dark, thin lines rising from the green grass below. He was surprised to see so much nature—he had imagined there to be more buildings and trains and industry near the highway; that's what highways meant. But for miles he saw only grassy hills with an occasional red barn embossed on the side, and this looked beautiful to him, the idea of all this nature in a place that was supposed to be so busy.

Beyond Napa, May began to feel tired, even worn out.

"I need to close my eyes," he told Jennifer.

His lids shut slowly. At once he felt a great relief.

"It's unrelenting," he thought to himself. "It's thrilling, but I'm exhausted."

May couldn't keep his eyes closed for long. Despite the fatigue, he could not abide the idea of some bit of life passing by when he had the chance to know it was there. He kept looking. A few minutes later, he made a startling discovery.

"Look!" he exclaimed to Jennifer, pointing out his window. "A Ryder truck!"

A half hour later, Jennifer took the off-ramp to Davis. They were five minutes from home. May looked around at the town where he'd attended college and had now chosen to raise his family and run his business. It felt powerful to see traffic lights and medians and buildings he knew would be there. And he couldn't wait to greet his boys, who would be back from school in an hour, to explore the yard with them, take a walk with them, look around the house with them, and it struck him that he hadn't given a moment's thought to what his sons might look like during this day he'd spent yearning to see them.

Jennifer pulled into the driveway. Suddenly, May realized that he was about to see his mother, this woman who had believed in him, who had allowed him to build his own eighty-foot ham radio tower in her backyard even though she knew it could hurt him, and he knew that in a minute he would tell her he was okay.

CHAPTER NINE

May gathered his travel bag from the back of the van, walked through the garage, and opened the door to his house. A cyclone of yellow sound and motion exploded from the kitchen floor and hurtled toward him, a massive object against which he had no defense. Before he had a chance to put up his arms to survive the impact, the storm crashed into his leg and . . . began to lick his hand.

"Hey, Josh!" May said to his dog. "Oh, man! That was fast! I'm glad it's you, boy!"

May knelt down and looked at his dog's face. Josh's golden coat shone in the sunny kitchen area.

"He's blond, too," May said to Jennifer. "But his hair isn't streaked."

May stroked Josh's head, body, legs, and tail. Immediately, the image before him transformed from a general golden mass into what was clearly a dog.

"I see you, Josh," May said.

May heard light footsteps approaching and felt a hand on his shoulder. As he stood up he could see a billow of white fall below him, and he knew that this was his mother's hair. He stepped forward and reached for her.

"I'm okay, Mom," he said.

"I know, Michael," she said.

"I can see."

"I know, Michael."

May hugged Ori Jean for another moment and then stepped back. He looked at her, the whole of her. And he thought, "She looks short." He stared again at the white puff of hair that surrounded her pink face. He could see that she bent over slightly.

"I'm old," Ori Jean said, smiling.

May took her hands. His first instinct was to look at those hands, to see what he was touching. But he would not look away from his mother's face.

"Thank you for being here," he said.

For a moment, neither of them spoke. Then May squeezed her hands gently.

"Thank you for everything, Mom," he said.

Carson and Wyndham were due home shortly. Jennifer walked across the backyard, toward their school, so she could accompany them home. May watched through the kitchen window as she disappeared through their brown wooden fence.

"Are you enjoying it?" Ori Jean asked.

"It's unbelievable," he said, still gazing out the window. "It's thrilling, incredible. I can't believe it."

Ori Jean watched her son watch the world outside, and in his easy grin and hopeful eyebrows she could see her baby again. That was how he'd looked at balloons during his first birthday party, how he'd looked at the backyard the morning he went to make mud pies, how he'd looked at her when he came home from the hospital even though his eyes couldn't look anymore.

A few minutes later, May saw the gate swing open. Two short people with blond hair popped through, their bouncy limbs like the sound of popcorn, one wearing a long-sleeved dark green shirt and carrying a stick, the other in a colorful short-sleeved shirt and swinging a backpack. May felt like he might bubble over—he couldn't wait to touch his kids, to tell them everything, to see them move, to share the story of how the bandages came off, to tell them about the close calls on the highway. He swung open the door.

"Hey!" he said, spreading his arms.

"Hi, Dad," they said, dropping their stuff, rushing past May, and scrambling upstairs to play. He hadn't even had the chance to look at their faces. Ori Jean and Jennifer roared with laughter, but no one laughed louder than May. He went to the bottom of the stairs and called up.

"Hey! I can see! Come back down here! I want to check you guys out!"

Carson came down first. He sat in May's lap at the dining room table, grinning and looking into his father's new brown eye. May put his face just a few inches from his son's. He'd always heard that Carson had deep blue eyes and Wyndham pale blue eyes, and he wanted to see what these blues were all about.

Carson held still for his father, which allowed May to absorb the color of his eyes, a blue different from navy or the sky, a textured blue, a thermal blue, a Carson blue. May kept gazing into his son's eyes, their noses almost touching, marveling at the glint of light that danced atop the color. He'd heard forever about the sparkle in a person's eye, about how eyes could appear to smile and even sing, only he'd never been able to fathom it, a body part with its own personality—did elbows sing?—but there in Carson's eyes he could see it, a flash here and a twinkle there, a slightly new eye with every blink, an eye that looked alive as it moved to connect with his own.

"Your blue talks," he said.

May moved his eye to Carson's face. Ordinarily, he didn't touch people's faces—it was too invasive, too personal—but this was his son sitting in his lap so he had at it, ruffling Carson's hair, flapping his ears, stroking his nose, scrunching his lips. Again, the touch seemed to electrify the visual image and make it easier to understand. Now he could see that the insides of Carson's ears were a bit pinker than the edges, that his hair was more consistently blond than Jennifer's, and that his face looked as delicate as it had always felt, a seven-year-old's face. Then, near Carson's nose, May made a discovery.

"Carson, you have freckles," he said.

Jennifer strained to hold back tears.

No one had told May that Carson had freckles. He gazed at the soft brown dots, trying to touch them but feeling nothing but skin—what an amazing thing to see something that could not be touched!—and falling in love with them because they were part of his son, feeling the luckiest man to have the chance, seven years into adoring his son, to discover a new bit to adore on top of it all.

Carson smiled at his dad. His mouth lit up mostly white.

"Hey!" May said. "There's a hole in there!"

"That's my missing tooth!" Carson said, putting his finger on the dark spot. "Right there!"

May put his finger on the hole as Ori Jean cackled with laughter in the background.

"Carson, go upstairs and get some of the pictures you've drawn," May said. "I'd love to see your artwork."

Carson scrambled off his dad's lap just as Wyndham raced in to replace him. May went directly to his eyes, which were a lighter, softer, more liquid shade than his brother's.

"So that's pale blue," May said. "They're beautiful, Wyndham."

May moved to Wyndham's hair, which was nearly as white as Ori Jean's. He could not get over the idea that each of his family members was called blond when there were such different colors on top of their heads.

May ran his hands over Wyndham's face. He searched for freckles but found none.

"You don't have freckles," May said.

"Nope!" Wyndham said.

"Okay, run upstairs and get some cool stuff to show me."

Wyndham leaped off his father's lap and bolted up the stairs, nearly colliding with Carson, who was shooting back down with an armful of artwork and picture books.

"Here's a painting I made," Carson said, jumping into May's lap.

May bent forward and put his eye near the large construction paper.

"That's excellent, Carson," May said. "It's got really nice colors—the yellow is fantastic. But what does it show?"

Carson took his father's hands, as he always did when he wanted May to see something, and moved them over the paint.

"The yellow part is a flower," Carson said.

He showed May other drawings—of a stone man, a pumpkin, and a face. May could not identify any of them. Carson didn't care.

After showing his paintings, Carson put an oversized picture book of animals on the kitchen table. He opened to the first page.

"Do you know what that is?" Carson asked.

May studied the picture. He could perceive the shape and the colors, and the image looked sharp to him, but he could not identify what the picture represented.

"It's an animal," Carson hinted.

May looked for legs and, after several seconds, found equal-looking parts that protruded from a central mass.

"Well, it looks like it has four legs, so maybe it's a dog," he said.

"Oh, no," Carson said, shaking his head. "That's a bear."

"Why is it a bear? What's the difference?" May asked.

"It's husky, it's got short ears . . . and, um . . . it's got thick fur."

May studied the photo.

"Okay, yeah, I can see some of that."

Wyndham streaked to the table and jumped on May's lap alongside his brother.

"What's this one?" Wyndham asked, flipping ahead several pages.

Again, May could not discern the particular animal, or even that it was an animal at all. It took him several seconds to figure out which part of the picture was the animal and which part the back-ground, or even to determine that the animal was right side up. But the most striking part about try-ing to identify these creatures was the idea that they were somehow flattened out on the page, and that seemed true no matter what angle they were shown from, and that mystified him because every object he'd ever experienced he had experienced in three dimensions.

"I don't know what this one is," May said. "Is it a cat?"

The boys laughed hard. Wyndham nearly fell off May's lap.

"No!" Wyndham said. "It's an elephant!"

May laughed as hard as they did. Carson showed him the trunk, the fat tummy, and the floppy ears, and explained that it was a side view of an elephant. May could not conceive how that was possible—in his mind, an animal experienced from the side should show only one ear, but in this pic-ture he could see part of the other floppy ear, too. How could that be?

The boys showed him another animal. May worked hard to assemble the clues, thinking about why part of the picture showed something very long and slender and part showed something rounder and bumpier, while all the parts had brown patches. He ran through the catalog of animals he had felt that might have those kinds of parts, but he could not match any to the image before him, so he thought about the concept of long—what kind of animal has something long?—and finally made his guess.

"Is this the giraffe?" he asked.

"Yes!" the boys exclaimed, laughing. May was happy to get it right. But he also felt the first twinge of frustration with his vision—why couldn't he just see the giraffe?—and the thought wisped past him that this could not be the way people really see—it couldn't be this much effort—and he wondered, for just a moment before returning to his kids' laughter and questions, how long it would take him to get better at this.

Wyndham opened a shoe box and reached inside.

"Here, Dad, this is a dragonfly," he said, placing the insect on the table. It was still alive.

May put his eye just inches from the insect. He was astonished to see that the wings were as big as the body—he'd always imagined a dragonfly to be just slightly larger than a housefly.

"This thing is huge!" he said.

"Look at this!" Carson said, pulling out a praying mantis. May touched the insect, lightly stroking its antennae and legs and delighting in its twitching motions.

"He's really delicate looking, even more than he feels," May said. "I don't want to break him."

The boys belly-laughed, then sprung off May's knees and charged upstairs to retrieve more things to put in front of him: a Lego theme park, comic books, Hot Wheels cars, a basketball—anything they could find. The next twenty minutes were a lightning storm of stair dashing and guessing games. May loved watching them run. Motion was easy to see. Joyful motion was beautiful to see.

Soon enough, the boys wanted to know if May could read. They found a book with big letters on the cover and put it in front of him.

"Do you know what this letter is?" Carson asked, pointing to a word.

May studied the first letter. He knew how letters felt from handling his kids' wood-block letters, and from using an Opticon years ago, a machine that raised a series of 144 pins into letter shapes on the finger as the user moved its optical sensor across a printed page.

"That's a **P**," he said.

"Yep," Carson said. "Okay, what's this?"

"Is that an **R**?"

"No, it's an **A**!"

May got the next three letters right. But by the time he'd come to the last letter, **Y**, he could not remember the first three, forcing him to start again. It took a full minute before he put the word **party** together. He was astonished that reading a

simple word required so much work. But that concern didn't last long. He was too busy loving his role
as his kids' favorite new toy.

Now that Carson and Wyndham had shown May
every object inside the house, they set out to show
him the rest of the world outside. They suggested a
walk through the schoolyard and to University Mall,
a scenic route—and one that led to Fluffy's, their
favorite doughnut shop. The family put on jackets
and thanked Ori Jean for starting dinner.

May was just a step out the back gate when the
kids asked if he could see some flowers. He bent
low toward the yellowish shape and put his hands
on it. He was astonished to see what his hands
could never tell him: that a so-called yellow flower
had several different yellows in it, each growing
richer as it neared the middle, with specks of green
along the way and a purple center—and yet people
simply called it a yellow flower.

The boys raced ahead to find more things to
show their dad. Though seven and five years old,
they were virtually the same size. May easily distinguished the two by the color of the clothes they
were wearing, and by Wyndham's white-blond hair.

The school playground made May talk. He
knew the area perfectly from a thousand of these
walks, so when he looked for the bathrooms he saw

a building with two bright doors exactly where he expected it to be.

"There's the bathrooms!"

He knew the concrete picnic tables to be off to the right about thirty steps. He looked in that direction and saw gray circles and rectangles.

"There's the picnic tables!"

That meant the swing set was the next thing to the right. May called that one right, too. But he stopped cold when he came to a patch of grass that looked to be a darker green than the rest of the grass around it. He thought about it for several seconds—did grass grow in different hues of green on the same field? Was this another thing that no one talked about? Then he remembered that shade was supposed to make things darker, so the dark grass he was seeing must be in the shade.

Soon the family had crossed the schoolyard and made it onto Linden Lane. May could see a dark horizontal line on the sidewalk every few steps, and when he dragged his foot across it he knew that line to be the crack in the sidewalk. He determined that the crack appeared darker not because it was a different color of cement but because the sun wasn't reaching it in the same way it reached the rest of the sidewalk . . . which meant it, too, was a shadow. He saw the same darkening cement when reaching intersections, and he realized that curbs must also appear a different color because of shadows, not because they were painted a different color. And he thought, "I'm going to have to remember all this business about shadows."

Around the block, May headed for the low-hanging tree branch his kids always warned him about. Before they could utter a word, he ducked under it without breaking his stride.

"Whoa! Cool!" the boys exclaimed. May seemed a bit astonished himself.

Down the street, Carson pointed overhead and asked, "Dad, do you know what that is?"

May saw a red shape over Carson's head.

"That's probably a sign for Linden Lane."

"Nope. Try again."

"A 'No Parking' sign?"

"No! It's a stop sign!"

May stood shocked. Stop signs were yellow. He knew they were yellow.

"No way," he said. "You're pulling my leg."

"It is, Dad!" Wyndham said.

May appealed to Jennifer.

"It's definitely a stop sign," she said.

"Where are the yellow stop signs?" he asked.

"There are none!" his kids chirped, laughing.

May could not believe it. For a lifetime he had believed stop signs to be yellow. Yellow had always seemed like it would be the brightest and most dramatic—and therefore the safest—color. School-buses were yellow, his traffic safety sign from fourth grade was yellow. So stop signs had to be yellow.

May still was trying to reconcile red with stop signs when he came across another curious object. He touched it and immediately recognized it as a fire hydrant. And yet the hydrant was yellow!

"I thought fire hydrants were red!" he exclaimed. "What's going on?"

The boys laughed again.

"A lot of them are red," Carson explained. "But sometimes they're yellow."

"This is going to be a lot of work," May thought.

He spent the rest of the walk trying to keep up with his sons' rapid-fire questions. They wanted to know if he could see this newspaper box, that gas station sign, those red berries. All of it was thrilling to May, all of it was wondrous, and all of it was new. But it was also everywhere and all at once, and as they neared their house he was eager to go inside and take a break from the excitement, to be in a place where he could close his eyes. Sliding open the kitchen door, he was greeted by the smell of Ori Jean's special meat loaf, and it comforted him because he knew automatically, in his heart, what it was.

With Josh by his side, May made his way to the master bathroom. He was overdue. Since boyhood, he had urinated while standing unless he was in another's home, where he was less familiar with the layout. This time, like every other time, he looked straight ahead. It wouldn't occur to him to glance downward for another few days.

May washed his hands, also without looking, walked into his bedroom, and fell backward onto the bed. He closed his eyes. Instantly, his body exhaled, the kind of "Ahhh . . ." that came when removing his ski boots after a full day on the slopes. And he had this thought: "Oh, my gosh. Is this really all the same day? Did I wake up this morning totally blind?" He reached for the radio and turned on NPR—he needed a reminder that the rest of the world was still out there. While the reporter spoke reassuringly about some foreign conflict, May disappeared between wakefulness and sleep. The next sound he heard was Jennifer's voice calling him to dinner.

It had been hours since May had eaten, so he was ready to dig in. He looked at the colorful plates in front of him and tried to figure out if the designs on top were food or decorations. He found his fork and pushed it toward the biggest shape, which he took to be the meat loaf. When he touched it he knew that he was right. And yet the meat loaf was brown colored, not red, which was strange since he knew that meat loaf was made from red meat. He

brought a bite to his mouth and saw the fork closing in on him, and he wondered, "How did I aim
before I could see?"

Reds, whites, greens, and yellows offered themselves for May's consumption. He'd rarely considered a food's color, yet here it was, each with a kind
of built-in visual advertisement. He picked up his
glass of milk and studied it. The liquid looked bright
white from the top but darker and more opaque
from the side, and this idea seemed a bit unreal to
him, that the same milk might be different whites
depending on one's vantage point.

"May I have more milk, please, Dad?" Wyndham asked.

May looked around and found a shape that
looked to be a likely candidate. He reached for the
milk carton, picked it up, and passed it to his son.

"Oh, my," Jennifer said under her breath. "Oh,
gosh. That was amazing."

She looked across the table at her husband. He
smiled as he watched himself push a cherry tomato
around on his plate. It hadn't occurred to her that
he still hadn't looked much at her face or his children's faces. All she knew was that she was proud of
this man, and that her sons were watching what it
meant to go out and try.

With their last bit of dessert, Carson and Wyndham knew they were in trouble.

"Dad, we have a lot more stuff to show you," Carson said.

"Yeah, I know where there's a spider," Wyndham said.

"Nice try," May said. "Bedtime does not change just because I can see. Get going."

The boys dropped their heads and trudged upstairs. May followed a few minutes later to tuck them in.

To May, the floor of the bedroom his sons shared might as well have been the surface of a new planet. Wherever he looked, a curious stew of colorful shapes melded into the beige carpeting, forming a cacophonous chasm between the door and their brown wooden bunkbed. May knew that he must be looking at the same sprawl of toys, balls, electric cords, art projects, clothes, and backpacks that he ordered put away every night, so he set out to see if he could recognize his favorite among them, a programmable electric truck.

He squatted and stared across the landscape of the shapes. A couple of minutes later, he found one that appeared long from side to side and seemed to have wheels. He reached to touch it. Instantly, he knew he'd found his truck, its form suddenly sensible to his eye, its red cab a revelation.

"I found it," he said. "It's red."

May loved this truck because it had buttons on the back that could be pushed to program its movements: go left, honk, turn around, and so on. May scanned the truck for those buttons. Near the rear he saw several small white globs.

May began to tap in instructions. A moment later, the truck's motor whirred and it began to move. He watched as it turned left, just as he'd instructed, then right, as he'd instructed, and as it went into a figure eight May saw beauty in its motion, not just for the elegant shapes it was carving out, but because he had made those shapes happen for his eye.

"Time to clean up in here," he said to the boys, then watched them move about the room picking up colorful shapes. A tall lamp in the corner lit the room—there was no overhead light—providing superior contrast between the objects he was trying to see and their backgrounds. On the other side of the room, where it was darker, objects seemed to blend into their surroundings.

Their room picked up, the boys changed into their pajamas and climbed into their bunkbed. May turned off the light, took out his guitar, and sang them a song. In five minutes they were out cold. May walked to their beds and kissed them good night. He never thought twice about being able to find them in the dark.

Now exhausted, May and Jennifer agreed to retire for the night. On his way to the bedroom, May saw a blond carpet on the floor in front of him. He knew there was no carpet there, so he bent down to examine it. The carpet turned toward him and panted. May stood up and stepped over the blond mass.

"Hey, Jen!" he said. "I just stepped over Josh!"

May had stepped on his dog countless times since they had teamed up. Though beautifully trained, Josh had an uncanny off-duty knack for plopping himself down wherever the notion struck him. Avoiding him seemed like a big deal for both of them.

May waited while Jennifer washed up for bed, then took his turn in the bathroom. He flipped on the light and began to look into the mirror. He'd felt conspicuous doing this in Goodman's office, but with privacy he was free to really look. He stared at the man in the mirror and again was struck by the tallness of the fellow who stared back at him, and it startled him that he hadn't realized how tall he was all these years, that this must be the visual equivalent of hearing one's own voice on a tape recorder for the first time.

He stepped closer and, in the way a radio station becomes clear as it's tuned in, the man looking back at him grew more distinct, he suddenly possessed more details, more clarity; there was more to him. May stepped back and the man in the mirror again became more general, a mass of shape and color that was more John Doe than Mike May. He played with this changing fellow for a minute, back and forth, closer and farther, tuning the radio in and out, until he felt the confidence to really lean in and look, and when he did that a bushelful of gossipy details spoke back to him. Blemishes, wrinkles, freckles, a mole, the gray in his beard—it all struck him as intensely personal, and it occurred to him that if he could read these stories on his face then others could, too, and he backed away and thought to himself, "Enough of that." He could not get over the idea that, for all these years, so much of him had been hanging out there for people to see, to simply like or dislike as they pleased.

Now safely distanced from the details, he raised his arm and moved it around, watching an identical arm copy that motion in the mirror. He took his hand and, relying solely on its reflection, tested how close he could move it toward his head without touching his hair. He never grew tired of turning sideways and watching the man in the mirror turn away from him.

The sight of his hands in the mirror intrigued May, so he looked down for a firsthand inspection. At arm's length, he could see the general shape of a hand and fingers, but as he drew it closer to his eye the veins and wrinkles emerged, and he wondered, "Are those lines a good thing?" A moment later he'd found his toothbrush. He posed from several angles while watching himself brush his teeth in the mirror. Then he closed his eyes to see if he could find a visual memory of what he'd just seen. Even with his eyes closed, he felt like he could see the toothbrush.

May went into the bedroom. Jennifer sat on the bed, held the back of his head in her hand, and reached in to apply medicine to his eye. Then they pulled each other close and hugged. One of them said, "What a day. Who would have thought . . ." But before the sentence was done they were both sound asleep.

A series of vertical lines lay across May's eye as he awoke in the morning. He knew he was looking at the ceiling, so he thought about why a ceiling might have lines drawn on it. He tapped Jennifer, who was just waking up herself.

"Jen, is that a heater vent up there?"

Jennifer rubbed her eyes and looked toward where May was pointing.

"Yes, sweetie. It's great that you can see that."

May looked around the room. Everything was still there; yesterday hadn't been a dream—it was still happening, right where it had left off. He tried to remember if he had dreamed during the night, but he couldn't remember a thing.

Yawning, May walked into the bathroom and examined himself in the mirror, this time without his clothes. Jennifer entered a moment later. She, too, was undressed. Hustle-bustle boy noises echoed from the kitchen, where Ori Jean was helping Carson and Wyndham get ready for school. Jennifer stood next to May, shoulder to shoulder, and they looked at their naked reflection in the mirror, neither moving nor saying a word for several seconds, arms and hands at their sides, Jennifer's skin a golden brown, May's a pale white, the gentle rise and fall of their chests distinctly visible to May's eye, each of them with the same calm body, each taking in the whole of the people in front of them rather than any individual parts, each realizing that they appeared to be a single person if they looked at their reflection in just the right way.

Jennifer leaned over, kissed her husband on the cheek, and left the bathroom. May stepped into the shower and turned on the water. Glistening strings flew from the showerhead onto his neck and chest, exploding on contact and throwing dots of clear wet shrapnel before his eyes. He looked toward the showerhead and could see the tiny holes from which the water flowed, a kind of living metal flower, and he watched those holes spray until the room seemed to start swirling gray in front of him. He reached out to touch the swirl and his hand went right through it, and he stood there for a moment with his arm inside this buzzing dull color until it hit him that he was seeing steam. And for the next two minutes he watched the steam, a magnificent, evolving phenomenon he believed he could look at forever, one that no one could have fully explained to him, this idea that something could be there and not be there at the same time, that one could see something clearly and yet put his hand right through it.

May reached for his shampoo. Ordinarily, he would have patted around to find it by touch, careful not to knock over Jennifer's countless other bath products. He knew that the shampoo came in a blue bottle. He saw the blue and took it. Vision like that was power.

After he dried off, May went to his closet to select his clothes. He found a pair of pants and a shirt he knew would match—most of his neutral wardrobe did—and looked to see if the colors were pleasing together, as he imagined people meant when they said that clothes matched. It all looked smooth to him.

In the kitchen, his boys abandoned their toast and rushed to put a cereal box in his hand, asking if he could read its name. The letters were big, which helped, but he couldn't read any of them instantly. He traced some with his index finger, perceived others as attached to each other, and struggled especially with those that were lowercase. Still, he identified the big first letter, an **R**, added in some deductive reasoning, and read his first two words: Raisin Bran. The boys cheered and ran to the pantry, pulling out all the other brands of cereal and asking their father to read those. May spelled out the words letter by letter, but again, by the time he'd reached the last letter, he'd often forgotten the first few, a source of great amusement to his boys.

As he did on most mornings, May walked his sons to school. But for their clothing and different shades of blond, he could not tell them apart. At the schoolyard, some of the moms noticed that May was looking around. They knew that he'd undergone surgery and asked if he could see.

"Well, I see you're wearing a nice red sweater and have blue jeans on," May said.

"That's right! Wow!"

"And I can see that you're both dazzlingly thin."

"You should teach our husbands how to see!"

In fact, May could discern that the women were petite because he could see them next to a row of others. And he thought, "Man, people really do come in all sizes."

Back home, May went to work for the first time since his surgery. He returned business calls, typed e-mails, and didn't bother trying to read his computer monitor—it was much easier to keep listening to his screen-reading software, as he had for years. In between, he described his new vision to Kim Burgess, a junior at UC-Davis whom he'd recently hired as an assistant. Burgess had long blond hair and, by all accounts, was a knockout. May found himself smitten by her hair and lost himself watching it cascade to the side when she answered the phone and fly back when she pulled it into a ponytail. He could see Burgess's mannerisms, postures, gestures, and it was all in front of him, all there for the taking by his eye, for as long as he chose to look.

During lunch at the backyard patio table, May delighted in his ability to use vision alone to reach for the milk carton and find his napkin after it fell to the ground. He could easily distinguish between Burgess and Jennifer based on their hair lengths and the color of their clothes. When the women spoke their heads bobbed, their lips flapped, their hands gestured. This bedlam at once amused and distracted him, and try as he might he could not keep track of what they were saying so long as their faces ran spastic like that, and he wondered, even as he continued to smile pleasantly at their stories, how they could keep track themselves of even a word that came from such facial commotion.

Ready to return to work, May stretched and looked up at the sky.

"Hey, Jen, what's that white thing moving up in that tree?" he asked.

Jennifer looked where he was pointing. She saw nothing. Finally, in a distant and tall tree, she saw the flapping white wisp of a kite's tail. She could barely make it out herself—from this distance it appeared the size of a thread.

"Wow, you can really see that?" she asked.

"Yep," May said.

Jennifer looked again at the tiny piece of the kite. A minute ago her husband had had to press his eye against the milk carton to read the letter **M**. Now he had spotted a bit of fabric in a distant tree. She had believed that things couldn't get more interesting than they had been yesterday. She was beginning to think she was wrong.

Late that afternoon, five-year-old Wyndham poked his head into May's office.

"Come play ball with me, Dad!"

May's heart raced. Many of his happiest days had been spent chasing, throwing, and kicking balls. Yet during the year he'd contemplated new vision, he'd never imagined that he'd see one.

"That would be great," he said.

Wyndham ran and got a red-and-white soccer ball, then joined his father in the backyard. They stood about fifty feet apart. Wyndham placed the ball on the ground.

"Ready, Dad?"

"Ready."

Wyndham kicked the ball on the ground. Instantly, May saw it rolling toward him, its bright white shape a perfect trill against the brilliant green grass below, and without thinking or planning he stepped to the left, shot out his foot, and trapped the ball under his shoe. For a moment, May simply stood there, astonished.

"Nice play, Dad!" Wyndham shouted. "Now kick it back to me."

Jennifer watched from the kitchen window as May backed up a step, looked down at the ball, then swung his leg forward, connecting perfectly with the ball and sending it hurtling back toward his son, who barely needed to move to trap it himself.

Wyndham kicked a few more on the ground. May moved and stopped them all. Then Wyndham got a new idea.

He took a big approach this time and sent the ball flying not on the ground but in the air, off to May's right. Instinctively, May moved right, lifted his leg, and knocked the ball down.

"Whoa! That was so cool!" May exclaimed. "Do more like that, Wyndham!"

His son obliged. May knocked them all down. Then, without either of them saying a word, they arrived at a new idea together. Wyndham placed the ball on the grass, took a couple of steps back, then ran forward, kicking the ball even higher to his father. May streaked back and to his right, stuck out his arms, and clenched his hands around the ball.

"Yes! Great catch, Dad! Awesome!"

May stopped and looked at his hands. The ball was still there, bright white with little red designs, in his control, like it belonged there, like they had rendezvoused from a long time ago.

"I caught it," May said.

He asked Wyndham to kick more. Soon May was catching four out of every five his son sent streaking his way, including some that sailed over his head or required a running leap to reach. Even when he missed, he ran after the ball like he was four years old again. For an hour, he and Wyndham lost themselves in the game, in keeping score, and in each other. Kids had never taken it easy on May when he'd played sports as a boy, and as he made another running catch of yet another difficult kick, he felt like the best part about this game was that Wyndham never thought to, either.

That evening, after his kids had gone to bed and the dinner dishes had been dried, May and Jennifer retired to their bedroom. She turned to the bathroom to wash up. He reached for her hand.

"I want to look at you," he said.

Jennifer stepped forward, took May's hands in hers, and kissed him, first lightly on the cheek, then more passionately, on the lips.

"I'm really nervous," she said. "But I want you to look at me."

She unbuttoned May's shirt, pulled it off his back, and let it fall to the floor behind him. She pulled her own shirt over her head, unhooked her bra, and let it fall to the floor, a white swoop he could see as clearly as the soccer ball. She lifted herself on her toes and leaned into May's ear.

"Stay here," she said.

Jennifer walked to the far wall and turned on the ceiling lights, then turned on the bedside lamps until the room glowed intensely bright. The light helped May find his clock radio, which he used to play some music. Jennifer pulled down her jeans. A moment later she was fully naked. And, she felt, fully bright.

"Are you completely undressed?" he asked.

"Yes," Jennifer said, crossing her arms over her breasts. "It's just me now."

May pushed off the rest of his clothes.

"This is great," he said. "I finally get to gawk at you."

Jennifer laughed and felt her face flush. She climbed into their bed and lay flat on her back.

"Okay, I'm ready," she said.

May knelt beside the bed and began to draw near for a closer look. Jennifer pulled the covers over her body and up to her chin.

"It's cold in here," she said.

"If I have to go under the covers I'll need a flashlight, and I think we're out of batteries. That really leaves me no choice."

Jennifer slowly crept out, pushed the sheets to the foot of the bed, and lay back flat, arms at her sides, legs pressed together. It had been a long time since she'd felt so nervous and aroused all at once.

Already, May found himself in a battle to keep his hands from Jennifer's body. Her shyness only electrified that impulse. But he wanted to see what vision delivered by itself, how this most glorious object in the world, a woman, entered his world when he touched her with eyes alone.

May walked on his knees toward the head of the bed. Suddenly, he could see Jennifer's streaked blond hair, a different species than she owned while dressed and washing dishes, no longer well mannered and patient but swooped across the pillow like a fanned deck of cards, its blond and gold streaks a call of abandon into which it felt like he could fall in a hundred different places. He moved his glance to her forehead. There, lost between her eyes, he saw a stray lock of blond hair, innocent to the idea that it had been separated from all the rest, a private accent mark even his wife couldn't see was there.

"Look at me," May said, still on his knees beside the bed.

Jennifer turned her head to the right. Now he could see her mouth—the light vertical lines etched into her lips, the hills that fell to a valley at the center of her top lip, a reddish pink unlike any color he'd seen. She began to breathe a bit more heavily, which caused her lips to part just slightly, a distance that looked to May wholly different from a smile, a distance that, when combined with the sound of her breath, looked sexy to him.

Jennifer tucked some fallen hair behind her head. May leaned in close.

"You have smaller ears than I thought," he said. "Why didn't you tell me before we got married that you had small ears?"

"I do not!" Jennifer laughed, fluffing her hair back over her ears.

May climbed onto the bed and knelt beside his wife, who remained on her back. He put his eye to her neck.

"I can see the hollow of your throat," he said. "Remind me to tickle that later."

"Michael! Oh, gosh, no tickling! I'm feeling wiggly enough already!"

"Hey, what's this?" May asked, pointing to a dark spot.

"That's a birthmark," Jennifer said. "I've told you about that a million times, remember?"

May did not remember, but judged it best not to admit it and keep looking. He lay on his side, stretched out, and set out to finally see what he'd been imagining, conceptualizing, and contemplating since age twelve: a woman's breasts.

He looked toward the middle of Jennifer's chest for the dark circles of her areolas, but found them instead lying to either side.

"That happens when you're past forty and you've had kids . . ."

"You're beautiful," May interrupted. His hands moved toward her breasts and finally he was powerless to stop them as they traced exploratory circles near her nipples and moved underneath for a fuller touch. Jennifer breathed deeply.

"What do you see?" she asked.

"It's incredible how the color changes from the nipple to the areola to the breast. There's so much going on. And I can see that your nipple is erect."

"You're looking too closely!" Jennifer said. "I feel like a cereal box!"

May continued to caress her breasts, molding, lifting, sculpting, and kneading. Jennifer fought the urge to dive back under the covers—she had never been inspected like this—but as she watched him hit and miss and gasp and exclaim, as she watched him try to understand her, she knew she was watching a kind of birth, and she tried to imagine the kind of love and courage it took to allow another person to watch you being born.

May slid his arm under Jennifer's neck and she snuggled into him. A single word now, a brush of the hand, even a hot breath would have pushed the moment into intimacy. Neither of them said anything. May still had places to explore. Turning over, he crawled backward until he was straddling Jennifer's waist with his knees.

"What do you see now?" she asked.

"It's amazing. I see your ribs. It's obvious what they are. Wow. Ribs."

May moved to Jennifer's waist and hips. Here she felt especially confident. In her forties, things weren't quite as perfect as they used to be, but she'd been working out, eating California healthy, and feeling better and more confident than ever in her body.

"I'm turning on my side now," she said. "That should really show you my shape."

Jennifer rolled onto her side. May was not yet fully able to direct his eye itself, so he began to move it over her curves like a roller coaster car, dipping from the top of her ribs down to the valley of her small waist, then slingshotting back up through the area's highest peak, her hip bone.

"Oh, man, Jen, you really are curvy!" May said. "This must be what the panorama looks like at Kirkwood!"

Jennifer laughed and fidgeted and laughed some more. May ran his hands over the same curves his eyes had just traversed. At the same time, he used his vision to inspect the curling skin twists of her belly button, the wisps of baby blond hair on her arms, the turn of her stomach, and a birthmark of which she most definitely had not informed him. Then he stepped back and took in the whole of her body, and it made sense to him; he didn't have to assemble her parts the way he had to add up letters in order to read. He thrilled to this multitiered access. Often, during lovemaking, he had wished for another hand. But here, with an eye that could touch anywhere and everywhere at once, he felt he'd been given the gift of as many more hands as he desired.

May crawled backward on his knees until he reached Jennifer's bikini line.

"Okay, I'm going to look at everything," he said. "I'm going to really look."

"Okay . . . I think," Jennifer replied.

May put his eye just above Jennifer's private parts. She strained not to wiggle or laugh or jump him.

"Well," May said, "I guess you really are a blonde."

"Michael!" Jennifer protested.

"I can see your tan line, too. Even though it's still winter I can see where it is."

May put his hands on Jennifer's knees and gently pushed them apart. She did not resist. He knelt in between and maneuvered his head for a very close and well-lit view. He resisted all urges to touch and used his vision to see what he could discern, corkscrewing his head into various positions, allowing the light to play off the most interesting parts, watching how delicate areas merged into other areas announced only by subtle shifts in color. Part of Jennifer wanted to run away and lock herself in the bathroom; the other part wanted to pull her husband close and forget about all this looking stuff. Instead, she remained still in just the way he needed, telling herself, "Just stay a visual object. Just stay a visual object . . ."

After several minutes, May worked his way down Jennifer's legs, continuing his spoken stream-of-consciousness play-by-play, providing insight on body vagaries even she had forgotten. Before this day, no one had told her she had cute knees.

By the time May reached Jennifer's toes, the couple had run empty on restraint. Jennifer pulled him to her chest, they began kissing, and the rest followed with a charge and passion that startled them both. Occasionally, Jennifer peeked to see if May was checking himself out—after all, his body was as new to him visually as was hers. But he never seemed to look. To May's thinking, it would have been a waste of resources to inspect himself; why squander his vision when there was a beautiful woman in front of his eye?

As their lovemaking continued, neither looked at anything at all, preferring to close their eyes, breathe deeply into each other's ears, and just feel. Then, when a crescendo began for both of them, May opened his eyes, and for a moment he could see that Jennifer's eyes were still closed, and she looked dear and vulnerable—should he be looking at her when she didn't know to look back?—but he didn't think for long because a moment later she opened her eyes and gazed directly into his, and it felt to him that her eyes had heard his eyes calling, that eyes could really do that, and now neither of them was willing to break the gaze, they just stayed locked into each other, and as the moment reached its peak Jennifer's eyes seemed changed to May, they were no longer just a color and a shape and a movement, they were a voice, and that voice seemed to say, "I'm with you."

May slept a bit late the next morning. By the time he reached the kitchen, Carson and Wyndham were just about out the door. May poured himself a cup of coffee and sat at the table. He looked first at Carson, who was pulling on his backpack, then at Wyndham, who was fidgeting with a red baseball cap. Jennifer asked if he might like a bagel, but May didn't hear her. Josh nudged his hand, but he didn't feel it. May just kept looking and looking at Wyndham. Since losing his vision, May had felt himself just a whisper from being able to see the red hat that his father had given him for their hunting trip; it was always just a hairsbreadth beyond his grasp— there but not there. He had asked himself, "Would I see that red hat if somehow I were made to see?" Now, as Wyndham waved good-bye, May could see that red hat, and as he waved back, it seemed for a moment like he could see himself, too.

CHAPTERTEN

Not one of Sendero's creditors cared that May could see. His voice-mail in-box was full. He spent day three of vision digging out.

That evening, he and Jennifer drove to a theater in Sacramento. A friend named Michelle and her husband, Clifford, had purchased third-row seats for the musical **Rent**. May was curious to see the play. He was very curious to see Michelle.

The couples met in the lobby and reached to embrace. May knew from previous hugs that Michelle was tall and curvy, so he readied himself to sneak a peek at whatever might be visible in close. But when she pulled him near, his eye raced up, not down.

"Whoa! You have red hair!" he said.

"That's true," Michelle replied, laughing.

"Do you make your hair that color or does it come that way?" May asked.

Michelle laughed some more.

Rent seemed built for new eyes. The actors came wrapped in colorful costumes, ricocheted off massive props, and matched their arms and legs to the music. May tried to count the number of dancers in the chorus line, but he struggled to keep track, especially when they were moving. With every shift in position they appeared a different picture to him, forcing him to restart his count each time.

It was no easier for him to follow the plot. When he looked at something, entire chunks of storyline escaped him. He simply could not pay attention to story—or to anything else, it seemed—while there was vision going on. And in this theater there was always vision going on.

Halfway through the show, May began to feel his mind lag.

"Man, this is exhausting," he thought. But he didn't want to miss a moment, so he told his eye to stay open, and a few minutes later he used his fingers to hold it open. Every shift onstage required a fresh analysis, and there were shifts every second, and it occurred to him that there were shifts every second outside the theater, too, out there in life. A few moments later he leaned back and closed his eyes, and this time he didn't fight it. The world went calm again. He could breathe.

Walking toward the theater exit, May felt as if he'd been through one of his college wrestling matches. In the lobby, hugging Michelle, he thought nothing about her curves or neckline. Instead, he told himself, "I know I'll get used to this."

Only ten days remained until the technology conference at which May would launch his portable GPS system for the blind. He spent his days immersed in preparation, his nights as the new toy for his kids. In between, he took his vision out for some test drives.

Dining with his family at a local Italian restaurant, he deduced that the white shape in the center of the table must be the basket of bread, the brownish-red thing that hovered nearby his glass of wine. He reached for each of them with the nonchalance of James Bond. During appetizers, he spotted a slice of lemon and a sprig of parsley haunting the edge of his plate. Finally, he understood why cooks put inedible but colorful food in one's meal. Even better, he was able to push the intruders to the side, a victory in a decades-long war he'd been waging against garnishes. Never again, he thought, will I gag on parsley.

The server delivered a portion of wonder with Carson's spaghetti. Steam climbed from the plate and swirled around his face, fleeing when the boy made blowing sounds. Strands of spaghetti danced in midair before being sucked into the splotch of darkness May knew must be Carson's mouth. He didn't say anything to his son about that style of eating spaghetti, but he thought, "I'm not sure I like how that looks—it doesn't seem very graceful—

though no one else seems to mind, so I guess it's okay."

At home, May admired the ease with which he found the newspaper at the end of his driveway, and reveled in the power that came with reaching cleanly for one's coffee cup. At dusk, he could walk to the field behind his house and take in the sunset, which appeared beautiful to him not just for its melding of colors, but for its high contrast against the pale sky.

One morning, while urinating, May heard himself missing the bowl. He looked down and saw a yellow stream. He shut his eyes and turned his head, straining to maintain his aim even as he told himself not to look. Seeing his urine felt to him like touching it, and he didn't know anyone who wanted to do that.

Around the same time, he visited a nearby medical office so that doctors could check his cyclosporine levels. A nurse asked for his arm, swabbed it with alcohol, and slid a syringe into a vein. May watched as a thick crimson oozed into a glass tube. For a moment he couldn't connect that color to anything he knew, but as the dark red smoothed higher it hit him that this was blood in the tube, his blood, that was him climbing up that tube, and the idea that he could see such a secret and life-bearing part of him flowing away turned him faint.

"This never bothered me before," he told himself. "Stay awake. Stay here."

But as May left the doctor's office, he knew it had bothered him. And he wondered about the things in the world he'd long passed by that he was not going to pass by anymore.

A local television station got word of May's surgery and asked to send a reporter to his house. The interviewer arrived with an African-American cameraman. May had never seen a black person before. He looked at the man very closely. He did not want to stare but needed to keep seeing him. May had been raised free of racial prejudice; equality had been among his mother's fundamental principles. He had lived his life presuming that there must be some staggering feature or characteristic that would explain the ugly reaction by some whites to African-Americans. Yet as he looked at this man, he could not see a single distinguishing feature other than the color of the man's skin.

"Man," May thought as he sat on his couch for the interview, "the guy looks exactly the same as everyone else."

A week into vision, May's sister Diane planned a surprise visit. She would have told her brother she was coming, but that would have ruined her scheme.

On the way to Davis, Diane and her young niece, Courtney, detoured to a costume shop, where they bought a set of Groucho Marx eyeglasses, nose, and mustache. In May's driveway, Diane affixed the disguise, walked to the door, and rang the bell.

May, who had been working in his office, answered the door.

"Hi, Uncle Mike, it's Courtney!" the little girl said. Then she broke out laughing. "Can you tell who it is in that funny face?"

May figured instantly that the bigger person with Courtney must be Diane, and a moment later he deduced from Courtney's words that Diane must have arrived in disguise.

"Diane!" he said. "You haven't changed a bit!"

Everyone laughed as May took Diane into his arms. She had been the last person he'd seen before his accident.

Diane stepped back and looked at her brother. She asked if he liked the disguise, but try as he might May could not see that she was wearing one. He saw the pink of her face, the shapes where her features should be, and her hairline, but her face area didn't coalesce into any meaning for him; he couldn't read "Diane" in it any better than a layperson could read the results of an electrocardiogram. And this is how it seemed to May for all faces—they appeared clear and sharp but just laid on the page without meaning, each interchangeable with the rest.

"I'll get better at this," he told himself. "If I practice with faces I'll know them."

Diane sat on the couch and reminisced with her brother. She choked back tears as they recalled sharing bicycles and his adventure driving her Datsun 510. Then, almost offhandedly, she told May how sorry she'd always been for giving him the glass jar of powder that had exploded and blinded him.

"You didn't give me that," May said. "I climbed into the rafters and found it myself."

"What?" Diane asked.

"That's right, Diane. I absolutely did it myself. I remember it as clear as I remember yesterday. You had nothing to do with it."

For a time neither of them said anything.

"How long have you been thinking you did that?" May asked.

"Since it happened," his sister replied, tears running down her cheeks.

"And you never told me?"

"No, Michael. I've just felt so bad."

After Diane left, May pulled on a jacket for a walk to Fluffy Donuts. He considered going without his Seeing Eye dog, Josh—he could do the path to Fluffy's in his sleep—but he didn't want to abandon this important family member just because he could see. He affixed Josh's harness, and the longtime team set out for doughnuts. May even chose another route, this one less familiar, in order to observe some fresh scenery.

Early in the walk, Josh hesitated for a moment to indicate a step up. May saw no curb or step in front of them, just a smooth surface, so he disregarded Josh's signal and kept walking. A moment later his foot bashed into the curb, nearly sending him sprawling. He looked down. To his eye, the curb still appeared flat, the same color as the street.

A few minutes later, Josh hesitated to indicate stairs. May looked in front of him and saw only a series of horizontal lines painted on the street. He slowed and then, taking baby steps, approached the painted lines. When his foot fell off the first line, he knew that Josh had been right again.

The rest of the walk was spent in a struggle between May's vision and Josh's vision. Often, when Josh indicated a step or a curb or stairs, May's eye told him it could not be so, and yet Josh was right every time. But when they approached Fluffy's and Josh signaled a step down, May saw that step—that one didn't look like a line—and he wondered if that step appeared obvious to him because it was the one step along the way he had expected to be there.

Carrying a box of doughnuts under his arm, May set out for home. Again, he balked at Josh's direction. May knew that Josh could sense that something had changed with him. A dog guide feels its owner's trust through its harness; it is reassured, even comforted, when the owner takes its cues. May knelt and stroked the scruff of Josh's neck.

"You're doing a great job, Josh. I'm the one who's a little haywire now, but I'm sure we'll get this squared away before too long. I still trust you."

At home, May undid Josh's harness and gave him a bowl of water. Then he headed upstairs to see the boys, and the stairs in his house did not look flat or like lines to him at all.

The next night, May placed a call to Bryan Bashin. As May's close friend, and as someone who might benefit himself from stem cell transplant surgery, Bashin was certain to be eager for the results.

"So?" Bashin asked.

"Where do I begin?" May replied, laughing.

Bashin wanted May to gush about the new experience of vision, to provide a free-association staccato about it. But he found May a bit reticent—he seemed to talk more in snippets than stories, in stops and starts rather than torrents.

"Well, tell me about the physical details," Bashin said. "Is the cornea taking? Is your vision clear? Are you in pain? What's your drug regimen? Give me the nuts-and-bolts stuff."

"The cornea seems fine," May said. "The vision is very clear and sharp. But I need to be close to see details, sometimes really close. I'm not in any pain at all. The drugs and hassle part you wouldn't like: I'm taking eyedrops in the morning and at night to minimize the risk of infection; I take teardrops every half hour to keep the eye moist; I've gotta take the cyclosporine orally twice a day and by drops into the eye. But listen to this, Bryan. Those eye-drops I told you about, they have to be refrigerated. That means I have to bring an ice pack with me when I travel."

"Man, what a hassle!" Bashin said.

Bashin asked about the parts of May's vision that worked best. That's when May gushed, telling him about playing catch with Wyndham, about being able to find things he'd misplaced or dropped, about the colors in Carson's art projects.

"It sounds like an adventure of the highest order," Bashin said.

"Yes," May replied. "It's that trail in the forest that no one has ever been on."

"What about reading?" Bashin asked.

May fell silent for a moment.

"I know the letters, and I can read words if I really concentrate," May finally said. "But reading per se somehow isn't coming to me. I'm not sure why. It's the same with faces. I'm not sure I'm getting them, although it's hard to say because I don't really know what faces are supposed to be like. I think I just need to give it all time."

May's voice brightened.

"You know what, Bryan? I think figuring this out and giving it time might be part of the adventure, too."

———

Though May scarcely had time for coffee, he went twice a week for blood work in Davis and three times a week for checkups with Dr. Goodman in San Francisco.

Goodman would ask May to read the Snellen eye chart, the one that starts with the giant E on top. From the standard testing distance of 20 feet May could not even see the E—it simply wasn't there. When Goodman moved him closer, to within five feet of the chart, May could read the E and the next two lines. Goodman estimated May's acuity at 20/800 for uncorrected distance, meaning May could see at 20 feet what people with excellent natural vision or corrected acuity (glasses or contacts) can see at 800 feet. People are considered legally blind when their vision is 20/200 or worse.

"I know that 20/800 sounds bad," Goodman told May. "But we have patients who are 20/1,000 and are independent. They get around without a dog or cane and can see enough to do the activities of daily living on their own."

Goodman also asked May to read the lines on a handheld card. From inches away, his vision was much better, about 20/100. That result encouraged May. He did not like to do poorly on tests.

"So what's wrong with my eye?" May asked.

"There's nothing wrong with your eye," Goodman said. "In fact, it's an almost perfect eye. Optically, I'd say you're 20/40. In California, that's good enough to drive."

"I'm not sure I understand," May said.

"I'm not an expert on this," Goodman said, "but I'm pretty certain the problem is in your visual cortex."

"My brain?"

"I think so. I mean, I can see your entire optical system, and it's excellent. An eye seeing as beautifully as yours should be able to read all the way down the chart. That leaves the brain."

Goodman's thinking made sense to May. Of course it would take the brain some time to get used to seeing, especially after forty-three years of blindness. May was already excellent at some aspects of vision, like motion and color. And he'd always been a quick study. Whatever his other shortcomings, his brain had always been good. The rest of his vision would definitely come soon.

Only a week remained before May's product launch at the Cal State University–Northridge conference in Los Angeles. He worked eighteen-hour days preparing brochures, establishing prices, and fine-tuning the GPS. CSUN would be the place where the world met Sendero.

On the afternoon before the launch, Jennifer drove May and Josh to the Sacramento airport. She would join him in a day to help decorate his booth and pitch prospective customers. Inside the airport, May located the colorful tile path to the boarding gates he'd known so well underfoot. Like Dorothy on her way to Oz, he followed the winding color to his destination, which he recognized, after several seconds of study, by reading the large letter and number above the gate.

He took his customary window seat with Josh at his feet and began to look around. He'd been on hundreds of airplanes, and yet everything seemed a revelation: the speckled colors of the seats, the small white towel on the headrest, the floor lighting, the matching outfits of the flight attendants—no one had told him about any of this. What an advantage, he thought, to be able to see whether the flight attendant was addressing him or the person in front of him, and whether there was a line for the lavatory.

May fastened his seat belt as the airplane thundered to its takeoff. When the pilot signaled that it was safe to use approved electronics, May opened his laptop and started working. After a half hour in the air, he looked up from the screen.

"Wait a minute," he thought. "I can look out the window."

He turned his head to the left and put his eye against the glass. Green squares crawled by below, dissected in places by crisscrossing dark lines that reminded him of the veins he'd seen in his hand. Puffs of gray, streaked white lines, and blobby stretches of blue lay atop the sliding squares. May's mind went into action. Green was likely farmland, since the stretch from Sacramento to Los Angeles was agricultural. The dark lines could be roads or maybe rivers—yes, they might be rivers, too. The blue, since it stretched as far as he could see, was much more likely sky than water. But what about this white—could it be snow? He'd heard that it had been snowing in the Tehachapi Mountains . . .

"Excuse me," May said, turning to the woman in the seat beside him. "I just got my sight back last week after being totally blind for forty-three years. Could you help me figure out what I'm seeing?"

The woman fidgeted in her chair but said nothing. May waited several seconds. Still she didn't speak.

"Are the white lines out there mountains?" he asked.

"No, honey," the woman finally said. "That's haze."

For the next half hour, the woman provided a play-by-play so detailed and impassioned that others might have mistaken her for the person with new vision. Much of what May saw had to be reconciled with his intellect. The ground below moved by very slowly, yet he knew he was traveling at five hundred miles per hour. The green squares were tiny, yet he knew they must cover many acres. He wondered if all of this seemed odd to sighted people, too.

When the plane landed and slowed to taxi, air travel seemed a bit less strange to May. For decades, airplanes had felt like a kind of time machine to him, a box into which one stepped, waited for a few hours, and then emerged in a different place. The sight of the world passing beneath confirmed that he had gone somewhere, and that seemed a powerful feeling to him. As he gathered his bag and took Josh's harness, he hoped that the GPS he was about to unveil, the one that would announce passing streets and points of interest, would give the same kind of feeling to the blind.

Standing at baggage claim, May watched dozens of pieces of luggage snake past on the conveyor belt. He didn't rush to find his own, preferring instead to watch the mechanical parade. Many of the bags appeared melded to each other, especially if they were of similar color. He pressed his pocket-sized remote control, which activated a beeper attached to the handle of his suitcase.

"Next time," he told Josh, "I'm going to put something bright green on the handle so I don't need this beeper."

For a moment, May wondered if that meant bright green was his favorite color. But as he considered it further, he realized that it wasn't so much the green as the bright that excited him. At least for now, his favorite color was bright.

He made his way to the elevator at the Los Angeles Airport Marriott, the site of the CSUN show. When the doors opened, he stepped out and scanned the lobby area. He could see bunches of people gathered in one spot—evidence of a front desk. When he walked to the area he could see that the people had formed a line, so he took his place at the end of it. Normally, he moved forward in lines by listening to feet or by sliding his cane forward. This time, the room was noisy and he had no cane. It didn't matter. When the line moved, he saw it and moved with it. He made a mental note to tell Jennifer about this feat. Then he went to his room and crashed for the night.

In the morning, May put out water for Josh and left for the show. Before vision, he would have used his cane to navigate the hotel's network of halls, passageways, and show floor. This time, he was going solo.

May walked tentatively. He felt alien without his dog or cane, as if he'd left his hotel room without an appendage, without his arm.

"Don't worry," he told himself. "There are no drop-offs here, I know there aren't. There are no drop-offs here."

Newborn worries flooded his thinking. What if a hotel employee or guest passed by and assumed he was fully sighted and expected more of him? What if they thought his eyes looked weird? What if they saw his measured walk and wondered, "What's wrong with that guy?" What if someone approached and expected him to recognize their face or read their badge? What if blind people at the conference thought he was trying to show off?

May wanted to turn back. He wished he'd made a sign to hang around his neck that read, "I can't see perfectly. I don't mean to give that impression." He kept going.

The convention hall played a symphony on May's eye, its colorful banners, labyrinth aisles, and high-design corporate logos elbowing one another for first position in his awareness. None of it made immediate sense. The colorful shape to his right was simply a blue rectangle until he considered that it was near the floor, which meant it likely wasn't a banner; it appeared to contain some large writing, which meant it probably belonged to an exhibitor rather than to the hotel; and it bunched at the bottom, which meant it could be a decorative skirt like the one he used to cover his own show table. Or maybe it was the side of a box. Or someone's jacket. Every colorful shape demanded analysis. He yearned to touch them all.

May began to walk the aisles in search of his booth. Along the way, he spotted a series of short horizontal lines along the ground. He stopped for a moment, remembering that stairs could appear that way to him. Could there be stairs on a convention floor? He remembered that some of the more elaborate convention booths used stairs in their displays. But was he near such a booth? And would an exhibitor at a conference for people with disabilities use stairs? He stepped lightly toward the lines. The ground was flat; the lines were just a design. He looked up for a moment to settle his mind. Bright and colorful shapes and lights and twirling fans yapped back at him.

Nearing his booth, May saw people walking with canes and dogs. He had never seen a blind person before. Right away he could see what he'd known forever: that blind people moved differently. Some walked tentatively, some plodded, some outright strode; all of those styles were obvious to his eye. He enjoyed watching the ones who dodged obstacles, a strong clue that they had some useful vision.

"That's how I'll look pretty soon," he thought. "It's kind of like seeing myself in the future."

Standing tiptoe on a chair, hanging balloons and banners, Jennifer was already at work on the booth by the time May arrived. She climbed down, gave her husband a kiss, and put him to work stacking brochures. May thanked her for making the trip.

"It feels like we're a team again," Jennifer said. "It's like our bun-warmer days in Oregon."

———

The Sendero booth buzzed from the opening bell. Prospective customers, distributors, suppliers, even the media lined up to talk to May about his product. Few people pitched their wares more naturally than May did, yet he found himself nervous to greet these people. He knew that word of his surgery had spread through the so-called blind vine, so this would be the first test of the blind community's reaction to his decision, and an unflinching barometer of things to come. If these people believed he'd deserted the cause, run from the life he'd embraced, leaped at his first chance to "hang with sighty," as some called it, it could cost him his business and, equally terrible, the respect he had earned over so many years. He reached out his hand and said, "Hi, I'm Mike May. What can I tell you about Sendero?" He dreaded hearing the word "sellout" in return.

No one said it. In fact, the response seemed universally supportive, full of excitement and interest. One after another, people used words like "explore" and "curiosity," and the best part was that May sometimes couldn't tell whether they were referring to his surgery or his GPS. Congratulations flowed. By midday, not a single person, including prominent members of the powerful blindness organizations, had expressed a doubt about him, his eyesight, or Sendero.

Their faces, however, were another matter. Especially when they spoke.

Mouths flapped, eyelids flickered, heads bobbed. Faces looked battery-powered. People had calisthenic lips. This random ballet demanded interpretation, but the moment May tried to figure it out—**Why does that woman's mouth make a circle whenever she sounds surprised?**—he lost what the person was saying and then had to struggle to merge back into the talk. It occurred to him to look away slightly, just enough to avoid the commotion, but then he'd see hands gesturing, torsos rocking, feet shuffling—people talking with their bodies!—and he'd wonder, "Are those movements individual or universal? Why does he wave his hand to ask a question?" and these questions again unplugged him from the flow of the conversation.

"It's so strange," he told Jennifer during a break. "Faces are so distracting. It's like when you're talking and you hear an echo of your own voice. It's impossible to ignore that echo. Seeing someone speak is just like that for me. I feel like I have to close my eyes to hear people."

"You can close them," she said. "I'll talk to people for a while."

"No, I can't," he replied. "It's all so interesting. I don't want to miss a thing."

That afternoon, May demonstrated his product in the field. It worked flawlessly, delivering people to a hotel door, to a nearby steakhouse, wherever they wanted to go. Some went to his booth and placed orders or signed up to become distributors. He recognized many by the color of their hair or clothes, and greeted them by name before they could say hello. It was the kind of victory, he told Jennifer, that made him feel like a kid again.

Near day's end, as May prepared to close his booth, he heard the whisper of a distant and sultry land.

"Hola."

A delicate pair of hands took hold of his. At once, he knew they belonged to the wife of one of the major foreign dealers, a woman who had been attending the show—and leaving men breathless in her wake—for years. She spoke only Spanish. May had always been happy to speak it with her.

She pulled herself closer to him, their chests just inches apart. Reports about the woman's heartbreaking figure flew through his mind. He moved his eyes toward her dress and could see at once that it was low cut—the colorful fabric seemed miles to either side of her bronzed skin. He glanced further downward. A thick, dark line divided her chest. May had once studied engineering. He knew that the dark line—a shadow—was being cast by something.

"Holy smoke," he thought, "there's a lot of woman there and not a lot of clothes."

They parted and the woman began to speak, telling him how nice it was to see him, asking how he'd been. She didn't realize he could see. He tried to stammer a response, but his limited Spanish vocabulary had left him.

May continued to soak in his friend. By all accounts she was gorgeous, and as she spoke May connected her reputation with the image in front of him, and very quickly that image began to look beautiful to him. He recalled men's descriptions of her shape and that, too, now looked alluring to him. He remembered that someone had said she had the face of an angel, and though he couldn't understand her face, it also looked beautiful to him now. Since boyhood, May had understood the power of imagination and suggestion and expectation on a blind person's concept of beauty. Now, as he struggled for yet another Spanish word, he wondered if things might not work that way for the sighted, too.

By the show's end, May had taken more orders and signed more distributors. At the airport, he and Jennifer celebrated the successful launch of Sendero and the warm reception for his new vision. On the airplane, Jennifer gave the window seat to May. This time during takeoff he was already pressed close to the window, ready to watch the world move by from another new perspective.

About a month after CSUN, May took his sons to Picnic Day, the massive annual parade and celebration put on by students at the University of California–Davis. Out of town on business, Jennifer asked them to remember everything so that they could tell her stories when she returned.

The men found prime seating on a curb as the parade began to roll. A giant and skinny creature or machine or robot wobbled down the road, its top disappearing and reappearing from the trees.

"Wow! What's that?" May asked his boys.

"That's a stilt walker!" Carson replied.

May began to ask for more details when a flailing shape streaked by atop a circle, stopped, then went backward on the same circle, parts thrusting to all sides.

"What's that?"

"That's the unicycle guy!" the boys shouted.

"Is he waving at us?"

"No!" The boys laughed. "He's balancing!"

For the next hour, an assembly line of mysterious creatures passed May's eye: hula hoopers, tall clowns wearing umbrella hats, short kids holding big balloons, men wearing animal costumes, animals wearing sunglasses, Native Americans in traditional clothing, posters written in tall Chinese characters, horses with writing on their bodies. And floats. Lots of floats.

May yearned to understand these magnificent color-shapes, but where was he to begin? This was not a hotel room, where he could deduce that the dark round shape near the sink was a coffeemaker. This was not his living room, where he could reason that the rectangular shape on the table was the TV remote. He stared at each passing curiosity. Which part should he look at first? Which parts were important and which could be ignored? Which parts would give him a clue? By the time he attempted to answer these questions, a new object had paraded itself before him.

Near the end, the Cal Aggie Marching Band swung into action. As the players passed in front of May and his boys, they stopped marching and held their positions. Some members were just three feet away. May inhaled their bright uniforms and studied their brass instruments, some of which looked bigger than the person who carried it. Someone yelled a command and the band broke into another song, their knees rising and falling, drummers lifting and pounding, trombones herking and jerking, kids whirling, every uniform matching, and May marveled at it all, and when he looked down he could see his children moving too, pointing at things for him to see, telling him what was before them, and May could feel tears running down his face, and it seemed strange to him to be crying in front of the Cal Aggie Marching Band when he hadn't cried the day his bandages came off, and it seemed right to him to be crying because when he looked down again his sons seemed to be looking at him.

One night shortly after the parade, May and Jennifer lay awake in bed. She asked how he felt about his new vision. He told her that he loved it, that he was relishing every crack in the sidewalk, every differently colored doorway.

"I pinch myself every day," he said. "Vision is a bigger deal than I thought it would be. It's just incredibly interesting."

"It looks like really hard work, too," Jennifer said. "Sometimes you look exhausted. Are you sure you're okay?"

"It is really hard work," May agreed. "It seems like I have to process every little thing consciously to understand what I'm seeing. Everything is interesting to me, but sometimes it feels like I can't do anything in peace. And yet I don't want to close my eyes. I don't want to miss anything."

"What do you mean you have to process things?"

"Well, I think the best way I can describe it is that, for me, trying to see feels like trying to speak a foreign language."

"What do you mean?"

"You know how, when you're learning a language, sentences don't just roll off your tongue? You have to think of the vocabulary words you want.

Then you have to conjugate the verbs. Then you have to figure out how to order the words. That's what seeing feels like to me. One way or another, either through touching or logic or clues or whatever, I've gotta think about what I'm seeing, I have to put it all together consciously. Only then do I understand what I'm seeing."

"You're not fluent."

"I'm not fluent. Except for color and things that move—that stuff just happens for me. It's like color and moving things are my native language."

"Are you worried about it?"

"No. This is all still new—it's only been about six weeks. I'm sure it'll get easier with time. I mean, who learns a new language in six weeks? I just need a little time."

Jennifer rolled over and kissed her husband. A few moments later she was asleep. May lay awake beside her. He had seen Dr. Goodman several times since the bandages had come off. Visit to visit, his vision was always the same. Goodman always told him, "No change."

"It's early," May told himself. "Good things take time. It's not like anyone said it's going to be like this for life."

CHAPTERELEVEN

Now that May had vision, people demanded to know what he would be rushing to see. Was it the Great Pyramid in Egypt? A giant panda in China? The new **Tyrannosaurus rex** on display in Chicago? He gave them half of his real answer: he couldn't wait to see the panoramas at the Kirkwood ski resort. He shared the other half only with Jennifer.

"I've gotta get to the topless beaches at Saint-Tropez," he said. "When are we going?"

"Look," Jennifer said. "You need to grab a couple of your buddies, book your tickets, and go have at it. You don't need me around."

"Yeah, but you could be topless, too. You're not topless enough at home. Saint-Tropez could inspire you."

Jennifer threw a playful punch. May delighted in seeing it coming.

As it was, Jennifer had already taken measures to address the second half of May's wish. A normally conservative dresser, she had been wearing tighter and more brightly colored clothes, especially tops, when they went out for the evening.

"You look great!" May would tell her.

"I don't go to work like this," Jennifer reminded him. "This hasn't been my style, so I'm still getting used to these clothes."

May was grateful for his wife's indulgence. But that still left a universe of other women to see. A friend brought a **Playboy** magazine to his house. May studied the photos and was especially taken with one that spanned three pages.

"I can't get over her," May said. "She's got a crease going through her body."

"You're looking at the crease?"

Photos with good contrast, bright lighting, and stark backgrounds unlocked a wonderland of forbidden delights. Still, fine details weren't clear to him, making it difficult for him to locate some of his favorite features. He could not judge depth—none of the ladies looked voluptuous unless they faced to the side. But oh, the skin and curves! They were everywhere, and they tipped the row of dominoes in May's fantasy centers, allowing his imagination and sensory memories to fill in the rest. He'd heard men say that the hint of a woman's outline behind a changing curtain could be more exciting than seeing the actual woman herself. He'd never quite understood that, but he did today.

May did not rush to see the great wonders of the world. But he practically ran to Peet's Coffee in west Davis, through which endless parades of beautiful women were said to pass. He arrived during the morning rush, took a position at an outdoor table, and cast his vision into the oncoming stream of people. What he saw approaching were walking enigmas.

Were they men or women? He didn't know how to begin to decide. Faces revealed nothing to him of a person's gender, so he looked next to hair length, a decent clue but one riddled with exceptions, especially in this laid-back university town. Women seldom wore dresses or scarves or other telltale clothing—in fact, it startled him to see how similarly the sexes dressed. He searched for the confessing shape of a woman's breasts, but unless she was wearing a tight and colorful top he could not detect a thing.

Wrestling with unreliable clues was just half the battle. Often, May had only five or ten seconds to work through the information he'd gathered—hair, clothes, chest—before the candidate had passed, forcing him to clear his head and begin twisting a fresh Rubik's Cube of clues for the next passerby.

"Man, I've had vision for almost two months," he told Josh while walking home one day. "Why aren't I getting any better at this?"

At home, he told Jennifer about his coffee-shop missions.

"I know there are beautiful women in these

places," he said. "But it takes forever to figure out if the person I'm seeing is even female. Then, just when I think I've got it, she's gone—or he's gone— and I have to start over again."

"It's still early," Jennifer said. "You're still getting used to your vision."

"It's been two months. Is that still early?"

"It might be, Mike."

"I don't know, Jen. It took me about five seconds to see colors. It took me a day before I could catch a ball on the run. I still can't read. I still don't know Carson's face from Wyndham's face. Does that make sense to you?"

"I know it's hard work. I can see you working."

"I don't mind the work. In fact, the work is an adventure itself, it's fascinating. But after a while you want to think that all the work is getting you somewhere. I mean, that's human nature, right?"

A few days later, May got ready to leave for an eye appointment in San Francisco.

"I think Goodman's going to see some improvement this time," he told Jennifer. "It seems like I've been recognizing things a little faster. I think I've been doing better at Peet's, too."

"Don't do too good at Peet's," Jennifer said. "Give Dan a hug for me."

"I think I'm going to impress him today," May said.

May took the ferry to San Francisco, then chose to make the half-hour walk with Josh to Goodman's office. He fired up his GPS and began to follow its spoken directions. Every few steps he glimpsed a line on the sidewalk and found himself trying to determine whether it was a curb or a shadow, a drop-off or some paint, and he had to remind himself to let Josh guide him forward and to use his own vision for sightseeing to the sides.

A few blocks into the walk, May hit his stride. His GPS was flawless, he and Josh were walking seamlessly, and he could see San Francisco's buildings climbing into the sky all around him. "I've got to tell my dad about this," he thought. Then he took a few more steps, closed his eyes, and thought about how strange it was to keep forgetting that one's father had died even though he'd been dead for half a year.

As he neared Goodman's office, May could see shapes of white and brown swirling on the sidewalk in front of him. He stopped for a moment to contemplate the scene. He knew such haphazard things could not be meant for an orderly sidewalk in an orderly city. That meant these shapes no one was chasing must be garbage, and at that moment the white and brown no longer looked like just shapes to him, now they made a feeling inside him, now their movements became careless, their colors turned drab, now they seemed wrong to him, now they looked like garbage, like something he hadn't seen the moment before, and now he was disgusted.

He kept walking. To his right, he could see the windows of a building. Some appeared vaguely yellow, others had crooked lines across their widths, still others appeared not to be there at all. He stopped and looked more closely. The yellowed windows seemed difficult to look through. He'd heard things could look yellow when dingy and dreary, when worn out, and he began to think that these windows went with the garbage he'd seen, that he was looking at something that had been let go, that wasn't cared for anymore, and when he knew that, the yellow windows weren't just yellow anymore, they were ugly. He stared longer at the crooked lines on the other windows. No one would have drawn lines like that, lines that zigged and zagged for no reason and went to nowhere. He knew, therefore, that they must be cracks, and he hoped that no one had to live inside a building that made such sad impressions on the eye.

A block later, Josh moved to avoid something on the sidewalk. To May, it appeared to be a large dark shadow or a big bag of garbage—garbage would make sense in an area like this. He bent down to take a closer look. Emerging from the center of the darkness he could see the shape of human arms and legs, and now his heart pounded, and he moved his eye above the arms and found a neck and then a head, and now the image coalesced in rapid fire in his understanding: this was a human being, this was a homeless person curled on his side, and he tried to look for a face even though he couldn't understand faces, and he felt his throat tighten and tears well in his eyes when he looked back at the person's arms and legs, because he'd seen countless arms and legs by now and every one of them had been moving, every one of them had been talking and taking people places, but these arms and legs weren't talking or going anywhere, they just lay there shouting to him in their stillness, and May wished for the night so that this person might have some privacy, and even though he could see that the person was bundled in clothes, May wished for the night so that the world wouldn't see this person lying in the street so naked.

May took Josh's harness and kept walking, holding back his tears. He had only a few blocks to pull himself together. For the rest of the walk to Goodman's office he thought about nothing but the person in the street. He'd known about homeless people. But until today, he had always been guided around them. Near Goodman's office, he closed his eyes to collect himself, but the image of the person was still as bright and sharp as ever.

Dr. Goodman's receptionist greeted May and Josh and led them to an examining room. The high-backed chair and octopus of equipment were a familiar comfort to May. He relaxed and remembered why he had left the house so hopeful today—he expected to hear that his vision had finally improved.

Goodman entered and reached to shake hands. May met his hand perfectly.

"Mike," Goodman said. "I wonder if you'd mind answering a question before we start."

"Sure thing, Dan."

"My sons and I were talking about you. I told them how well you see colors. They wanted to know if you dreamed in color when you were blind."

"I don't know," May replied. "I don't know if there was any visual component to my dreams when I was blind. But here's the really strange thing. When I was blind, Jennifer used to ask if I saw colors or pictures or images in my dreams. And even then I didn't know. I always knew the storyline, like if someone was chasing me. But when she'd ask if there was a visual element, I'd say, 'I don't know. I just know what was happening.'"

"Do you have vision in your dreams now?"

"Yes. And the vision is just like when I'm awake. I connect with a thing's texture first and its visual component second. I can't see faces any better than when I'm awake. But I did have this dream recently where vision was really dominant."

"Tell me about it."

"I was in this room and I could see a lot of giraffes rolling and flailing around on the floor. And I could see Wyndham sleeping nearby. So I pushed one of the giraffes away to keep it from squashing Wyndham. I saw the danger and acted on it, all by vision."

"That's fascinating."

"Yes. And I thought about it the next day. I've never seen a giraffe move, but I think I got that flailing and rolling motion from watching Josh in real life."

Goodman began the examination. He held an eye chart up to May's nose and had him read the letters. He put various lenses over May's eye and had him read again. He asked him to count fingers. He ran tests on the eye.

"No change," Goodman finally said. "You're very consistent visit to visit."

"No change? Are you sure?"

"I'm sure. You've still got a beautiful working eye. You should be able to drive with this eye. But you're nowhere close. The issue must be your visual cortex, your brain."

May's stomach tightened. Blood rushed to his face. He wanted to shout, "How can that be? How can I have an eye good enough to drive a car but I can't even see the eye chart from twenty feet? Why do things look sharp but I can't see details? What's happening here? Start connecting, for God's sake! Start connecting!"

"Thanks, Dan," May said. "Thanks for everything. Maybe I'll surprise you next time around."

That afternoon at home, May went into the kitchen to fix himself a sandwich. Scattered across the counter he could see a book, a cutting board, car keys, Jennifer's fabric samples, an open jar of peanut butter, school projects, Jennifer's sunglasses . . .

"Jen? Jen! Where are you?"

Jennifer walked into the kitchen.

"Hi, sweetie. When did you come in?"

"Look at this stuff!" May said.

"Oh, I meant to move some of that—"

"Why is there a book in the middle of a cutting board? Why are your keys in a different place every day—except for in your purse, which is the one place they belong?"

"Don't tell me where my keys belong."

"Well, I know they don't belong in the peanut butter. Can we agree on that? Keys don't belong in the peanut butter?"

"They're not in the peanut butter. What's your problem?"

"I don't have a problem. I'm organized. I hate clutter. You know I hate clutter. You've known for fourteen years that I hate clutter. Yet here it is, again and again. It's like you put it there to get me."

"Why do you have to inspect everything so closely? You look for clutter, Mike. You want to find it. You're on the hunt for it all the time. We're just living here. Just let us live."

May started to move the piles on the counter.

"Don't move my things."

"I'm just putting them into piles, a little organization."

"That's an attack on me, Mike."

"No, it's just a little organization."

"Why can't you just live with it?"

"Because now I can see it."

One afternoon, May told Jennifer that he was going for coffee at Peet's.

"Are you going girl watching?" she asked.

"I'm going to try," he said. "I'm still not very good."

"Want some help?"

May looked at her.

"Do you think you can?" he asked.

"Oh, I know I can," she replied.

The couple found a table at Peet's, near the sidewalk.

"Before we start, show me how you look for women," she said.

May looked down the street. When a long-haired candidate strode past his table he made mental notes on her appearance.

"Whoa!" Jennifer said. "You can't do it like that!"

"Like what?"

"You were rubbernecking. You turned your entire body around to follow her! You'll get busted doing that. Here, feel this."

She took May's hands and put them on her face. She turned her head slowly in a forty-five-degree arc.

"You can turn your head that far, but going all the way around is leering—someone will punch you. Try to move your eye instead of your head. You have to be subtle."

May practiced on the next several people. He had to concentrate to move his eye rather than his head, but he improved with each attempt. Next, Jennifer asked what clues he used when trying to size up a woman. May explained that he looked for hair length, clothing, and evidence of breasts, but that each of them could be misleading or unreliable.

"There are other things to look for," she said. "Look at this woman coming toward us with the short black hair. See her shoes? No guy would ever wear shoes that colorful."

May registered the note in his mind: **Colorful shoes are probably women.**

Thus began an hour-long lesson on new clues. While May practiced keeping his head still, Jennifer taught him to look for:

- **Swinging hips** ("Women walk with a bounce; men don't.")

- **Purses** ("Men don't carry things over their shoulders, at least not in the United States.")

- **Tight pants** ("Women sometimes paint them on; men's are more baggy.")

- **Skirts** ("They flap in the wind more than shorts do.")

- **Bellies** ("Women show them a lot these days. Men almost never do.")

- **Jewelry** ("Some men might wear necklaces, but very few wear shiny bracelets.")

These clues were a treasure map to May. He memorized and contemplated them at home, then returned to Peet's with his wife a few days later.

"Okay, I see a person: medium-long blond hair, I think she's got a purse, and her walk is bouncing," May said. "It must be a woman. And I think she's hot."

"Good job, Mike, she is hot," Jennifer said. "Okay, now look to your right at ten o'clock. What do you think?"

May gazed for several seconds, forcing his head to stay still.

"Very nice. Bright shoes. Definitely cute."

Jennifer looked mildly annoyed.

"I'm cuter than she is," she muttered.

"Hey, Jen, what about that one? Long hair, belly showing, good walk, nice sound from her high heels. Looks good to me."

"That's a guy, Mike."

"It is? What about the high heels?"

"Those are flip-flops. But he does have a sultry walk, I'll give you that."

Armed with his quiver of new clues, May began haunting Peet's daily, assessing the women and thrilling to the idea that he could touch so many of them from a distance without ever touching them at all. Often, he brought Jennifer along; it took just a few minutes for her to assess his progress and then help him refine his technique. Sometimes she feared that she had burst his bubble, as when telling him that women he thought to be Miss Americas were in fact dowdy and drab. He reassured her it was no disappointment at all; in fact, he was coming to think himself lucky for his inexact ability to detect a woman's every defect—it made him much less picky and therefore populated the world with more beautiful women to savor. Other times, she worried that she confused him, as when she told him that a woman with a gorgeous face also had a naturally angry expression. He said he couldn't imagine such a thing—how could a face be beautiful and ugly at the same time?—but the paradox fascinated him and made the prospect of every face more interesting.

May continued to practice. Soon he could guess a passing person's gender with 80 percent accuracy. Jennifer celebrated his daily progress reports. When he reminded her that most wives wouldn't help their husbands delight in other women, she told him that she knew he was going to look and wanted him to be good at it. At home, he noticed that Jennifer had started to wear the kinds of tight-fitting clothes he responded to when they sat together girl-watching at Peet's.

At the end of April, May asked Dr. Goodman for permission to ski. Kirkwood was the one place he'd dreamed of seeing, and it was closing for the season. Goodman wasn't thrilled: May could get poked in the eye, hit with flying debris, cracked in the head. Ultimately, he left it up to his patient, which meant that May was going.

May never moved his eye from the window during the three-hour drive to Kirkwood, soaking in the tiny gold-mining towns and slushy S-curves he'd known by story and feel for more than twenty years. Near the snow line, the family competed for the title of "First to See Snow." Carson won, but May was in the game. It was the first time he'd ever seen snow.

May squirmed in his seat as Jennifer pulled into the resort's entrance—he couldn't wait to see this old friend. She drove slowly, and he gazed at everything. Every side street was where he knew it would be and every speed bump on the road looked familiar. Yet other parts seemed invaders to his eye. Orange cones steered cars to the lodges, while glowing yellow people took money at the parking lot.

"Why are those people so bright?" May asked.

"They're wearing fluorescent vests," Carson said.

"Why didn't anyone tell me about all this orange and yellow?" May asked.

"I guess we just didn't think of it," Wyndham said.

May still could not get over the number of amazing things sighted people never bothered to mention. It seemed the same as if he'd forgotten to mention to his family that he had a brother or that he played guitar.

The family geared up in their rented condo, then made their way to Chair One, a gentle beginners' slope. Riding the lift, May watched an escalator of trees pass to his left and the ground fall away beneath him. Jennifer looked like a cloud in her ski suit, except for the bright orange bib on her chest that read GUIDE—a signal to others that she was helping another skier. A moment later, they'd reached the top and had begun coasting downhill, a stroll more than a run down this docile incline, and it took May's breath as he found the corridor of trees he'd expected and watched the line-etched snow streak past his glinting yellow-and-red skis. Jennifer called out directions, but May didn't need them at these leisurely speeds. Everything was coming together, and he looked into the blue of the sky and felt goose bumps rise over his body, and it occurred to him that he needn't stop there, that he could look farther than the sky, and as he raised his head he saw a crown of jagged dark edges atop the blue. And he thought, "Those are the mountains. That is my panorama."

Jennifer knew the next part was coming. She knew it was hopeless to protest.

"Let's ski Chair Six," May said. "Let's go for it."

Chair Six was perhaps the most difficult and treacherous run at Kirkwood, a plummeting black diamond run pocked with moguls, the mounds of hard snow that turn a skier's legs to pistons. Speeds could reach thirty miles per hour on this mountain, and falls could send a person's body cartwheeling—an event called a "yard sale" for the mess of equipment the poor soul usually left behind on the mountain.

The lift carried May and Jennifer above the trees, and it didn't stop there. It seemed to rise above the mountains themselves, and for the first time in twenty years May felt himself gripping the handrail to make sure he didn't fall out.

The view from the top froze May in his skis.

The mountain dropped into a sea of trees and collected in a meadow, then caught its breath and rose up again on the other side and climbed and climbed until it became a roaring skyline of rock that romanced the clouds. He yearned to reach out and touch the panorama—it looked that close to him—but he knew, of course, that it was miles away. When he reminded himself of its distance it looked farther to him, as it should have, and he understood that in order to touch it he would have to fly to it, and for a moment he felt like he could.

Instead, he allowed the sunshine to cut through the chill air and soothe his face. Then he looked to his wife, who hadn't moved, who seemed ready to wait as long as he needed, and he told himself, "Lock in this feeling. This is what you came for."

Just before the run, May reminded Jennifer that he would need to concentrate on her guidance this time—there would be no more playing and talking as on Chair One—and asked her to remember to call out "Traffic!" if other people skied close to them. They pulled on their goggles and set off down the hill.

The steely white snow streaked underneath May's skis. This was a much different motion from before, this was speed, raging speed, maybe twenty-five miles per hour, and when he looked up angry dark

lines whizzed toward him from every direction—
were they people?—yes, they must be other skiers
rushing in too close: **Move away! Move away!**
Where was Jennifer, where was her orange bib, why
wasn't she saying anything? There she is, there's the
orange, but here comes another skier. Jen! Jen! Why
is she leading me into another skier? I can see his
shape, he's coming right toward me, HE IS COM-
ING RIGHT TOWARD ME!

WHOOSH!

May passed right through the skier. His heart
sledgehammered inside his chest.

"Jennifer! Stop!" he yelled.

Jennifer skidded to a halt. May pulled up beside her.

"What's wrong?" she asked.

"Jesus, Jennifer!" he said, panting. "You're supposed to yell 'Traffic!' "

"There wasn't any traffic."

"Then what was it?"

"What was what?"

"The person . . . the dark shape moving at us
so fast."

Jennifer looked around.

"That's the shadow from the chairlift."

"Why didn't you warn me about that?"

"I didn't even notice it, Mike."

May looked down the hill. Dark lines jutted

out across the mountain's white canvas. Some were moving, some were not. A skier whooshed past them, his dark suit indistinguishable from the chairlift's shadows.

"There's moguls coming, Mike. Can you see them?"

May squinted and surveyed the slope.

"I don't think so. Maybe when I get closer."

"You should stop, Mike. You can't even see the moguls. We can stop here."

"Let's keep going," he said.

The pair headed down the hill. Soon they were back to speed. May fixed all his powers of concentration on the shadows—if he just reasoned through their angles and shapes and direction he could distinguish real from imagined threats, people from trees, and here in front of him, this must be just a shadow because—

WHOMP!

May's skis plowed into a mogul, collapsing his knees and sending his limbs flailing. He fought to stay upright, but his jackknifed torso whipped him to the snow, where his arms and legs ragdolled and the world rushed by in torrential paint strokes of sky and snow. When his skid ended he wiped the snow from his goggles and looked back for the mogul that had crumbled him. He saw nothing but flat white snow. Jennifer stopped but gave her husband space to decide what to do next.

May got to his feet and kept going.

"Look for the bumps," he told himself as he gained speed. "Forget the other shadows."

He saw a patch of snow rushing at him; it looked like a patch because it was lighter on top than on the sides, and it occurred to him that this might be a mogul and—

BOOM!

The mogul exploded into May's knees, short-circuiting his balance and catapulting him face forward into the snow. Adrenaline choked his throat as he uncrumpled and pushed himself back onto his skis. He had to figure things out faster. He needed to tell shadows from trees, people from moguls, bright from almost bright, but the thought of working through all that at these speeds made his stomach tighten and his arms lock, the opposite of the liquid cool he'd become at Mount Jahorina during the Olympics. Again, he pushed himself forward with his poles and continued downhill. This time he didn't last ten seconds before another ambiguous shadow torpedoed his legs.

May looked for the color of Jennifer's bib. He saw only an orange dot in the distance. He began to push himself up, his face red with snow and tears, but he could feel the series of crashes that were still to come, the collisions with nothing and everything he couldn't avoid, and he stopped trying to push himself. He watched shadows dance around him, and he thought, "I'm done. I can't make it the rest of the way."

May closed his eyes and the world went still. He was safe here. In the darkness, he could hear his heart pounding. It was the only sound on the mountain. He'd never heard it move like that. He was safe here.

May lifted a pole and pushed it into the snow. He breathed in as far as his lungs would go, then pushed himself up, first to one knee, then to his feet.

"There's a way to do this," he said.

He opened his eyes.

"There's always a way. If I have to crash through, I'll do it."

He thrust his poles backward and began moving down the mountain, tentatively at first, then faster, then as fast as he could go. Over the next twenty minutes he fell thirty more times. Each time, he pushed himself up and started again. By the time he reached the bottom he could barely stand.

Jennifer rushed to her husband.

"Oh, my gosh. Are you okay?" she asked.

May just stood there for a moment, inhaling and exhaling.

"I think I'm done for the day," he said.

A few weeks after skiing at Kirkwood, May was invited by a friend to speak to a fourth-grade class near San Francisco. He told them about the unusual nature of his vision. Their questions were among the best he'd heard:

"Can you see your dog's tail wagging?"

"Definitely. I'm really good at seeing things that move."

"Can you see his tail if it's not wagging?"

"Yes, but that's only because I know dogs have tails."

"Can you see when your kids do bad stuff?"

"Yes. And I can see when their room is messy, too."

"What company makes the drugs you take? My dad will want to invest money in it."

"I don't know. That's a good question."

"Did they put needles in your eye?"

"I think so. I've got stitches in there."

"How many stitches?"

"I'm not sure. That's another good question."

"What am I holding up?"

"I can't tell; I need to touch things before I can really see them."

"Can you drive?"

"Would you want a guy driving a car who has to touch things in order to see them?"

"Will you ever be able to drive a car?"

"Well, I'm trying to teach my dog to look out the window to help me steer. And I'm trying to teach my kids to turn the wheel while I press the pedals. Why is everyone laughing?"

———

After talking to the fourth graders, May hopped a ride with a friend to Baker Beach, popular for its crashing waves and panoramic view of the Golden Gate Bridge. For several minutes he stood at the lip of the beach, watching the frothing white bubbles atop the water, astonished to see that sand changed from light to dark when lapped by the water. He removed his shoes and began walking in the wet sand, and a moment later he looked up and found the orange silhouette of the Golden Gate Bridge, its suspension towers aglow against the gray sky. For a time he walked toward this bridge, this structure he'd known all his life in his imagination, certain he could not reach it by foot but walking to get there still, a bridge that had called to him by legend for forty years and now called to him by orange.

After a time, he stopped walking and turned around to see how far he'd gone. There, lying atop the sand, were shapes that hadn't existed moments before, which meant he must be looking at his footprints. He had never conceived of footprints as visual; to him, they were the press-grind-and-pivot feel of sand on his feet—a texture, not an image. He looked at the trail and immediately felt connected to the footprints; they were a part of him, each step connected to the next until they arrived at and became him. He bent down to feel them, but the first one mushed away under his touch, and though he always wanted to touch things, he didn't want to touch his footprints anymore. It didn't feel like a good thing to do, so he stood up and left the rest of himself undisturbed.

On a lovely summer day, May met his brother Patrick in Palo Alto. Busy work schedules had kept them apart for much of the time since May's surgery. Today would be different. Today, Patrick brought the Limo.

The Limo was a long, sleek, black tandem bicycle built for performance and guts. The brothers had made countless rides with it down the Pacific Coast, always with May churning in back while Patrick steered in front.

"Let's do it different today," Patrick said. "You ride up front. You steer."

"You sure?" May asked.

"I'm sure I'm terrified," Patrick said. "I'll have no control. You have no experience. The bike is built for speed. But let's do it."

May smiled the way he had when he was six.

The men climbed aboard the Limo. Hydrants of adrenaline opened inside May's body. The brothers began pedaling. The front seat felt foreign to May, wobbly and heavy, like he was trying to wag a dog by the tail.

"Aim for the white line in the center of the road," Patrick called. "Easy left . . . left . . . okay, hold steady!"

Soon the tandem's speedometer read twenty-one miles per hour. May kept the bike pinned to the white line. He felt like he could keep riding forever, wind in his face, brother as his engine, this ferocious and beautiful machine his servant.

The road, however, was ending, and the Limo needed to be turned around, a tricky maneuver even for sighted riders.

"Want to try the turn?" Patrick asked.

"Definitely," May called back.

May began to lean left, looking to the outline of trees on either side of the road for guidance. He leaned harder left. The bike bent with him. Each man pedaled harder to defy gravity and calamity. The Limo banked farther, the brothers' knees churning to keep it aloft, until May again saw the white line that meant the center of the road, and a moment later he was guiding his brother back to where they'd started.

At ride's end, May and Patrick checked the odometer. They'd covered three miles. They embraced and vowed to go even faster the next time out. On the way home, May replayed the ride in his mind. It seemed curious to him that he hadn't seen the edges of the road narrowing in the distance the way sighted people always described it; to him, the edges looked parallel for as far as his eye could see. The disparity didn't bother him much, but he wondered if, after almost four months of vision, he shouldn't be seeing things more normally than this. Still, it had been a thrilling adventure, and he couldn't wait to get home to tell his family about pulling a U-turn even some sighted riders couldn't manage.

Enchanted Hills Camp turned fifty during the summer of May's new vision. This was the place of his boyhood adventures, where he'd wooed Jennifer, where it always seemed he could run without stopping. He took his family to celebrate for the weekend.

Late on Saturday night, after hiking the upper camp, he and the boys began the long trek back to their cabin. The sky was jet-black, and Carson and Wyndham said they were scared.

May wanted to distract his sons, to divert their attention until they reached the lower camp. Instead, they diverted his.

"Dad, do you see the stars?" Carson asked.

"Yeah, they're so bright!" Wyndham added.

May did not want to break their distraction by stopping to look, so he asked them as many questions as he could about the stars until, before they knew it, they'd reached their cabin.

After the boys and Jennifer had fallen asleep,

May took Josh to Recreation Field, a clearing in the woods at Enchanted Hills. He had fallen asleep here many times after listening to sighted counselors describe the night sky. Tonight, he wanted to see the stars for himself.

He wrapped Josh's leash around his leg, lay flat on his back, and closed his eyes. He could hear echoes of counselors from decades back yelling "Go!" to start a race. He could hear them telling him about the sky.

May opened his eyes. Electric dots of silver-white, as many as the sound of a rainstorm, ran to every space in the world, and when he tried to see where they led there was no world anymore, they led everywhere, across a blanket of night that had no edges, and for a moment May didn't know where he was among these stars, if he was under them or around them or beyond them, they were everywhere and he was everywhere, he was where he wanted to be.

He lay there for an hour or maybe two. Past midnight, he heard the worried voices of female counselors who seemed to think that he and Josh might be wild dogs or bobcats. He sat up and waved his hand. It was chilly and time to go back to the cabin. He lay back one last time and looked to the sky. He still didn't know why his vision wasn't improving, still had no clue to its strange nature. More and more, he'd been wondering if this vision might somehow be his vision for life. But he could think of none of that now. As a million stars danced onto his eye, he could think only of how lucky he was not to have looked at the night sky until his sweet sons had urged him to do it.

CHAPTERTWELVE

Four months had passed since the launch of Sendero's GPS system. Customers seemed thrilled with the product, but it remained too expensive—$995 **plus** the price of a laptop computer—for any but the most well-heeled individuals. After an initial flurry, sales began to wane. May had to face something he had suspected from the start: that the company's survival would depend on convincing various departments of rehabilitation and other agencies to buy the product for their blind clients. He continued to work long days making sales calls, planning business trips, and providing tech support to existing customers. Money grew tighter for the May household. May figured he had six months to make the business fly. He had no backup plan.

Late one afternoon, Jennifer and May made a trip to the grocery store. She headed for the deli section, leaving May on his own to explore. He pushed a cart slowly down the first aisle, gazing at shelves in which every item appeared collaged to the next.

This colorful melding of things occurred often in unfamiliar settings, and it could flummox and frustrate him. Boxes on shelves looked sharply in focus, yet he couldn't tell where one began and the next one ended—how was a person to make sense of that? He found it hard to muster sympathy for shoppers torn between brands of mayonnaise when he would have been happy just to see the individual jars.

This didn't happen at home or at Peet's coffee shop or at the handful of other places in the world May knew intimately. For him, context and expectation were everything; they literally produced better vision. So when he spotted a long, silver, rectangular shape on his family room coffee table, he saw it as the robust, three-dimensional television remote control he knew it must be. But if someone had taken that same remote control and put it on one of these grocery shelves, or even on his car seat, it would have appeared to him just a colorful, flat, meaningless shape. The problem for May was that for every place he knew as intimately as his family room coffee table, there were countless places in the world—like this grocery store—he did not.

That meant May had to figure out what he was seeing in a different way. To do this, he relied on an arsenal of clues he had to assemble on the spot. They were:

- Touch
- Color
- Context and expectation
- Other senses

Over the next ten minutes in this grocery store, he turned to each of these clues repeatedly. As he walked the aisles, here's how it worked:

Touch. Overwhelmingly, irresistibly, May's first instinct was to touch the items on the shelves; more than anything, an object's feel revealed its identity. Items like bread, eggs, frozen pizzas, and fruits were easily discerned by his hands. Many others, especially things in nondescript packaging, like boxes of crackers or cans of soup, remained mysterious. In cases where touch fell short, he looked next to:

Color. A two-liter bottle of soda became Coca-Cola for its iconic red-and-white swirls. The dark green Heineken sign signaled the store's beer section. A purple box with black lettering was a dead giveaway for Kellogg's Raisin Bran. Still, the colors of many items revealed nothing about their identities. In those cases, he turned next to:

Context and expectation. The heavy brown jar he was handling in the bread aisle was not likely to be spaghetti sauce, which would be shelved near the pastas, not the breads. But it might well be peanut butter, which he knew belonged near the bread. The small rectangular box he touched next to the eggs in the refrigerated section was almost certainly butter rather than Pop-Tarts. If, by this time, his checklist of clues still hadn't given meaning to the shapes he was seeing, he would try to engage his:

Other senses. Coffee could be smelled from a distance of three aisles. Nothing sounded quite like dry spaghetti when shaken in its box. And as a last resort he could pull an item to within a few inches of his eye and try to read the label, though that could take a minute or more—if he could do it at all.

This was the cognitive heavy lifting required of May virtually everywhere and always. He saw almost nothing automatically. He assembled clues around the clock.

Jennifer tracked him down, and together they went to check out.

"How'd you do?" she asked.

"Man, it's a lot of work," he said. "But a grocery store is okay for me. At least there are some clues here."

"I see you found the Raisin Bran. That's great."

"If the world were made up of nothing but Raisin Bran boxes," he said, "I could see forever."

———

Jennifer needed to make another stop, this time at Costco. May long had been fascinated by this warehouse club store, which sold, under a single gargantuan roof, stereos, computers, blue jeans, office furniture, rotisserie chickens, toys, vitamins, and virtually anything else a human being might use, usually in bulk sizes and stacked on palettes that could reach three stories. He hadn't been to Costco since his surgery and was eager to take it in.

He and Jennifer grabbed one of the store's oversized shopping carts and began walking the aisles. The items on the shelves blended into one another before May's eye. As always, he ached to touch things, so he began to put his hands on the objects within his grasp. Many items were contained in commonly shaped boxes or in a blister pack, the object sealed between cardboard and a stiff plastic bubble, thereby short-circuiting his touch. He yearned to tear open these packages to discover their contents, especially the blister packs, in which the product was tantalizingly visible but untouchable through the plastic. Many of the blister packs showed a picture of the product on the cardboard, but to May the picture often looked like part of the actual item on top of it—he simply could not separate illustration from object. Many other things in the store were stacked high and beyond his grasp. His touch, in effect, had been turned off.

May went to his other clues. He looked for revealing colors, but in this warehouse setting an item's
packaging was often more utilitarian than come-
hither. He tried to draw on context and expectation, but sections in this store seemed randomly
placed, and the categories were endless—it was possible to find a flannel shirt for sale across the aisle
from toys. Even the size of a product's packaging—
usually a potent context clue—revealed little about
its contents here, as many of Costco's boxes held
bulk amounts of the things inside.

May searched harder for clues but found few.
Boxes on shelves melded further together. Items
flattened. Things still looked sharply in focus but
had little meaning, and without meaning what was
he seeing, really? He redoubled his efforts but
quickly felt overwhelmed. And it occurred to him
that much of the world was like the world of
Costco—a massive place in which the true nature
of things seemed just beyond his eye. As Jennifer
found him in an aisle and put her arm around his
shoulders, he knew that this might be the way the
world appeared to him forever. When Jennifer
asked how he was doing, he told her that he was
tired.

Not long after his trip to Costco, May attended a
board meeting of the Society for the Blind in Sacramento, where his friend Bryan Bashin was the di-

rector. The meeting started and voices began flying. Ideas were served and volleyed, objections noted, minutes made. In the hallway afterward, Bashin asked May what it looked like to see so many people moving and speaking and gesturing. May told him that it was a lot to see, an overflow, and that after a time he'd been forced to close his eyes.

Late that night, Bashin called May at home to inquire of his well-being. A part of May wanted to confess to Bashin that his vision hadn't improved since the surgery, that seeing continued to require intensive mental effort, that he didn't want **every . . . single . . . thing** he encountered to be a project. And he wanted to confess that he was starting to wonder if this struggle might be for life. But that didn't sound like Mike May. That wasn't Mike May. Instead, he told Bashin, "I'll find a way."

May wanted another go at Costco's shelves. He asked Jennifer if she needed anything else at the store. She said she could always use another gallon of ketchup. A half hour later they were in the aisles.

He stared, touched, stroked, reasoned, expected, imagined, deduced. Much of the store remained a canvas of bright and colorful shapes. He still could not tell the illustration on the blister pack from the product inside its plastic bubble. Costco still seemed a lot like the rest of the world.

Near the back of the store, May spotted a large

object at the end of the aisle. He moved near it and put his reasoning powers to work: The object wasn't moving. It was large and squarish. It was positioned near pallets.

"Is that a forklift?" he asked Jennifer.

Her face went white. She waited for a moment, then leaned in to May's ear.

"No," she whispered. "That's a very, very heavy woman. She might weigh four hundred pounds."

May didn't believe it. Then the object reached for something on a shelf. To him, the heavy woman looked like two people stuck together.

May could barely reconcile the image with the idea; he had never touched a person anywhere near that size. Ordinarily, his impulse would have been to move closer, if not to touch then to get a better look—anything to cement this new impression. This time he wanted to move away, not because he desired to know less about the heavy woman but because the woman disgusted him. He told himself, "No! Stop feeling that way! She's a human being and her size is irrelevant. She's a person!" but he could not stand down his contempt, the sense that her shape equaled sloth and laziness and maybe even slovenliness, that her shape equaled her. As the woman labored down the aisle May could really see her, and in the huff-and-puff of her walk he could envision her struggling to climb stairs, squeezing in beside him on an airplane, breathing. He raced to remind himself that he was the kind of man to empathize with such a plight, but his feeling overwhelmed him, and it said of the woman, "She disgusts me."

On the way home, May told Jennifer that he was ashamed.

"I'm sick about it," he said. "I formed an emotional reaction to this person strictly based on her appearance. That's an ugly thing to do. People do that with the blind, too. I never wanted to be a person like that, Jen. And I never thought I was. I've gotta work on that. I don't want to be that."

"You're not that, Mike."

"Maybe I am, Jen."

"Have you always felt that way about very heavy people?" Jennifer asked.

"That's the thing," May said. "I never did when I was blind."

As the summer rolled on, May focused even more of his energies on pitching his GPS to government agencies. Still, six months after his sales efforts had begun, Sendero had not sold a single unit to any of them. The agency decision makers seemed happy to buy a twenty-five-dollar cane, but they didn't seem to think a blind client needed much else to find a job. Money grew tighter in the May household.

By this time, word of May's cutting-edge surgery had attracted some media attention. A television crew asked to film a short interview in his home, to which May consented. Jennifer borrowed some furniture from friends for the shoot—as a designer, she did not want viewers to see that she couldn't afford to decorate her house to her own high standards. May tried to apologize for the family's constricting budget, but Jennifer wouldn't hear of it. She reminded him that they were old hands at start-ups and that their own new furniture would come in due time.

The crew set up and began filming. May knew what their first question would be before they asked it, because it was everyone's first question: "How did it feel to see your wife and kids?"

He knew what they wanted to hear. They wanted him to say that seeing his wife and kids was the single most important and beautiful moment of his life, that it was like a religious experience, that he'd cried and finally felt that he knew them completely. Instead, he told them what he told everyone, and it always sounded something like this:

"Seeing my family was great, but not for the reasons you might think. It was a very special moment we'd been leading up to, and when the bandages came off it was a chance to share it with them and describe it to them and just be around them for their reactions. But I already knew them better than I knew anyone else in the world, so I didn't need to see them in order to know them or love them any better. I already felt like I could see them when I was blind. And, actually, the first time I cried, it was from seeing a float in a parade."

That answer always killed the buzz in the room, and it did this time, too. The interviewer rephrased the question to give May another chance. May gave him the same answer.

Later, the reporter asked if May had seen anything that had bothered him since gaining vision. May related how upset he'd been to see a homeless person, that the sight of clutter and disorganization troubled him, that even car exhaust and smog appeared unpleasant for their implications. He didn't dare mention his reaction to obese people—he was nearly too ashamed to discuss it with his wife.

Jennifer was next in the interview chair. Straightaway, the reporter asked if she felt threatened by May's new ability to see women. She replied that she did not. The man chuckled knowingly, leaned in for a just-between-you-and-me, and asked again. She gave him the same answer. He tried a third time. May listened intently from the other room. He knew Jennifer had been nervous about being interviewed on camera.

"I don't know what you're driving at," Jennifer finally told him. "I think it's great. I want Mike to see other women. I want him to see everything."

May's face flushed warm.

"She knows who she is," he thought. "And she loves me."

May traveled to San Francisco in early July for another eye appointment. Goodman gave him the same assessment he always did: No change. On previous visits, May had asked if his vision might improve in a few weeks or a month. This time, he felt like asking if this vision might be forever, but instead he asked nothing at all.

That night, he poured a cyclosporine tablet into his hand. He could see the tiny pill on his pink fingers. And he wondered, as he did every night when he took this medicine, what the long-term effects would be, if he'd be made to pay for this journey into light.

Sendero delivered May to Louisville, Kentucky, for the Fourth of July. At night, he met up with friends at the Buckhead Grill, just across the Ohio River in Indiana, where the group sat down to dinner and awaited the fireworks. At first thunder, everyone rushed to the restaurant's deck for a riverfront view. May's stomach tightened. The sound of explosions always returned him to his backyard in Silver City, New Mexico, to the moment the world ignited and blinded him at age three.

It was safest to keep one's eyes covered during

explosions. May looked. Flying crayons of light mushroomed over his head, dripping neon greens and reds down the black sky and dropping blue knit umbrellas onto the river. Every explosion was sudden and unpredictable and impossible not to see, which is to say that they thrilled him in ways he hadn't known, which is to say that they terrified him in ways he'd known forever. During the grand finale his exhausted eyes begged to close, but he kept them open because even when he was three he had always needed to know what things were like.

Certain that the explosions had ended, May finally closed his eyes. A friend suggested that the group walk back to the hotel across the historic Second Street Bridge. Ordinarily, May would have looked the bridge up and down, but this time he was content to keep his eyes closed and join in discussions about the rhythm of the fireworks and the beauty of the night. Near the center of the bridge, he drifted out of the conversation and into his surroundings. To his left he could feel the shadow of the wind and the stillness of the Ohio River. To his right he could see the onrush of cars, their headlights darting, horns shouting, tires tracking. He walked in a straight line over the rest of the bridge. It felt like he could fall if he leaned to either side in just the smallest of ways.

After May returned from Louisville, he told Jennifer about his ambivalence about fireworks and about his narrow walk along the Second Street Bridge.

"How are you doing, Mike?" she asked.

May yearned to tell her what he'd been thinking lately: that it had been more than four months and this vision should have sorted itself out by now; that in ways his vision was getting more overwhelming rather than less; that the words **lifetime** and **unending** had begun to enter his thoughts. He choked off the idea of giving voice to these ideas. He was Mike May. He always found a way. So he told her that he was fine and they put their heads on the pillow, but May didn't sleep. Instead, he thought about how strange it felt to have no answers, to know of no one who could explain what was happening to him, to have no one in the world who could say whether this was going to be forever.

A few days later, the phone rang in May's home. A lively young woman with a lilting British accent asked to speak to Michael May.

"This is Mike May."

"Hello, Mike, if you don't mind me calling you Mike," said the woman. "My name is Ione Fine. I'm a research scientist at the University of California–San Diego. My colleague saw you on TV. I don't know if you know this, but cases like yours are extremely, extremely rare. But it's the sort of thing I study. I'd like to ask you a few questions, and I imagine you might have some questions for me. I wonder if you'd be willing to talk to me for a few minutes."

CHAPTER**THIRTEEN**

Dr. Ione (pronounced Eye-*oh*-nee) Fine had proposed to fly May to San Diego for three days of observation and testing. It sounded like a rigorous schedule, but he agreed. It seemed there might be answers in San Diego. May needed to know.

Fine picked him up at the San Diego airport in late July. From the moment they shook hands in the terminal May knew he'd better be on his toes. Fine's conversation danced like Ping-Pong balls in a lottery machine, ricocheting from descriptions of her vision lab to her love for dogs to the structure of the brain to a great Mexican restaurant she knew in the area. He worked to decipher her accent, an elegant British taffy flecked with girlishness and, when she delivered a quip, a bit of mischief. He could tell she was pretty. He could see it in how she moved. He could hear it in the way men spoke when she asked directions to the parking lot.

Driving to her lab, Fine introduced herself. She was twenty-nine years old and was working at UCSD with a renowned vision researcher, Professor Donald MacLeod. She'd become interested in the

effects of long-term visual deprivation after working on a case of vision restoration with a subject
who'd had limited vision but hadn't been close to
being totally blind.

"You mean I'm special?" May teased.

"You're so special I almost didn't call you," Fine
said. "The bloke I live with, Geoff, who is also a vision scientist, saw a little report about you on TV.
He said, 'Ione, you've got to come here and watch
this!' Now, I know these kinds of cases are never for
real, and I was a bit annoyed with him anyway because he wasn't helping with the cooking. So I kept
turning the asparagus, got a little snappy with him,
and said, 'No thanks, very much. I won't watch.'"

"So how did you end up calling me?"

"My supervisor, Don, and another colleague
watched the same report, and they nagged me. So I
finally figured, Okay, to get these people off my
back I'll call this Mike May character and confirm
that his case doesn't qualify as blind-for-a-lifetime.
Then I can have some peace and quiet."

"Why did you think I wouldn't qualify?"

"People never do. They either went blind later
in life, or they had some useful vision while blind,
or they had their sight restored not long after going
blind. To find someone like you, who was totally
blind since early childhood and had his vision restored so many years later, is incredibly rare. There

are probably fewer than twenty cases like yours known to history."

"How many?"

"Fewer than twenty documented in the history of the world. The first case goes back to ancient times. People like you just don't happen."

May sat there dumbfounded. He'd had the sense that he was alone in his journey. Now he knew it.

For her part, Fine didn't mention the deep depression that seemed inescapable among his predecessors, though she was aware of it from reading the literature. She'd made a mental note to stay on guard for signs of it.

Fine asked May about his life. He told her about his accident, about the force of his mother's example, and about his new GPS product, which he'd placed on her dashboard so he could know where they were going.

"Do you still hold the downhill speed-skiing record?" she asked.

"Still do," May said.

May asked about Fine's life. She told him that she was born and raised in Edinburgh, Scotland, and went to college at Oxford when she was seventeen. She was the daughter of Kit Fine, a renowned philosopher, and Anne Fine, the author of many of Britain's most beloved children's books, including **Mrs. Doubtfire.**

"That's one of my favorite movies ever," May said. "I like the story, the humor, the goofiness of Robin Williams. It didn't need much description—it's so much about his dialogue. Even his facial expressions are usually echoed by something he says."

Fine made a mental note about the facial expressions. Then she looked toward May.

"The book is even better," she said.

Fine parked her car and walked with May to her office. Inside, she laid out her plans for his visit. She told May she was going to subject him to a battery of tests, each designed to assess the quality and nature of his vision, each with the goal of answering—for the first time ever—the following questions:

- What effects does a near lifetime of visual deprivation have on the brain?

- Why is May good at certain visual tasks but poor at others?

- Can May improve?

The questions resonated in May's gut. These were the ones he had been asking himself, in various ways and at various levels, for months. Now a young woman from Scotland who hadn't even believed him to be real was proposing to answer those very questions.

"Do you think you can do it?" May asked.

"Well, this stuff has rarely been studied," she said. "The case histories are pretty sketchy. We can't blind people at birth to experiment on them— ethics boards get fussy about things like that. And there aren't any other subjects like you around. But we can try. We can definitely try."

Before anything, Fine wanted to measure May's acuity—his ability to see the detail in the world. She knew from talking to Dr. Goodman that May's eye and optics were near perfect, but that his visual acuity was poor. She wanted to see how poor.

She seated him at arm's length from a computer monitor, then sought to determine the accuracy with which May could discern alternating black and white bars in a patch of screen half an inch wide. People with normal sight can see the pattern until there are between sixty and one hundred bars. May could see only one black and one white bar. Any more than that and it looked gray. Other tests showed similar results. His ability to see detail— what Fine called "high spatial frequencies"—had fallen apart. That's why he had to be close, some- times inches away, in order to make out the detail in things. Fine gave May the results, and she didn't mince words.

"You're terrible at detail," she said.

"Is it my eye?"

"No. It's almost certainly your brain. And you seem such a bright chap."

May laughed. He asked why, if he was so poor at seeing detail, things didn't look blurry to him. She explained that when the brain encounters the high spatial frequencies that imply an edge, it sharpens them on its own. The sharpness of edges is basically an illusion performed by the brain, she said, and everyone's brain did it.

"But I still don't see the detail inside the edges. You do."

Fine explained to May that his brain was like a camera that took very low resolution photographs, even worse than the cheapest convenience store security camera. If someone was asked to touch up one of those security photos, they could probably sharpen all the edges in the photo, because the edges would be easy to guess. But they could never hope to fill in the remaining details—say, the burglar's face or the pattern on his shirt—because the camera hadn't captured that level of detail in the first place.

May sat for a moment in silence.

"That's exactly how I see," he said finally. "Thank you for that."

Fine next wanted to test May on his ability to do simple form tasks. May asked if it made sense to test him on anything now that she had determined that he couldn't see details. She reminded him that he could still see some details from up close, so she would simply enlarge the images on the test screen so that his acuity wouldn't be the issue.

He sat very near to the computer monitor for a new series of tests. He was able, with little effort, to name letters of the alphabet; recognize if something was to the left, to the right, above, or below something else; detect the change in orientation of a bar; and identify simple shapes like squares, circles, and triangles.

Next, Fine showed him a series of common objects, including a boot, a guitar, a bucket, and a frog. Instinctively, he tried to touch the objects, despite knowing that they were simply images on a flat screen. He struggled with all of them, searching each image for clues, drawing on all his powers of reasoning, assembling hypotheses and then straining to make his best guess. He identified just 25 percent of the objects. People with normal sight routinely identify them all, even when the fine detail that was invisible to May is removed. Fine noticed that the few he got right—like the guitar and boot—seemed to have a very particular shape that was recognizable from almost any angle, while those he missed—the bucket and frog—depended strongly on the angle at which the photograph was

taken. May had trouble with any image that required a sense of the depicted object's depth—as
well as its outline.

Fine scribbled some notes. She was struck not
just by May's seeming inability to perceive an object
in depth but by the immense amount of work he
exerted in trying to identify those objects. She could
see that none of it came automatically to him. And
she could see him laboring.

"How are you doing, Mike?" she asked.

"I'm a little tired but I'm fine," he said. "I'm
proud that I recognized the guitar."

The day was growing late, so Fine closed her lab
and drove May to a restaurant for dinner, where
they met her soon-to-be husband, Geoff Boynton,
a vision researcher at the nearby Salk Institute. They
were joined by Don MacLeod, a brilliant and soft-
spoken Scot who supervised Fine's work at the university. May found the men as engaging and warm
as he did Fine. Over a long dinner they talked about
May's GPS, their fondness for dogs, and the strange
nature of May's vision. None of them sounded surprised when he described the disparities in his visual abilities. None of them seemed shocked when
he said that faces meant little to him. It felt good to
be among people who seemed, in ways, already to
know him.

Near the end of the meal, Fine asked May if he

knew about a man named Molyneaux. May said that he did not.

"He was a Dubliner, and a friend of the great philosopher John Locke," Fine said. "His wife had a sudden convulsion coming out of church and getting into a carriage. Within a year she was totally blind. In the late 1600s, he posed a question to Locke that was debated by some of the great philosophers of the time. He asked Locke to imagine a man, blind for life, who had learned to distinguish a cube and a sphere by touch alone. If that man were made to see, Molyneaux asked, would he be able to tell, by sight alone, which one was the cube and which one was the sphere? Locke and others argued that he could not."

"I could see the difference between a square and a circle right away," May said.

"Well, Mike, you might be the answer to Molyneaux's question," Fine said. "My father is a philosopher, so my whole childhood was spent with philosophical arguments. Just once, I'd love to end one, shut them all up! But there might be a problem or two with proclaiming you the answer."

Boynton and MacLeod smiled. They loved it when Fine got on a roll.

"First, you weren't born blind. We don't know if your three years of vision aided your ability to distinguish shapes when the bandages came off. Second, maybe you could tell the cube from the sphere because of their two-dimensional shapes—same as you can tell a circle from a square. But what if Molyneaux had asked if the newly sighted man could distinguish between a triangle and a pyramid? Or a square and a cube? In other words, would the newly sighted man see the pyramid and the cube in depth?"

"That might be different," May said. "I don't know if I could."

"Well, we have a lot more tests to do," Fine said, raising a glass of wine for a toast. "Here's to finding out."

May stayed the evening at MacLeod's house, then drove with Fine to her lab the next morning. When they arrived, she told him that she would be testing him on faces.

"Uh-oh," May said.

Fine positioned him perhaps a foot away from a large computer monitor.

"I'm going to show you a series of photographs of faces," she said. "Tell me whether they are male or female."

The slides began. May studied each face. Again, he seemed to be laboring, to be consciously and deliberately assembling clues, building a theory, and thinking through his decisions. He scored only 70 percent in judging gender. Subjects with normal vision score 100 percent. Fine suspected that he was using clues like hair length and jewelry to judge a face's gender, so she showed him another series of faces, this time with hair and jewelry removed. His scores dropped to near random.

"I'm just guessing on these," he said.

Next, she asked him to judge whether a person in a photograph looked happy, neutral, or sad. As before, May struggled to find clues, this time trying to determine if the corners of the mouth were positioned higher or lower than its center—a clue to whether a mouth was smiling or frowning. He scored only about 60 percent on this test, not much above chance. Subjects with normal vision would get them all right. Fine then showed May short movies of people smiling to see if motion somehow helped him detect facial expressions. It didn't.

Finally, Fine showed May a series of photographs in which a person's face had been scrambled or inverted—perhaps the eyes, nose, and/or mouth had been flipped upside down or put in the wrong place. Such images are almost always disturbing to normally sighted people.

May studied the faces for several seconds. After a while, he reported that something seemed wrong about them, but he could not say what it was. He had no emotional reaction to them.

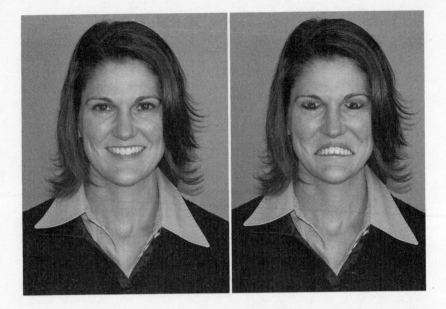

May cannot readily distinguish between the first (normal) face and the second face, in which the eyes and mouth have been inverted. The second image is typically disturbing to normally sighted people but is not for May. (Note that when the images are flipped upside down, the second face becomes more normal looking and less disturbing. That's because we are used to seeing faces right side up and are exquisitely sensitive to any disturbance in faces when they are right-side up. But we have much less experience with upside down faces, so we don't have anything close to that kind of sensitivity when they are upside down. In fact, we hardly notice very obvious distortions. Monkey species that spend a lot of time hanging upside down don't have the same sort of specialization for right-side-up faces that we do. It is likely they wouldn't find the second face above disturbing from either orientation.)

Fine studied May's body language. He looked spent. She remembered her commitment to watching for signs of depression.

"Are you okay, Mike?" she asked. "How do you feel?"

"I'm frustrated. I really want to do well on faces. I want to understand them. But I'm just guessing here."

Fine next tested May's ability to perceive motion. In test after test, he performed flawlessly, detecting and describing the motion automatically and without conscious effort. His results were the equal of the normally sighted. It was, with respect to seeing motion, as if he'd never been blind. He sat high in his chair with pride. The results startled Fine. One of them fascinated her.

She had shown May a collection of lighted dots set against a dark background such as the one below:

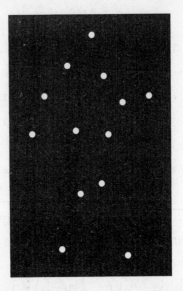

When she asked if the dots had meaning to him, he answered that they did not. Then she put the dots into motion. Immediately, May responded.

"That's a person walking," he said.

He was correct. Fine had shown him a "point-light walker," a person who had been filmed in the dark with just a few small lights attached to critical joints in the body.

She showed him another point-light walker.

"That's a woman walking," he said.

He was correct. Fine showed him several more. Often, he was able to identify the gender of the point-light walker.

"That's really impressive," Fine said. "That's quite a complicated and subtle bit of visual processing, Mike."

"Well, I'm very good at motion," he replied. "And in the name of scientific accuracy, I must acknowledge that I do my share of watching women."

The next test was to measure color perception. As with motion, May performed automatically and superbly. MacLeod, an expert in the study of color vision, judged that May's color vision might be even better than his own. May was rolling.

Fine suspected that the next set of tests, designed to measure depth perception, might prove more difficult. May had struggled with depth when trying to identify common objects.

On one of the first tests—for occlusion—May did well. He could judge which object was behind another object based on how one blocked the view of the other. After that, however, his performance collapsed. When asked which of three spheres bulged out (two were concave), he could not answer—this was the equivalent of not being able to perceive the moguls at Kirkwood. He struggled with perspective and other important pictorial cues to depth—cues that were essential to seeing the world in three dimensions.

Then Fine showed him this and asked him to identify it:

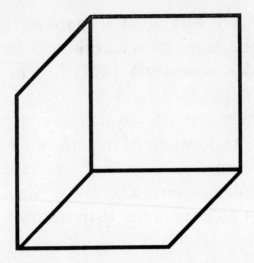

May studied the image.

"It's a square with lines," he said.

Those five words seemed the answer to Fine's variation of Molyneaux's question. She had asked whether the newly sighted man could distinguish a square from a cube. It appeared that May could not, even after six months of vision. All he saw was a square in two dimensions with extra lines.

For no particular reason, Fine pressed a button on the computer that put the shape in motion, rotating it in and out, in and out.

May shot up in his chair.

"That's a cube!" he said.

Fine couldn't believe what she was witnessing. Up to this point, she'd believed May to be virtually unable to see in three dimensions. Somehow, motion had produced in him the sensation of depth.

"That is absolutely incredible," she said. "That was just the coolest moment I think a scientist could ever hope to experience. I don't think I'm ever going to forget this, Mike. And I think it's really important."

That night, May and MacLeod went to dinner at the San Diego condo where Fine and Boynton lived. Before May arrived, Fine told Boynton about the day's fascinating test results, and about how frustrated her subject seemed when trying to perceive faces. Fine worried—she was a laboratory scientist and had no experience in helping people deal with stressful situations. Living in such a confusing visual world had to be frightening. She wished she knew how to help.

Fine served wine and cheese when May arrived. The conversation surfed from baseball to graduate students to local politics.

"Anyway, Mike," Fine said during a brief lull, "how's it going? How are you feeling?"

"I'm fine," he said. "But I'm curious about something, Ione. Why do you keep asking if I'm okay?"

"Umm . . . uh . . . umm . . ."

Fine could not find the words. She looked to Boynton for an assist. None was forthcoming.

"Well," she said finally, "it seems like there's a high incidence of depression in other sight-recovery subjects. We just want to make sure you're okay. We don't want to push you on this stuff."

May smiled. "Don't worry about me," he said. "I thrive on pushing. Push away."

Fine said that she'd been telling Boynton and MacLeod about the results of the face testing.

"Did she tell you I stunk?" May asked.

They confirmed that she had.

"It's really a mystery to me," May said.

"Do you know that perhaps one in a hundred people in the general population—maybe even more—can't recognize faces?" Boynton asked. "They can't even recognize the faces of people they know and love intimately."

"What do you mean? Why not?" May asked.

"It's a condition called prosopagnosia, or 'face blindness.' It's thought to relate to a problem in the part of the brain that does a lot of face processing. You don't hear much about it because often people are embarrassed to talk about it, and others don't even know they have it."

"How can a person not know they have it?"

"Because those people have always used other clues to recognize people, like a person's walk, hair color, clothes, that kind of thing."

"That's what I use. Do you think I have this condition?"

"You do have prosopagnosia, but it seems to be part of a more general difficulty in understanding

the visual world. In most people with prosopagnosia, their problems are limited to faces. Yours
seem to go way beyond faces."

The conversation turned to the subject of facial
beauty. What was it, May wondered, that made a
person's face beautiful? He'd forever heard about the
mysterious allure of the eyes, the drama of high
cheekbones, the power of a strong chin. But what
did all that mean? He couldn't understand those
things even when he got close enough to see them.

Fine, MacLeod, and Boynton told him that re-
searchers believed that attractiveness in faces seemed
to be based on two factors.

The first was symmetry—people seem to prefer
faces that are as closely matched as possible on the
left and right sides. There might be evolutionary
value in choosing such a person, since symmetry
provides evidence that the person has good genes
and that everything went right during early development.

The second was averageness—people seem to
like faces that are the average of their gender. If one
were to average the features on, say, one thousand
female faces, the result would be a slightly pixieish
woman that nearly everyone in the culture would
find pleasantly attractive (though few would find
gorgeous). It would work the same for male faces.

"But isn't beauty a cultural thing?" May asked.
"There was a time when men preferred a Rube-

nesque woman. Now they prefer a thinner build. Maybe it's just the culture of the time."

"Ah, but the waist-to-hip ratio stays constant," Fine countered. "You can have a society that likes thin women or plump women, but men seem consistent in their preference for a .67 waist-to-hip ratio, or thereabouts. Essentially, that means the woman's fertile."

"What's your ratio, Ione?" Boynton asked.

"A lady never reveals her ratio," Fine said. "But I will tell you that when I was in graduate school and heard about this waist-to-hip thing, I ran right home from class and measured. And I was right there at .67. I was very proud of myself."

They talked long past dinner. May savored the conversation. And he liked these people. In their tone, in their laughter, and in their ease, he could hear that they wanted more than just to study him. He could hear that they wanted the best for him.

May was scheduled to fly home the next morning. Fine brought him to her lab for a few quick tests before his flight. In her office, she became annoyed by the swirling and bouncing patterns of the screen saver on her monitor.

"That is incredibly distracting!" she said, sliding her chair toward the screen and turning it off.

"That's how vision feels to me all the time," May said.

Fine's last tests were on visual illusions. May's reaction to one of them struck her as particularly illuminating. She showed him these two tables:

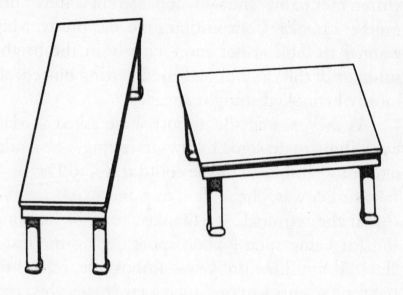

To normally sighted observers, the tabletops appear to have entirely different dimensions. To May, they appeared identical. May was correct—the tables are made from identical rectangles. He did not perceive the illusion.

May could hear Fine writing notes. Occasionally, she would murmur something to herself. He could sense her putting together the strange nature of his case, connecting the results and sorting the ambiguities to form an explanation, and maybe even a prognosis. Yet he did not want to push her for answers. "She'll tell me when she's ready," he thought.

———

On the way to the airport, Fine told May a bit more about growing up in Scotland as the daughter of a philosopher and a famous children's book writer. Her name, she said, appeared in some of her mother's books. Certain that Fine was pretty, May wanted to look at her more closely in the bright sunlight of the car, but he feared getting busted, so mostly he looked straight ahead.

As they neared the airport, Fine asked if May was willing to do some follow-up testing—he could return to San Diego or she could travel to Davis.

"Either way," he said. "I'm game."

At the terminal, she thanked him for his time and for being such a good sport during the tests. She told him how unlikely—impossible, really—it was for a scientist to find such a rare case as his, and such a bright and willing subject. She called it "once in a lifetime," and May knew what she meant. It was how he had come to think of his encounter with Dr. Goodman, the adventure he'd undertaken over the last five months, and about his feeling for these scientists in San Diego who were trying, with a few ghosts from history as their guides, to understand him.

May went back to work the same day he returned from San Diego. At night, he told Jennifer and his kids about his tests, about Fine, and about the idea that the scientists might put together some interesting theories about his case.

"And remember this," he warned his kids. "I don't fall for illusions. So don't try to pull any fast ones."

The next day he told his friend Bashin about the tests. Bashin couldn't get enough of the information.

"It's even more fascinating than we realized," Bashin said. "What's their thinking on this?"

"They haven't told me yet," May replied. "I think they're still trying to figure me out."

In San Diego, Fine tested a control group of subjects on the same tests she had given May. She removed the detail to simulate May's low acuity. They still got everything right. They still perceived illusions. That meant May's results were not due to poor acuity. They were due to something else.

Fine kept puzzling over May's case. He could perceive motion beautifully but was shockingly bad at other critical aspects of vision. Late one night, she wrote an e-mail to MacLeod:

I keep thinking about Mike suddenly seeing the cube in depth when it was put in motion. It's a little like the way a cat chases a ball of string when it's moving. Maybe Mike has a cat brain? Am I going crazy?

She was horrified a moment later to realize she'd sent the e-mail to May rather than to MacLeod. She received a reply a few minutes later.

> Glad to know I have a cat brain. Must go out for cat food now. Mike.

In subsequent discussions, Fine and MacLeod came to think of May's visual world as much like an abstract painting, filled with colorful and mostly flat and meaningless shapes. When people asked what Fine thought it was like for May to see, that was the best description she could give—that it was like looking at an abstract painting, that he had Picasso eyes.

Except when things moved. Motion, it seemed, lent a sense of depth to May's visual world.

Over the next several weeks, May traveled to San Diego and Fine traveled to Davis for more testing. The results were always the same: he was excellent at motion and color, terrible at understanding faces, seeing in depth (except if something was moving), and recognizing objects.

To May, this dichotomy remained as mystifying as ever. To Fine, however, it was all starting to fall into place. As she further contemplated the test results, reviewed cases that dated back to the 1700s, and lay awake at night thinking, she began to understand not just why May saw the way he did, but about the implications for his future, about whether he might improve. Her insights were grounded in a new way of thinking about how vision works—a way of thinking that just a few scientists were beginning to explore.

CHAPTER**FOURTEEN**

Before the middle of the nineteenth century, vision was widely thought to be a passive experience, one in which objects were simply "out there" to be seen. Various explanations were put forth to describe the process, including the idea that the eye shot "fingers" of light onto objects in order to "touch" them, or that objects broadcast images of themselves to the observer. These accounts supposed the world and its objects to be self-evident; seeing them did not require the brain to make inferences or engage in problem solving or do any of its usual cognitive work. And that made sense. Seeing felt effortless and automatic, if it felt like anything at all.

But then, starting in 1850 with the renowned German scientist Hermann von Helmholtz, and continuing in the middle of the twentieth century with psychologist Richard Gregory and others, scientists offered a startlingly different explanation for the brain's role in vision. Human beings, they argued, depended to a great extent on knowledge in order to see, to make sense of what Gregory called the "shadowy ghosts" that were the retinal images in our eyes.

The idea seemed preposterous on its face. How could knowledge make it possible to see? Surely, the most uneducated person saw as well as the most learned. But Helmholtz, Gregory, and the others were not referring to a knowledge of facts and figures of the kind found in encyclopedias. By knowledge, they meant **a set of assumptions about the world and the objects that exist in it.** This set of assumptions, they argued, was so deeply ingrained in the human brain that people imposed them instantaneously, automatically, and unconsciously on the visual data streaming in from the eyes. No one realized they were using knowledge to interpret the visual scene, but everyone did it all the time.

There was powerful evidence to support this theory. Among the most compelling examples was the existence of visual illusions. If objects were simply out there to be seen, visual illusions wouldn't occur—people would see things properly, as they actually were. Yet there were numerous visual illusions. What caused them?

Gregory and others argued that many visual illusions resulted when a person's implicit knowledge—that instant, automatic, and unconscious set of assumptions about the world and its objects—dominated over contrary evidence from the eye.

The hollow face illusion provides a powerful

example of this dynamic. It can be demonstrated by showing an observer the front of a simple plastic Halloween mask—say, one of Charlie Chaplin. As expected, the observer sees the face as convex— Chaplin's features protrude outward. When the mask is rotated to show the reverse side, however, Chaplin's hollow features also suddenly appear to protrude outward; they look as robust and convex as they did when viewed from the front.

What explains this illusion? Gregory argued—and every vision scientist now agrees—that it is due to the observer's very powerful knowledge of faces: every face he has ever seen has been convex. Therefore, despite the visual evidence, he must perceive the hollow face as pointing outward. His implicit knowledge of faces is so powerful that he cannot defeat the illusion—even if he consciously tells himself that he is seeing a hollow face.

Consider another illusion, "Terror Subterra" by Roger Shepard. Which monster in the picture is larger?

Nearly all observers perceive the monster in the rear to be much larger. In fact, they are identical in size—hold your finger against the picture to check. Again, the role of knowledge—one's set of assumptions about the world and its objects—is critical to the perception. But what knowledge causes us to perceive one monster as so much larger than the other?

In human experience, an object's perceived size depends on two factors:

- Its size on the retina

- Its perceived distance

That makes for a simple formula:

$$\text{Perceived size} = \text{size on the retina} \times \text{perceived distance}$$

If these monsters were the same size, the one that appears farther away should cast a smaller image on the retina. Since it doesn't, the brain hypothesizes that the more distant monster is larger than the closer monster. And that hypothesis is so strong that the observer truly sees it that way.

But that's not the only bit of knowledge the brain imposes on this scene. Look at the monster's faces. The one being chased appears terrified. The one doing the chasing appears aggressive or angry. In fact, their faces are identical. In human experience, people being chased almost always appear frightened, while people doing the chasing almost always appear aggressive or angry. Our brain imposes that knowledge on the scene and therefore "sees" what it expects to see. (Illusions like this can even be affected by the particulars of our own experience—children of abusive parents, for example, are more likely to see a neutral face as angry, even at a very early age.)

This idea—that knowledge and vision are highly related—can be demonstrated in myriad examples that do not involve visual illusions. What do you see in this picture?

Some observers see a duck; others see a rabbit. Then the perception quickly shifts—those who saw the duck now see the rabbit, and vice versa. The brain's knowledge of these animals—its assumptions about them—causes it to form two hypotheses about the image. Since each hypothesis is equally likely, the brain continues to entertain them both, resulting in the "flipping" of vision between duck and rabbit. (Note, however, that if an observer is told beforehand that he will be viewing a picture of a duck, it is unlikely that he will first see the rabbit. In that case, the brain has been given some extra knowledge that it will bring to bear on the picture, and this will dominate what is seen.)

Recent advances in the ability to measure specific kinds of brain activity confirm that knowledge and vision are highly related. It is now thought that more than a third of the human brain is involved with vision, an indication of the magnitude of the task. Today, it is virtually impossible to find a vision scientist, researcher, or psychologist who does not agree that knowledge and vision are highly related, and that without our knowledge about the visual world our ability to understand visual scenes would fall apart.

This current understanding of vision seemed to have great implications for May's case. If knowledge and vision are highly related, and there's nothing wrong with May's eye, it seemed distinctly likely that May had a knowledge problem.

To get at the nature of such a problem, we must understand how human beings come to attain this knowledge in the first place.

A newborn's eyes are flooded with visual information—colors, motion, and shapes that come from objects in the world around it. Yet newborn babies have no experience with any of these things, and few assumptions about them.

What must it be like to see things about which you have no experience or knowledge? We can scarcely imagine it—by adulthood, we have experience with nearly everything. If we do experience something completely foreign to us, we find it nearly impossible to impose a meaning or interpretation on the image.

Consider this photo. What is it?

Very few people would be able to tell that the object in the photo is a fossil. Even fewer know that the fossil is of a swift-swimming turtle from Germany. Certain archaeologists, however, would understand it immediately. Their visual experience of this image, as a result of their knowledge, is richer and more certain. Most of us have that sort of richness and certainty only when we see a fossil to which we can attach meaning, such as the one below:

Notice how our visual experience of the first fossil feels very different from our visual experience of the second. That is because we have knowledge of fish, but not of German swift-swimming turtles, especially in fossils. We can imagine that to the infant, almost all visual experiences feel like our experience of the first fossil rather than of the second.

Here are two more objects for which we don't have a sufficient knowledge for true vision:

Wire-stretching device similar to the type found in some hardware stores.

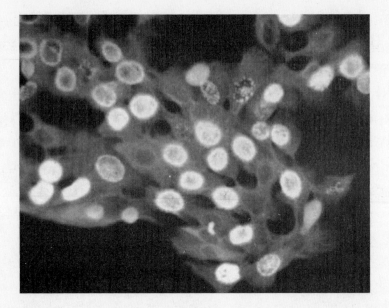

Corneal epithelial stem cells of the kind
transplanted into May's eye (as seen under
electron microscope)

To the infant, who lacks knowledge of the world
and its objects, the universe must seem a vast collection of these colorful, meaningless shapes, a
panorama of fossils and strange tools. One can
imagine that it must feel overwhelming to the infant, this overflow of visual information he cannot
even begin to sort.

How is the very young child to make sense of
this jumble of visual data? How is he to translate
these shapes into three dimensions and give them
meaning, to make them more than just a collection

of colorful blobs? How is he to build the knowledge of the world and its objects that is so essential to vision? It's not as if anyone can explain it to him.

There is only one way for the very young child to do this. He must interact with the things he sees. He must experiment with them, investigate them, explore them, probe them, play with them, touch, taste, smell, and hear them. He must handle everything, manipulate everything, go to and reach for everything. He must make his nursery his laboratory, a place in which his endless tests and trials with things—especially by touch—lead to a knowledge of their textures, shapes, purposes, and functions, to an understanding of their natures. Without that constant and direct interaction and experimentation with things, he cannot begin to form his set of assumptions about the world and its objects. Without touching a glass of water—tipping it, dropping it, breaking it, spilling it, shaking it, hearing its sounds, watching its water levels, observing the change of light and shade on its side as it's lifted, seeing it used to take a drink—he can't know a glass of water as anything but just a shape, a random fossil, and he might not even interpret it as a shape in three dimensions. In the laboratory of the young child, it makes perfect sense to eat carpet because that's yet another way to know the carpet's visual nature.

Interaction with the world and its objects is so

critical during early development that without it a person might never see properly. In a landmark experiment, Richard Held and Alan Hein at MIT raised two kittens in total darkness. For a short period during each day the kittens were placed in baskets that hung just above the ground from opposite ends of a pole. Holes were cut in one basket to allow one kitten's paws to reach the ground, but not in the other. The apparatus was constructed such that when one basket moved, the other moved identically.

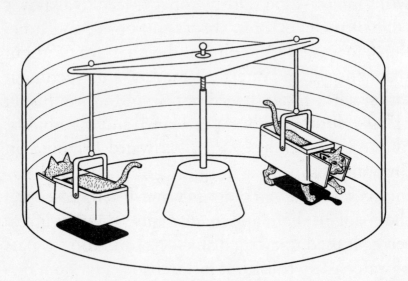

When the lights were turned on, the kitten in the basket with holes was allowed to run along the ground, causing its basket and its mate's basket to move identically, and giving each of them an identical visual experience.

At the end of the experiment, only the kitten that had been allowed to actively move the basket could move around the world using vision. The passive kitten—though it had exactly the same visual experience—was functionally blind. Seeing the world passively was not enough; interaction with the world was essential for vision to be useful.

Other studies show similar results. There is evidence that people brought up in iron lungs—in which their interaction with objects is severely restricted—cannot see things properly beyond the range of their body movements, beyond what they could touch. In one strange case, a boy was raised in a pawnshop and surrounded by all manner of objects. To ensure that he didn't touch the items or meddle with their tags, he was kept in a playpen. When removed, he simply could not judge distances beyond what he'd experienced by touch in the playpen.

The lesson in all this is clear: interaction with the world and its objects is critical to building the knowledge necessary for useful vision.

Mike May had that crucial interaction with the world. He had built his knowledge and formed his set of assumptions. By the time of his accident, at age three, he could see nearly as well as an adult.

Yet after his stem cell transplant surgery, he found himself with a strange and different kind of vision. He could perceive motion and color almost perfectly, but he could not make sense of faces, perceive things in depth (unless they were moving), or readily recognize objects. What explains this dichotomy? Is there something about perceiving motion and color that's different from perceiving faces, depth, and objects? And how does that relate to knowledge?

Ione Fine set out to answer that question by examining how people learn to perceive these things. She believed the answer might go a long way toward explaining May's vision. And maybe toward helping him improve.

FACE PERCEPTION

To most people, human faces appear distinctly unique, the most personal and nuanced objects in the world. In reality, they are very similar to one another. Differences of just a millimeter or two in symmetry or space between the eyes or in the eyebrow curvature or cheekbone angle or forehead height can make two quite similar faces look vastly different.

Animal faces are distinguished by the same kinds of tiny variations. Yet to us, chimpanzee faces look alike and sheep faces seem identical. Why do we see such profound difference in human faces but not in animal faces?

The answer lies in learning. Through intense practice that begins in early childhood, we make ourselves into experts on human faces. Practice and learning are everything. That's why shepherds can identify their sheep by faces—they've practiced all their lives with sheep faces, and now they're experts. And that's why people sometimes struggle to distinguish among faces from different ethnic or age groups—they haven't sufficiently practiced and interacted with them.

Practice with human faces doesn't just help a person identify and recognize faces. It also makes it possible to judge a person's gender, read her expressions, assess her interest in us, predict her mood. Often, the difference between a smile and a frown is just a tiny change in the angle of—or even the shadow on—the corner of the mouth. A one-millimeter shift in the pupils of a person standing across the room can tell us whether that person is looking at us or just over our shoulder; a one-millimeter shift in her eyebrow can tell us if she's interested or angry—all this at a distance of thirty feet. People would never be able to attach meaning to those minuscule differences without the benefit of massive practice—and massive learning.

That kind of learning takes years of intense

practice; children are still developing their face-perception skills at five or six years of age.

DEPTH PERCEPTION

When we open our eyes, a two-dimensional image falls on our retinas. Yet we perceive the world robustly and in three dimensions; its depth feels absolutely real to us, not at all a trick of the brain. How does that happen? How do we translate our flat retinal images into the majestic three-dimensional world in which we move and interact so confidently?

There seem to be three kinds of clues that the visual system uses to perceive depth:

- Pictorial cues

- Motion cues

- Stereopsis

Pictorial Cues to Depth

Pictorial cues are features in a photograph or painting or other two-dimensional representation that can produce the impression of depth. They are the ones Italian painters discovered in the early Renaissance. The most important are:

Occlusion

When an object hides another object, that object is seen as being closer.

Relative Height

The closer an object is to the horizon, the farther away the object appears.

Note that this is true both for the ships in the illustration (which are below the horizon) and for the balloons (which are above the horizon).

Cast Shadows

Shadows can indicate an object's depth. (The two photos are identical but for the addition of shadows in the photo on the right.)

Relative Size

The farther away an equal-sized object is, the less room it will occupy on one's field of view.

Familiar Size

Our knowledge of an object's size affects how we perceive that object's distance—and the distance and size of other objects around it.

The familiar size of the dolphins in the photo affects how we perceive their distance. Most of us would estimate that distance to be about ten feet. If, however, dolphins were the size of football fields, we might estimate that they were several thousand feet away in this photo. If dolphins were the size of insects, we might estimate their distance in this photo to be just a few inches.

Aerial Perspective

The air contains minuscule particles of water, dust, and pollution. The farther away an object is, the more particles we must look through, and therefore the hazier that object appears.

(Incidentally, aerial perspective doesn't occur on the moon, which has no atmosphere and therefore no particles. Astronauts struggled to judge distance on the moon.)

Linear Perspective
Parallel lines converge on the retina as they recede in depth.

Texture Gradient
As a surface gets farther away from us, its texture gets smaller and appears smoother.

Shape from Shading
When an object has a three-dimensional shape, some surfaces will be in the light and others will be in shadow.

These are just a few examples of the cues our brains use to transpose the two-dimensional images on our retinas into the perception of a three-dimensional world. One can hardly imagine the immense amount of knowledge about the world required to process these pictorial cues to depth, and to do it instantaneously, automatically, and unconsciously.

It turns out that these pictorial cues are **themselves** based on knowledge—a kind of statistical knowledge about what the world is like most of the time. Such pieces of knowledge are called "priors." They represent what we believe about the world when we come upon a new visual scene. Here are some examples:

- Adults are between five and seven feet tall.

- Light tends to fall from above.

- Physical objects create shadows.

- Certain objects are a certain color.

- The lines in our culture are often at right angles to each other (as with buildings).

Consider this photo:

The inclusion of a barn, a boat, and a creek in this photograph greatly helps us judge the windmill's size and distance. That's because we possess prior knowledge—that barns, boats, and creeks are almost always a certain size. If the windmill were the only object in the photo, we might think it a toy, or we might judge it to be several times larger than it really is.

How does a person go about learning these pictorial cues and priors? By now, we've seen that much of visual learning is done in early childhood, through constant interaction and experimentation with the world and its objects. It's the same with learning depth. A baby reaches, crawls, observes, tests, falls short, and goes too far, constantly calibrating visual clues with its tactile experience until the two-dimensional image on the retina translates automatically into a visual experience of depth. Infants aren't even sensitive to the pictorial cues to depth until they're about six months old—the age at which they start grabbing for objects. After that, the process of understanding and using pictorial-depth cues takes years to perfect. The task is astoundingly difficult—engineers still can't build a machine that can compute depth as accurately and robustly as humans compute it. Yet the child does it without any help from the parents and over just a few years—all from interacting with its environment.

Motion Cues to Depth

Pictorial cues, remember, are just one of the ways in which the visual system goes about perceiving the world in depth. Another set of cues becomes available when the observer or the object is in motion. These are known as motion cues. Two of the most important are:

Motion Parallax

Nearby objects move faster on the retina than distant objects do.

Motion parallax can be observed by watching the passing scene from inside a moving car. Nearby objects—like houses—appear to fly past, while more distant objects—like mountains—seem hardly to move at all. We perceive the faster-moving objects to be nearer to us than the ones that are moving more slowly.

Kinetic Depth Effect

The motion of a two-dimensional representation can create a perception of its three-dimensional form.

It was the kinetic depth effect that occurred when May saw a square on Fine's computer monitor leap into three dimensions as a cube when it began rotating on-screen.

Motion cues also rely on priors, though they are much simpler. Babies learn them more quickly and at a younger age than they do the pictorial cues for depth. Babies can perceive moving objects in a few weeks. Depth in motion is understood by the age of four months or perhaps even earlier.

Stereopsis

Stereopsis creates an impression of depth by comparing the small differences in the images produced by each eye.

Look at a nearby object. Cover one eye, then the other, then the first again. The object appears to move back and forth. The brain compares those two slightly different images to compute—and then perceive—the object's depth.

Stereopsis, of course, occurs only in people who have two working eyes, and so is not applicable to May's case. Stereopsis is not thought to be critical to good depth perception in humans, as it is useful only for objects that are about a yard from the body or closer. Beyond that the distance between the two eyes is so small compared to the distance to the object that the images in the two eyes are essentially identical. Many people think that stereopsis is the reason people are able to see in depth, but if you shut one eye you can still reach out and pick up a coffee cup, and you can still drive. About 10 percent of the general population doesn't have good stereoscopic vision, and even professional athletes have been known to lack it.

OBJECT RECOGNITION

Human beings must be able to recognize objects in order to interact with them. That alone requires massive learning—there's an endless number of objects in the world to know. But it's even harder than that. We must also recognize each of the objects in the world from every possible viewing angle. How can that be possible? Consider this picture. What does it show?

We recognize that object as an elephant. It is the most readily recognized view of an elephant—called by some its "canonical" view. Now consider the next picture. What does it show?

We also recognize this object as an elephant—despite its decidedly noncanonical view. How do we recognize something from a noncanonical view? After all, the picture above presents a very different two-dimensional form; it has a very different shape. Why don't we see it as a different object from the one shown in the first photo?

It is thought that a primary reason we can identify an object from its various noncanonical views is because we already understand its depth from its canonical view. Once the brain understands an object's depth—its robust and three-dimensional form—it can make the inference about how that object would look from different angles.

That ability is critical because most of the objects we encounter in our daily routines are not conveniently positioned for us at their canonical angles. And even if they were, their shapes would change the moment they moved or we moved. Our ability to see in three dimensions allows us to understand objects from virtually any viewpoint. If a person could see only in two dimensions, he would need to learn to recognize not just the objects in the world but myriad different views of each of those objects—an impossible task.

There are many other factors involved in recognizing objects, but without depth perception the rest are moot. Object recognition, like much of depth perception, develops later in the infant and can take years to perfect.

Motion

Infants perceive motion as early as two weeks after birth. By the time they're ten or twelve weeks old they can smoothly follow moving objects. They seem able to do this almost instinctively, without much need for experimentation or interaction with the world. It seems that motion is simply there to be perceived, and making sense of motion is a relatively easy task that seems to be nearly complete by six months of age.

Color

Infants have considerable color vision by the age of about two months. Development of color vision seems merely to depend on seeing color in the world, and doesn't require the baby to interact with the world. Color, like motion, seems simply to be there to be seen.

This understanding of the various parts of vision raises a critical question: Is there a difference between the things May perceives well (motion and color) and the things he perceives poorly (faces, depth, and objects)?

It definitely looks as if there is.

Motion and Color:

- **are simpler.** Motion is simply an object's change in position over time. Green is green.

- **don't require a complicated knowledge of the world to be perceived.** Infants understand motion and color within the first few months of life.

Faces, Depth, and Objects:

- **are more complex.** They are often characterized by tiny and subtle variations, cues, and clues that change frequently and are often dependent on context.

- **require a massive and complicated knowledge of the world to be perceived.**

This knowledge is derived in early childhood from constant interaction and experimentation with the world and its objects. It takes infants several months to understand faces and depth and to recognize objects.

———

The differences between the two categories are stark and fundamental. They also seem to suggest that the broken parts of May's vision can be fixed—maybe even made perfect.

Remember that knowledge and vision are highly related. If May can't perceive faces, depth, and objects, that might be because he forgot or otherwise lost the knowledge of how to do it. That makes intuitive sense. Perceiving faces, depth, and objects are among the most complicated tasks the visual system must learn—just the kind of complex knowledge we know that brains forget all the time. (Few of us, for example, remember those lengthy algebra formulas from school.) It makes equal sense that he'd retain the knowledge of how to perceive motion and color; they are among the simplest tasks for the visual system—just the kind of basic things that brains seem to remember forever. (Most of us, for example, remember basic arithmetic for life.)

This sounds very hopeful for May. If he forgot or otherwise lost the knowledge of how to see faces, depth, and objects, then surely he can relearn it. Who better than May to undertake some challenging learning?

But Fine wasn't sure he could learn it. To understand why, we must know a bit about neurons—the cells that calculate and contain all the knowledge we have—and how they work in the brain.

The human brain contains approximately 100 billion neurons. Neurons are a particular type of nerve cell designed to process and transmit electrical impulses. Some of these neurons transmit signals from the world outside, bringing signals to the brain from the eyes, ears, fingers, and even the stomach wall ("Oof—I ate too much"). But the majority of neurons receive, modify, and pass along signals from other neurons. Each neuron forms thousands of connections with other neurons, meaning that the number of possible combinations between them is greater than the number of elementary particles in the universe. It is thought that the brains of higher primates, and their network of neurons, are the most complex structures in the universe.

Particular connections between neurons are what give rise to particular sensations, perceptions, feelings, thoughts, memories—everything a person experiences, remembers, and feels. When a person perceives a banana, it is the result of electrical impulses traveling first from the eye to the brain, and then through a very particular network of neurons that have been formed to recognize and react to bananas. These "banana neurons," as we might call them, are created and strengthened by our experience with bananas. Neurons and connections for recognizing Uncle Joe are created and strengthened by experience with Uncle Joe. Forming particular neural networks is what we call learning. We form particular neural networks to represent everything we experience in the world, including faces, depth, objects, motion, and color.

To learn something as staggeringly complex as vision—with all its subtleties, shadows, cues, clues, priors, exceptions, contexts, and confusions—a person needs massive amounts of neurons available and ready for that purpose. But who owns a supply like that?

Young children do.

Consider the enormous learning of which young children are capable. Compared with adults, for example, they learn language at a staggering rate. Such learning is made possible in the very young child by huge stores of available neurons that are awaiting assignment. In fact, children have an **overabundance** of available neurons for learning; those that don't get used actually die as the baby becomes a small child.

Adults, however, don't have that kind of ready supply of neurons available for learning. Nor, it seems, do adult neurons form connections with other neurons as quickly and easily as do young-child neurons. That's why adults simply can't learn like children do.

A powerful example of this is language learning. An adult who learns a language will never be as fluent as a person who learned that language in childhood. In most cases, a native speaker can tell the difference between another native speaker and an expert later learner. A linguist can tell in every case.

Another example can be seen in cases of early brain damage. Frighteningly large chunks of brain are often removed from small children because of tumors or epilepsy—sometimes almost half the brain. That kind of brain loss in an adult would cause a severe handicap; the person might never walk or speak properly again. But in small children the brain can reorganize to make the best use of the remaining neurons (remember, there are 100 billion of them). Often, after a few years these children show no signs that a large part of their brain is missing.

This all seemed to be bad news for May. If he was to relearn the complex parts of vision he forgot or lost during his forty-three years of blindness, he would need the massive supply of neurons that children possess to do that kind of learning.

Maybe May still had his supply. After all, he possessed those neurons when he went blind, at age three, while he was still learning. Shouldn't his supply still be available for learning faces, depth, and objects? Shouldn't he be able to pick up where he left off?

Fine was skeptical that May's face, depth, and object neurons were still available for those tasks.

She had serious questions about whether he could resume his learning at all.

She knew from recent research that when certain neurons lose their input, they change what they represent in the world. If they can't do the job they were meant to do, they get up from their current jobs and go to represent something else. A neuron's ability to change its representation is known as its plasticity. Plasticity was one of Fine's particular areas of interest.

What determines if a neuron, deprived of its input, goes on to do something else? What determines its plasticity when its signals stop arriving—as happens to some vision neurons when a person goes blind?

It turns out that when neurons lose their input they are more likely to change what they represent if:

- they are deprived of input during childhood—especially early childhood

- there's a demand from another part of the brain for their services

- they represent complex tasks

Some of May's vision neurons—namely, those that process faces, depth, and objects—fell into all three categories, making them prime contenders to have gone off to represent something else.

Other of May's vision neurons—namely, those that process motion and color—seemed to satisfy only the first two categories, making them far less likely to have gone off to represent something else. The third category was key.

If that's what happened, Fine thought, it boded badly for May. It suggested that the neurons and networks he used as a child to perceive faces, depth, and objects had gone to do something else, perhaps to read braille or to aid in echolocation or to help him recall telephone numbers he couldn't write down. They were plastic enough when he was blinded to learn other useful skills, but they would not do that again; they would not come back to do vision now that he was an adult. Brains, for complicated evolutionary reasons, are not built to make many new neural connections in adulthood. If that was the case with May, it was likely he would never perceive faces, depth, or objects normally because he, like all adults, no longer had the available neural networks to learn them.

Still, Fine was not certain that this was the case. After all, no one had done the studies—almost all research on the effects of visual deprivation had been carried out on animals, like cats and mice, that are very different from humans. So this idea was purely speculative. She stayed up late into the nights, turning May's case over in her head, contemplating it, hypothesizing about it, testing it against all that science knew about vision and neurology. Textbooks provided no answers. The case histories gave no insights. There were no other subjects in the world like May. It was a full-blown mystery with particulars unlike any a scientist had ever tried to tackle. How was anyone to know whether May's vision neurons had irreversibly reassigned themselves?

There was, Fine thought, one way to know for sure.

She called May and asked if he'd be game for a new test, one that was very unusual and very new. It was one, she said, that some people would never consider.

CHAPTERFIFTEEN

On the telephone with May, Fine explained the deep connection between knowledge and vision. She described the magnitude of the knowledge required to see properly, and how much of vision was subtle, complex, dependent on context, based on tiny clues and rules of thumb. She related how vision slowly developed during early childhood, when the brain was capable of such massive learning, and how this huge amount of unconscious knowledge is imposed on the visual scene instantaneously and unconsciously—an astonishing feat of computing power. She told May that he'd once had this knowledge but must have forgotten or otherwise lost it after his accident. She said that without that knowledge a person couldn't see normally no matter how good his eyes.

For six months May's vision had been a mystery to him. Now it began to make sense. If a person couldn't bring this massive bank of knowledge to a visual scene, it stood to reason that he would bring whatever knowledge he could. That's why he yearned to touch everything. That's why he strained for context, leaned so heavily on color, motion, and his other senses. It was all to bring whatever knowledge he could to the raw data streaming into his eye.

"That must be why it's exhausting," May said. "I'm doing it all consciously. I've got to think about it. You don't."

"Precisely," Fine said.

"And that's why it feels overwhelming."

"Absolutely. By the time you're finished thinking through one visual image, others have jumped into the scene, each of which demands the same conscious, deliberate deciphering. I can imagine that would feel overwhelming."

Fine said that she suspected that to May vision felt like speaking a second language, a deliberate process similar to conjugating verbs, recalling vocabulary, working out tenses, and then assembling the parts into a whole.

"That's just how it feels," May said. "Imagine doing that every waking moment of every day."

Fine didn't need a crystal ball to know May's next question.

"Okay, I forgot how to see. How do I learn to do it again now?"

She explained to him about neurons and plasticity—about how some neurons, when deprived of input, will go off to do other jobs while others seem perfectly happy to remain at their original posts.

She told him that it was distinctly possible that the neurons he needed to perceive faces, depth, and objects—the ones he needed for so much of normal vision—might have gone away for good.

May sat in wonder at the simplicity of Fine's explanation. This single idea—that his brain might be wired for some parts of vision but not others—explained his world. It was why stairs looked like lines but he could catch a ball on the run. It was why he couldn't recognize his children's faces but could perfectly sort the laundry. It was why he could navigate his way around a cluttered room but could not find his shoes in that same room.

"Can I get those vision neurons back?" he asked.

"If they're gone, then we don't think so," Fine said. "It's like when you build a new house. Say you want to move the master bedroom from upstairs to downstairs. If it's early in construction—in the house's early childhood, so to speak—it's not a big deal to move the bedroom. But if the house is an adult already, it's too late—the bedroom is there to stay. That seems to be how plasticity works with certain neurons. They can shift early in a person's life, but shifting late is much rarer."

May's throat tightened. He understood the implications of Fine's explanation. If his vision neurons had permanently changed their representations, he would never improve; vision would always be a nonstop process of heavy cognitive lifting and information overflow.

"Does that mean I can't get better?" he asked.

For a moment Fine was silent.

"I'm not sure," she said. "We don't know if the parts of your brain that once perceived faces, depth, and objects are still wired to do those things. But there's a fairly new technology that can go a long way to telling us what's happening in your brain."

Fine told him about a special type of brain scan known as functional magnetic resonance imaging, or fMRI. An fMRI scan could look at specific areas of the brain and detect whether those areas were responding to specific stimuli. It could do that because active areas of the brain use oxygen, giving them slightly different magnetic properties than inactive areas. The fMRI could detect those differences.

Fine explained the process: She and some fMRI specialists would slide May into a large scanner, one that filled the better part of a room. While he was inside, they would show him pictures of faces. If the parts of his brain responsible for processing faces showed activity when presented with images of faces, then Fine would know that May still had the neurons and networks necessary to process faces. If they did not respond, she would know that his brain simply did not work for faces anymore. She would do the same with objects, simple forms, and motion. That would give the scientists the best chance to understand what was happening in May's brain. That would give them the best answer to whether May could learn to see again.

"What are the chances that the neurons I need are still there?" May asked.

"I don't know," Fine said. "No one's done a case like this before; it's totally unique. I wouldn't bet ten dollars on it either way."

"But there's a chance they're still there?"

"There's a chance. And that would prove you've got something to work with."

"When do we start?" May asked.

"Well, I should tell you that these scanners can be claustrophobic. They can be quite noisy. You're put inside them and asked not to move at all. Some people aren't comfortable—"

"When do we start?" May asked.

May's fMRI scan was scheduled for late September at Stanford University. He had two weeks to wait. He spent much of the time searching for new Sendero investors, and began to apply for federal development grants. His GPS-Talk product still performed beautifully, but May knew that the government agencies he hoped would buy it for clients still couldn't get their arms around paying several thousand dollars for a device that guided the blind from the heavens when they could pay twenty-five dollars for a cane that guided them from the ground. More and more, he believed that his company's survival depended on securing a new influx of investment or a major grant to allow him to shrink the product's form factor and reduce its price. Time was growing short.

Flush with a new understanding of his vision, May dialed his friend Bashin and invited him to a steak dinner in Sacramento.

"I know how things work," May said. "Dr. Fine explained it all to me."

"Forget steak," Bashin said. "We need a place where we can really talk. I know a Thai restaurant where they let you sit all night—they forget you're even there."

"What day should we do it, Bryan?"

"The question isn't what day, Mike. The question is, do we meet tonight at six-thirty or seven o'clock?"

May loved the boy in Bashin's voice. After months of questions, thrills, struggles, and uncertainties, Bashin still conceived of May's new vision as an adventure.

"Let's make it six," May said.

Over pad thai and imported beer, May recounted Dr. Fine's explanation for his vision. To a man of science like Bashin, the information was thrillingly cutting-edge. He asked strings of questions, most of which May found he could answer, a testament to the clarity of Fine's exposition.

As the restaurant emptied and the ice in their glasses melted, the men's conversation took a different turn.

"It's fascinating," Bashin said. "Dr. Fine says that a lot of what people see is based on their assumptions and expectations about the world, right?"

"Yes, that's how I understand it."

"Don't you think that's true in the emotional sense, too? How much of a person, I mean of their heart and soul, do we see or don't see because we have certain assumptions about them? Or how much beauty are we missing in things like this spoon or, say, the old wood on a park bench because we don't assume we'll see beauty in them?"

"That's true," May said. "You know, Ione talked a lot about how the brain imposes knowledge in order to see. But I think there might also be beauty in not imposing knowledge—"

"In being open to everything—"

"Yes, in being open to everything, in being open to every possible interpretation. In ways, there's something liberating about my vision, in the sense that so much of what I see can be anything. It's fascinating to think that an object, or even a person, can be anything. It means that almost anything can be beautiful."

Bashin and May talked deeper into the night. Each was fascinated by Fine's characterization of depth perception as an interpretation of the world, an intuitive leap by the brain. What other things in the world, they wondered, seemed ironclad but were merely interpretations? They laughed as they entertained possibilities both silly and serious.

Near closing time, a waiter blew out the candle on their table and took their water glasses. The men rose and reached for their wallets.

"You know," May said, "Ione told me about a famous study from the 1960s. I think you'd find it interesting."

He described the experiment in which two kittens were raised in the dark except for short periods during the day when they were placed in connected baskets and the lights were turned on. One kitten was allowed to put its paws through holes in the basket so it could reach the ground and move both baskets along. The other kitten had no holes in its basket and could only watch. Visually, their experiences were identical. At the end of the experiment, the active kitten had normal vision. The passive kitten was functionally blind.

"That's remarkable," Bashin said.

"It makes sense to me," May said. "I think exploration is everything. I think that's why I never grew up feeling like I couldn't see."

In late September, May squeezed into Fine's rental car for the hundred-mile drive from his home to the neuroimaging center at Stanford University. When they arrived, they joined another postdoctoral researcher, Alex Wade, professor Brian Wandell, and graduate student Alyssa Brewer. Together, these scientists would use a colossal magnet to journey deep into May's brain.

After exchanging pleasantries, Fine and her colleagues scurried to collect bite bars, stimulus equipment, swipe cards, and computer disks. And bawdy jokes. The jokes were part of the deal. May would be expected to remain in the scanner for long stretches, often with nothing to do. Reading him off-color jokes during downtimes was the least Fine could do to help him pass the time.

Wandell showed May to the scanning room, where he was read a lengthy disclaimer, asked if there were any bullets in his body (metal interferes with the machine's magnetic fields), and told to remove his personal belongings. He was surprised to learn that he needn't do anything inside the scanner except lie still, stay awake, and look at the images shown to him, which would be projected onto a mirror angled over his eye.

May peered at the scanner, a massive white rectangle that reached nearly to the ceiling and seemed to occupy most of the room. A patient would lie on a connected conveyor table that would slide him inside the machine through a narrow round bore at the scanner's front end. Operators sat in a nearby control room. May had heard tales of scanner claustrophobia and panic.

"Can I touch it?" he asked Wandell.

"Sure, go ahead."

May ran his hands over the bore's opening, the attached projector, and the conveyor table. To the scientists, he appeared to exhale after this tactile exploration. To them, it appeared that touch had switched on his vision.

May lay down on the table and prepared for his trip inside. He was given headphones, through which he would hear instructions. A projector, a screen, and a mirror were clamped across his neck, making him look like an invading alien from a 1950s science fiction movie. Though he wasn't told it at the time, the screen was nicknamed "the guillotine." When he was finally ready to go, the scientists moved to the observation area.

"Wait a minute!" Fine called out. "Where are my dirty jokes?"

Brewer ran in clutching several pages of randy puns, limericks, and blonde jokes. Fine inspected the lot.

"No, no, no!" she said. "These are too funny! He'll laugh too hard and move his head. Run back and find some that are only moderately funny. And hurry!"

The conveyor table began to move, and in a moment May was inside the scanner. Metal banged and magnets whirred—WAKACHUCK! WAKACHUCK! WAKACHUCK!—as Fine first showed May a series of movies showing stationary and moving dots. Next, she showed him a series of human faces—one per second for 20 seconds—followed by twenty seconds of blank screen. Then, she projected a panoply of images of everyday objects. After a lunch break, she showed him several different motion stimuli. All the while, the scientists watched May's brain for changes in oxidization and recorded the results.

Two hours later, the scientists thanked May for his time and for the opportunity to do such pioneering work. They told him it would be several days before they finished the first look at the data. Fine drove May back to Davis and said she would call him with the results. He stopped for a moment before leaving her car.

"Can I ask a final question?" May said.

"Of course," replied Fine.

"Do you have any leftover jokes I can take with me?"

The fMRI specialists went to work on May's scans. The results were unmistakable. The areas of his brain responsible for motion lit up like a pinball machine in response to motion stimuli—they were as robust as those areas in the brain of a normally sighted person. But the areas of May's brain responsible for processing faces showed no response to faces. The areas responsible for recognizing objects showed no response to objects. The areas responsible for perceiving simple form did respond—weakly—but they seemed strangely disorganized in a way the scientists had never seen before. Fine took a deep breath and got ready to call May with the news.

The phone rang in May's office. Though he'd handled dozens of business calls that day, he had a feeling this one might be Dr. Fine. He was right.

Her voice sounded subdued as she reported the brain scan results. The bottom line was this: May didn't seem to possess the neural structure necessary for normal vision—it just wasn't there anymore. That meant he was unlikely ever to see in the automatic way of the normally sighted. Fine's best guess was that May's vision would remain a process of heavy cognitive lifting, assembling clues, figuring things out, and managing the constant overflow of information and its resultant fatigue.

May went numb. He wanted to speak but his mouth didn't move. He looked out his window, still holding the telephone to his ear. The world outside looked flat to him.

"Are you saying I won't see normally for now, or I won't see normally ever?" May asked.

"However hard you work at vision, Mike, I don't think you'll ever see fluently, the way normal people do. It will always be incredibly hard work."

May thanked Fine for the results, and for the kindness and effort shown to him by her and the other vision scientists. He agreed to return for more testing but hardly heard his own words. A moment later they said good-bye.

In the kitchen, as May poured himself a glass of water, Jennifer asked about his day. He told her that he'd received the test results from Fine and that she'd said they weren't good, that his brain wasn't wired for normal vision and likely never would be.

Jennifer took his hand. He didn't feel it.

"They have to be wrong," he said.

"Mike, it's okay—"

"They must have made a mistake," he said. "If I give it another year or two it will all sort itself out."

The next day, May called Fine at her office. He asked if she was certain about the results—was she sure it was his brain and not his eye that was the problem? She told him that she was.

A day later he called back. This time he asked if the "forever" part of the prognosis applied to perceiving faces.

"Your case is totally unique, Mike," she said. "But I think it's very unlikely that you'll ever recognize faces normally."

The next day, he called again and asked if his poor depth perception and object recognition were forever, too. Fine confirmed that they were.

May called his close friends Bashin and Jerry Kuns, two of the most sober thinkers he knew. He described the brain scan results and waited for them to reassure him that the scientists had made a mistake. Instead, they listened quietly and then, each in his own way, told May that it sounded like Fine had got things exactly right, that it all seemed to fit with the case histories, with modern brain science, and with this hard truth: that nearly eight months had passed and May had shown almost no improvement in his vision, despite being the one person they knew in the world who could improve at anything.

That night, lying awake in bed, May stared at the ceiling heating vent he'd seen the first morning of his new vision. It appeared to be just a series of lines.

"Ione's right," he thought. "This is forever."

For a lifetime, May had lived ready to crash through. Now he seemed to move in slow motion, as if the oxygen around him had gummed. He hardly spoke to Jennifer, placed no more calls to Fine or to his friends. When he looked out the window during work breaks, he let the jumbled clues be what they wanted to be.

Late one evening, about a week after receiving his test results, May went to the bathroom and reached for his nightly cyclosporine pill. He could not read the writing on the bottle—it was just another color in the pink blob of his hand. He did not remove the cap. Instead, he stared at the bottle and asked himself, "Why am I still doing this?" He knew that he need only drop the remaining pills in the toilet and push the handle; his cornea would be rejected soon enough and he could go back to the full and rich life he'd known and loved. He stood for a minute looking at the colors on top of his hand. Finally, slowly, he shook out a pill, placed it in his mouth, and swallowed. It took a long time before he put the rest of the pills back into the medicine cabinet.

For the next week, May lay awake deep into each night. His style was to see the best in things, but no matter which way he considered his situation he could not think of a reason to keep taking those pills.

By making the journey into new vision he had stayed true to his principles: speak to your curiosity;

have adventures; be willing to fall down and get lost; there's always a way. He could always look at himself in the mirror and know that, at the moment he'd been offered this one-in-a-million journey into vision, he'd remained loyal to those principles, he'd leaped aboard, he'd been himself. And he had done what fewer than twenty people known to history had done: he had seen what this vision stuff was all about.

But that's not all he'd done. He'd also answered questions—about life and about himself—that few people get the chance to answer. He had wondered if his decision to pursue vision meant that he wasn't as content in his blindness as he'd always believed himself to be—if he wasn't who he thought he was. He had wondered if, by becoming sighted, he would become ordinary, if the world would still recognize him. And he had wondered if the blind community would still accept him.

Now he had those answers. Vision had not changed how he felt about himself or about his blindness. Now he could say from experience that life without vision was great because he'd lived life as a sighted man, too. He did not feel ordinary for gaining vision; in fact, he felt himself to be exactly who he'd always felt himself to be. And the blind community, far from rejecting him, had embraced him; they'd understood him and his journey.

And he had one more answer. He had always

believed that knowing and loving someone had nothing to do with seeing that person. He had told people he didn't need vision in order to see his wife and kids. Now that he saw them, he knew he'd been right.

So he had his answers. Now he was being told that his strange vision would never improve. That meant he would never drive. That meant he would never read. That meant he was in for a lifetime of heavy lifting, hard work, overflow, and fatigue, that his visual world would always be a confusing world.

And, on top of it all, he had to continue risking his life for this vision. He had to continue inviting cancer in order to see.

One night, about two weeks after talking to Dr. Fine, May again stood over the toilet with the bottle of cyclosporine in his hand. He had taken his journey. He had been himself. He could always tell his sons that he had tried.

CHAPTER SIXTEEN

May stared at the bottle of pills in his hand.
Slowly, he lifted his head and found his reflection in
the mirror. A tall man looked back at him. It did
not feel to May like he was invading the man's personal space. He could tell because the man did not
move away from him; he just kept looking back at
May and waiting.

For a lifetime, May had defined himself by one
principle above all others: there's always a way. It
had pushed him up a 175-foot ham radio tower as
a teenager, made him a world champion skier, delivered him to a mud hut village in Ghana, launched
his businesses. It was what he did. It was who he
was.

But it had never asked of him the impossible.
He could be forgiven now for letting go of vision
because now he knew that vision was impossible.
There wasn't a way.

May looked at the figure in the mirror. He
found the dark patches he knew to be the man's
eyes. He'd heard since boyhood that eyes could
speak, but he'd never understood what that meant.

This time, the two dark patches spoke. And when they spoke they said this: There's always a way.

May unscrewed the cap on his medicine bottle.

It struck him as crazy to try to find a way when something was impossible. He remembered Einstein's definition of insanity: doing the same thing over and over again and expecting different results. Yet some small part of him yearned to see what this man in the mirror would look like—if he'd look different somehow—after May had tried to find a way to do what couldn't be done.

He shook a pill into his hand, put it in his mouth, and gulped some water.

In between business meetings and conference calls and bedtime stories, May began to think through the problem of how a man missing the vision parts of his brain could teach himself to see.

Nearly a week passed without a breakthrough. Then he devised a plan. He would concentrate harder on the visual data streaming into his eye. For eight months he had waited for the rest of his vision to catch up with the parts that worked beautifully—motion and color. That kind of waiting around must have meant he hadn't tried hard enough. If he brought to vision the kind of onslaught of effort that he brought to his business, maybe then he could improve, maybe the other parts of his brain might kick in and help do the work of vision. If it took fourteen-hour work days in order to see, then that's what he was prepared to commit.

May began to pay very close attention to visual scenes, trying to block out the rest of the world so that the images before him had no choice but to disrobe and reveal their meanings. The results were disastrous. Objects melded together even more severely. Faces turned even more generic. He nearly fell down the stairs in a hotel after dedicating his full attention to looking for stairs.

"This really is impossible," he told himself.

He devised a new plan, which also failed. As did the next. In each case, he tried to figure out a better way to analyze the visual data before it became a confusion to him. In each case, he never got there in time.

Then he began to think differently. For eight months he'd been asking, "How do I get better at vision?" Maybe the better question was, "What am I good at already?"

He'd barely finished asking when a stream of answers poured into his head.

"I'm good at touch," he thought. "I'm good at sound and echo. I'm good with my other senses. I'm good with a dog and a cane."

What if, May thought, he went the other way around with vision? What if, instead of focusing first on the visual and then using his good senses to fill in the blanks, he used his good senses first—the things he'd excelled at when he was blind—then used vision to fill in the rest? "What if," May wondered, "I try to see by being blind again?"

The idea sounded crazy. How could a person learn to see by being blind? And yet he couldn't shake the notion. He began to form a plan.

He would go out into the world and tell his vision to back off, to play the supporting role while his other senses attacked the scene first. It's not that he would close his eyes; rather, he would first pay attention to his hands, ears, dog, and cane. He did not announce this plan to anyone. It still seemed crazy to him.

On the way to a business meeting, he got an early chance to test his new idea in the airport lounge. Rather than walk into the room and try to figure out the avalanche of visual impressions that were sure to assault his eye, he would move about the room, touching things and listening for echoes first. Only then would he contemplate how the visual data matched these more certain impressions.

He entered the lounge. As always, shapes and colors leaped onto his eye. He ordered his vision to stand down and wait but it would not wait, it was all around him before he could move to touch or hear anything. "Wait!" he told his eye, but suddenly vision would not be told to wait, it would not stand down, it all flooded in because vision was meant to be first, it was biblical. By the time he ordered his bottled water, May was more exhausted than ever.

"Keep trying," he told himself. "Keep doing what you're good at."

He tried next in the hotel conference room where his meeting was to be held. On entering the room, he swept his cane across the carpet, chairs, table, and walls. He moved his hand over telephones, pens, and notepads. He stroked the wires that connected the telephone and listened to his voice as it echoed off objects. And he tried to do all of this without thinking about the visual data streaming into his eye. He just let his other senses happen, and quickly he began to see the area not just as a box of shapes and colors but as a room, a conference room; it made sense to him, and he felt his adrenaline race because he hadn't strained much to see any of it, he'd just let himself see it the way he had when he was blind, and now he could see it visually, too.

Over the next few weeks, May continued to practice cooling his vision while moving his other senses to the forefront of information delivery. He started to see things faster and more accurately. Some days he stumbled in these efforts. Some days he stumbled to the pavement. He kept practicing. Seeing the world kept getting easier. He wasn't automatic, and he wasn't close to normally sighted. But he was better. He was thrillingly better. And, as he told Jennifer one night, he'd done it in the most unlikely of ways—he'd helped himself to see by being blind again.

"You sound like a little boy," she told him.

"I feel like it," he said. "I'm proud."

So long as May could integrate vision with his other senses, he could see better. But that still left a world of objects beyond his reach, things he could detect only through his eyes. How was he to identify the strange wonders that moved past during the Picnic Day parade in Davis? How was he to distinguish a flight attendant from any other passenger on an airplane? How was he to tell what was for sale inside those plastic blister packs at Costco?

Again, May put his mind to the matter. Again, he asked, "What am I good at?"

His first answers were of little use. He was good at skiing, but that wouldn't help. He was good at playing guitar, but that wouldn't help either. He was good at a lot of things, none of which could help him see things he couldn't reach by his other senses.

One day, while stewing as he waited yet again for Jennifer to find her car keys, he had a new thought.

"I'm good at being organized. And I've got a good memory."

Organization and memory had been the linchpins of his ability to construct the mental maps he had used so effectively as a blind person. Why, he wondered, couldn't he use organization and memory to build maps of the things he saw?

He figured it this way: When he encountered important objects, he would memorize some identifying clue or trait that would help him recognize that object in the future. Dr. Fine had told him that his brain was broken for vision, but no one could tell him he couldn't catalog and remember—he was better at that than anyone he knew. The project would be a massive one—there were countless objects to know in the world—but if he stuck to those that mattered to him, he might better learn to recognize the world beyond his grasp.

Armed with his plan, May fired up his GPS-Talk and walked to a shopping area near his home. Inside a hardware store, he began to handle things and catalog clues. He knew that flashlights were often built with on-off buttons in the middle of their handles, but he'd never noticed until now that those buttons were often rectangular and a different color from the flashlight itself. He filed that information under "flashlights" in his brain. In the tools section he inspected a collection of saws. He had used saws before but had never looked at one since gaining vision. He studied the patterns made by the jagged teeth, the wide rectangles of the blades, and the tool's silver color, then cataloged that information under "saws."

Near the checkout counter, he handled a small and heavy blister pack. He asked the clerk what was inside. The clerk told him that they were batteries. May studied them. Most of the batteries were the same color—black on the bottom two-thirds, a reddish-brown on the top third.

"Some batteries are black on the bottom and a rusty orange on the top," he told himself. "Remember that, too."

May had written his first page of clues. His next goal was to expand it to the size of the Sears catalog. When Jennifer remarked about an object that seemed interesting or important to him, he asked, "How did you know it was that thing?" or "What's the best clue?" When his assistant, Kim Burgess, drove him to San Francisco for his appointments, he asked her to show him the important trucks on the road, then memorized the shapes and colors of their logos. At Wyndham's soccer games, he recorded the clothing habits of the other parents. Before long, his kids didn't need to be asked, "How'd you know that?"—when they found something cool they just told him the clues.

He didn't hesitate to enlist strangers in his mission. On a flight to a business conference, he realized he still couldn't tell a flight attendant from ordinary passengers. So he asked the man seated next to him for help.

"How do you know which people are the flight attendants?"

"Excuse me?"

"I have low vision, so I'm trying to figure out who's who. What are the clues?"

The man thought it over for a bit.

"Well, let's see. The flight attendants sit facing toward us when the plane takes off. They're the only ones standing during the seat belt instructions. And they all dress the same."

"That's great," May said. "Those are excellent clues. Thank you."

During the safety announcement, May searched for the standing people. He found one a few rows ahead and memorized her clothes. During takeoff, he looked to the front and found a person seated facing toward him. She was wearing the same clothes as the one who'd been standing. Later in the flight, he rose from his seat, walked down the aisle, and found someone dressed in those clothes.

"What time are we landing in Chicago?" he asked.

"We're due a few minutes early, at six forty-four P.M.," she replied.

Walking back to his seat, May had to keep himself from shouting, "Yes!"

He spent the next weeks memorizing clues and

building his catalog. One day, Jennifer invited him on a trip to Costco. Inside the store, he roamed the aisles and looked for clues. Many of the items still appeared melded together, and most were generically packaged. In the electronics section, he saw a large rectangular box—just the shape that could hold anything. This box, however, looked different to him—black on the bottom two-thirds, copper on top.

"Those are batteries!" he thought.

He picked up the box. The objects inside were heavy and made a rattling sound.

He picked up another box and began to walk away.

"I'm buying batteries today," he said.

Standing in the checkout line, May told Jennifer about his score.

"I did it in a second, Jen. It was amazing. That would have taken me twenty or thirty seconds before. I didn't have to think about it at all—I kind of just saw it."

"Mike, that's wonderful."

"And the best part is that it was natural, it just came to me. It wasn't work. It was just there."

"Why do you think it took so long to figure out this new way to see?" Jennifer asked.

"I know why," May said, placing his batteries on the checkout counter. "I was waiting around for my vision to improve. I was waiting for all the parts that didn't work to catch up with the parts that did. It made perfect sense at the time. But I'm not going to wait anymore."

May flew to San Diego to see Dr. Fine. She hoped to write a paper on his case and had asked him to undergo more tests. In her lab, he told her about his efforts to find other ways to see, and the thrill he felt when it worked.

"I'm so happy for you, Mike," she said. "You really are a pioneer."

"Well, I feel like we were a team in this," he said. "You did me a great kindness by being straight with me. I needed that in order to move on."

In between tests, May told Fine that he'd tried to improve his reading and depth perception, too, but decided after much consideration that he already had better ways than vision to do those things.

"Braille and my screen readers will always be much faster for reading," he said. "And my old cane and dog are much more adept at depth."

"What about faces?" Fine asked.

"That's what I wanted to talk to you about," May said.

That night, Fine's was the only car in the science building parking lot.

"I'm in the clue business now," May said. "I

know I'll never understand faces as a whole or automatically. But what clues can I find in faces, with my abilities, that will tell me something about them?"

Fine sat May in a chair just a foot from a computer monitor. For the next several hours, she sat beside him and showed him every photograph of every face she had, pointing out the clues to gender: the difference between plucked and unplucked eyebrows, how shades of lipstick differ from natural colors of lips, how a woman's upper lip curves more dramatically, the revealing angles of cheekbones. At the end, she tested him. He scored 90 percent. They both knew that May would never get close enough for long enough to discern most of these clues in the real world. Neither of them seemed to mind. It was enough to know that they were there. Later, she worked with him on identifying common objects, helping him extract new kinds of clues.

At the airport, May hugged Fine good-bye.

"Thanks for being part of my adventure," he said. "And thanks for being there for me."

When he returned to Davis, May called Dr. Goodman. Since his first surgery nearly a year ago, he'd been concerned about the potential side effects of cyclosporine. Goodman had told him there might come a time when he could stop taking the medication. May asked Goodman if perhaps that time had come.

"Let me check with the nephrologist and get back to you," Goodman said.

A day later the doctor called back and told May he could stop taking the cyclosporine.

"This is fantastic," May told Jennifer after he hung up the phone. "I'm on a roll here."

Despite his desire to practice full-time with his new approach to vision, May had a business to run. Sendero continued to struggle to convince government agencies to buy the product. May knew he had to shrink the GPS and its price, but he needed more development funds to do it. By now, the company had been turned down for several small grants. May got word of a big grant—one worth a million dollars—and began to write an application with the help of Burgess and some colleagues. He knew of no others available after that. Things were starting to get scary for Sendero.

May used the breaks between doing business to refine his new approach to vision. More and more, he was able to integrate vision with his other senses. More and more, he was able to draw on his bulging catalog of clues to decipher objects. He told his friends Bashin and Kuns that the best part was that he was doing it more automatically every day. The era of brutal heavy lifting, he told them, seemed nearly bygone.

One day, while walking into town for a haircut, May found himself instantly able to watch the passing visual scene without thinking at all about moving along—a thrilling example of integrating his senses.

"I'm good at this," he thought. "I'm really good—"

WHOMP!

May's body hurtled over a concrete bench, and his face smashed into the ground. The bench was the same color as the sidewalk. He never saw it coming.

"Oh, man, I'm bleeding pretty good," he said aloud.

May hobbled into the hair salon, where the receptionist gasped at the sight of him. Blood flowed from his forehead and lip, down his cane and his leg, and into a pool on the floor. Someone led him to a sink, where he watched the red liquid swirl before disappearing down the drain. It was the first time he'd seen his own blood outside a test tube.

"This is a good reminder," he told himself after his haircut. "I got cocky."

A few days later, while on a flight from Washington, D.C., to Denver, May struck up a conversation with a young blond woman seated next to him. Eventually, he told her about his surgery. She asked if he could see the color of her eyes. He replied that he could only do so from up close. She leaned forward and put her forehead just an inch from his. Her eyelashes fluttered up and down so close he believed he could feel their breeze. May had never before looked closely into a stranger's eyes. He was overwhelmed with emotion and could not speak, not even to tell her that her eyes were a singular blue. He could only sit there and keep looking.

Late that evening, he remained shaken from his encounter with the woman. Before he turned off the light next to his hotel bed, he opened his computer and typed, "This was a very intimate experience for me and I can't fathom how sighted people go around seeing each other's eyes without being flustered too. I understand a bit better now why so much is made of expressions in the eyes as it is talked about and written about passionately and poetically. I will certainly remember Ms. DC to Denver for introducing me to yet one more mystery of the sighted world."

In mid-November, May went hiking with his college friend Ann Turpen, her husband, and their two daughters. He had never seen them. Before they set out for the woods he made careful mental notes about the family's clothing—part of his program to catalog and remember. By the time they returned, several dozen people had gathered just outside the woods for a wedding. May quickly lost his companions in the throng. He scanned the crowd, looking for Ann and her family. Moments later, he'd picked out each of them, all from a good distance, and gathered them together.

"Wow, how'd you find us in that crowd?" Ann asked.

May did not know how he'd done it. He hadn't looked for their colors. He hadn't looked for their shapes. He hadn't done anything. A smile inched across his face.

"I don't know how I did it," he said. "That's one of the most incredible things that's ever happened to me. I didn't try to see. I just saw."

May was due in San Francisco for a checkup with Dr. Goodman. He was eager to tell Goodman about his work with the scientists and about his mission to improve his vision. The men shook hands and May found the examining chair.

Goodman held open May's eye and started to remark about the latest San Francisco 49ers game. He stopped in midsentence.

Looking through the biomicroscope, he could see that May's transplant was swollen and that clumps of white blood cells on the back of the eye's surface were attacking the transplant. May's immune system was rejecting his cornea. He was going blind. And fast.

"Mike, we have a terribly severe rejection occurring," he said. "I've seen lots of them, and it's probably the worst I've ever encountered."

May sat stunned. For several seconds he couldn't process Goodman's words. Rejection? For nine months he'd been coming to these checkups, and the one thing that was always beautiful was the health of the eye itself.

"Am I losing my vision?" May asked.

"It's bad," Goodman replied.

May's heart pounded into his rib cage.

"Did it happen because we stopped the cyclosporine?" May asked.

"Very likely," Goodman said. "This rejection came on like a storm."

May could barely speak. How could this be? Nothing was blurry or painful. How could this be?

"What can we do about it?" May asked.

"I'm going to level with you," Goodman said. "It's very unlikely that we can do anything about it; it just looks too far gone. There are ways we can try to fight back, but they involve desperate measures—a flat-out assault—and they're not pleasant. And even then it probably won't work."

"What kind of measures?" May asked.

Goodman sat on his stool and made his list. To fight this kind of rejection May would have to:

- Ingest heavy doses of immunosuppressive drugs

- Apply topical immunosuppressive drugs to his eye

- Ingest oral steroids

- Apply topical steroids to his eye

- Receive a series of steroid injections directly into his eye

Each of the measures carried significant risk. May would have to ingest both cyclosporine and an additional immunosuppressant—all at higher doses than before, all with even higher risks for toxic and potentially deadly side effects. The oral steroids could cause bleeding ulcers that could hurt or even kill him. The steroid injections could blind him.

May took a deep breath.

"How long would I have to stay on the drugs?" he asked.

"We don't know. It could be a long time."

"Are you saying I would need injections directly into my eye—not near my eye, but in the eye itself?"

"Yes."

"Is that painful?"

"Yes."

"Is there a chance this rejection can heal on its own?"

"No. It's one hundred percent certain that, if left alone, the cornea will continue to swell, the transplant will be rejected, and you'll go back to being blind."

May took another long breath.

"Do I have time to think this over, Dan? This is a lot to digest."

"I'm afraid not," Goodman said. "If we're going to war, we've gotta go now."

May sat motionless in the examining chair. He knew what vision was. He'd found a way when things were impossible. There was nothing left to answer. There was nothing left to see.

CHAPTER SEVENTEEN

The glinting silver needle at the end of Goodman's long syringe bore down on May's eye, he could see its silver flashing, a metal too cold and hard to push into an eye and yet Goodman would not let him blink, he would not let go of May's lids, and the needle grew nearer and larger and brighter, May had nowhere to go but into that needle, and the sharpness now was everywhere and then on top of him, metal did not belong in an eye, but it kept coming and he could not blink.

The needle pierced through the surface of his eye and then pushed deeper inside. May's hands clenched the armrests on his chair as waves of pain tore into his head, down his neck, along his hands, feet, ears, tongue, hair, and breath. He wanted to scream but could not remember how. He needed to jump but dared not move because there was a needle inside his eye. For several seconds he could not breathe.

"It's done," Goodman said.

May couldn't speak. He'd broken bones before,

smashed his face. This was different. This pain was primitive. It was prehistoric.

Goodman gave May a minute to gather himself, then explained what was next. May had to ingest and apply a series of potent antirejection and immunosuppressive drugs. And he would have to return for more injections.

"How many more?" May managed to ask, dabbing at his tears and checking for blood.

"We don't know yet. It could be three, five, maybe more. It depends on your progress."

May could not imagine even one more of these offenses.

"When is the next one?" he asked.

"Tomorrow," Goodman said.

"I'm leaving for Phoenix in a few hours," May said. "I'll need to be back tomorrow?"

"As early as possible," Goodman replied.

"How long before we know if this is working?" May asked.

"About two weeks," Goodman said. "I think we should know by then. But this is a long shot, Mike. Remember that."

May's assistant, Kim Burgess, drove him to the airport. He was to be the keynote speaker at a business conference that evening and was to make presentations the next day. She knew he was shaken and asked if he could still travel. He nodded but did not speak. On the way to the airport, May called Jennifer and told her the news—about the rejection, the risky medicines, the injections, and the bad prognosis.

For a time, the only sound in the car was the tinny rhythm of Jennifer's voice coming through May's cell phone. Burgess wondered if Jennifer had finally had enough.

Near the airport, May briefly spoke again.

"Thanks, Jen," he said into his phone. "I knew you'd be with me on this."

Flying to Phoenix, May did not bother integrating his vision or cataloging clues. Instead, he looked out the window and thought, "This is it. You'd better remember those fields down there. You'd better remember the shapes of those clouds and the blue of that sky. You might never see them again."

For an hour he kept his eye pressed against the plastic window. And it hit him, as hard as the injection, that he'd better start seeing the big things in the world that he should have seen by now, the things he'd somehow presumed would always wait for this new eye of his. A doctor had given him vision—**vision**—and still it had never occurred to him to see the Galápagos Islands, the village in Ghana where he'd helped build a school, the Great

Pyramid in Egypt, a topless beach, the Taj Mahal, a bald eagle, an elephant. He hadn't even taken time to see an elephant.

May gave his presentation that night, then caught the first morning flight back to San Francisco. He could think of nothing but the gleam on Goodman's needle as it would press through his eye, and the chromosomal-level pain he was due in an hour. He'd been willing to risk cancer in order to continue his odyssey with vision, but as the plane landed he wasn't sure he was willing to take another of those injections. It sounded like someone else speaking when he gave the taxi driver Goodman's address.

May sat in the examining chair, and this time he clutched the armrests in advance. Goodman pulled open his eyelids and at once May could see the glinting needle because this time he knew it would be there, and it hung before him growling in the light until Goodman began to push it toward his eye. May had just told Goodman that motion helped him see in depth and this needle was now in motion, and he watched it move into his eye until shards of pain flew across his nasal cavity, into the bone in the back of his head, and then made an S-shape of his spine. If anything, this injection was worse than the first.

Goodman rubbed May's shoulder.

"Same time tomorrow," he told May.

At home, May told Jennifer about his time in Goodman's office but spared her the gory details. He said that it would be two weeks before Goodman could determine if the rejection had reversed, but that the odds were very poor. And he said it was his instinct to go see the major things in the world before he couldn't see them anymore. A few minutes later, the kids rushed through the kitchen door. May hugged them, inspected the school projects stuffed into their backpacks, then sat them down at the table.

"I'm back early from Phoenix because Dr. Goodman found a problem with my transplant," he said. "So now I'm getting these needles in my eye to try to fix things. There's a good chance I'm going to lose my vision."

"Needles?" Wyndham asked.

"Yep," May replied.

"Right in your eyeball?" Carson asked.

"Yep, straight in there."

"How much did it hurt?"

"Remember I told you I once had cavities filled without novocaine? It was worse than that."

"Worse than your explosion?"

"Yes."

"Was it gushing blood?"

"No, but believe me, I checked."

"Did you cry?"

"Almost."

"Was it worse than when I fell on a stick and got stitches in my arm?"

"I think so. This is an eye—the needle just goes right in."

"Ewww!"

"Ugggh!"

"If you lose your vision," Carson asked, "do you get your money back?"

May laughed so hard he nearly fell out of his chair. Then he looked at his boys for a very long time and told himself, "Remember this."

May's next injection, the following morning, was even more painful than the first two. Sitting on the ferry going home he felt as if he'd been beaten by a gang of thugs. He had to pull himself together. If he was going to see the big things in the world, he'd best start making travel plans now.

At home, Jennifer fixed him a sandwich and asked about his appointment. He described some of the details but was most interested in watching her move around the kitchen and seeing the bounce in her streaked blond hair as she whirled to throw things in the garbage can.

"Want to go to Peet's?" she asked.

May had travel agents to call. His assistant was waiting with the phone numbers in his office.

"Sure," he said. "Let's go."

That evening, Carson and Wyndham knocked on the door to May's office. They could see he was busy but asked anyway: Would he take them to the Graduate, an area sports bar and restaurant?

"Do I need a coat?" he asked.

The boys didn't mind that May walked a little more deliberately than usual on the way to the restaurant, or that he slowed down to look at the wild plants near Villanova and Sycamore, or that he stopped to inspect the house painted bright purple near the mall, or even that he took an extra minute to study the rainstorm of white bird droppings on the sidewalk outside the Graduate.

"Those are gross," Carson said. "Come on, Dad."

"Yeah, they are kind of gross," May said. "Let's go in."

May gave the boys money for the air hockey table and went to the bar to order drinks. A tall young woman with long black hair, shiny earrings, and a low-cut top came to take his order.

"What can I get you?" she asked.

May knew exactly what he wanted—two root beers and a Guinness.

"I'm not sure yet," he said. "What's good?"

The woman began to recommend beers. May watched her gold necklace dance just above the V of her tanned neckline, her hands trace shapes on the menu, her hair fly across the room when she moved it from her eyes.

"I need a little more time," he said. "Can you come back in a minute?"

When she returned, May watched her all over again.

In the games area, he challenged Wyndham to an air hockey match, nearly knocking their drinks to the ground as he lunged to make saves, sending the flat plastic disc on ricocheted pathways unknown in geometry books. He and the boys played pool (solids were easier to see than the stripes, but he loved all the colors regardless), watched NBA players dunk on the ten-foot television screen, and relaxed at a wooden table that had swirling patterns on top. May needed to go home to work, but everyone agreed to stay later when they discovered a new video game in the back of the room.

May wasn't due back in Goodman's office for another four days. He spent much of that time catching up on work. During one of his breaks, he walked to the big school playground behind his house, where he watched kids whirl around on the merry-go-round, traced his foot along the painted lines on the basketball court, and followed a man's remote-control airplane as it carved shapes into the sky. Near home, he surveyed the giant field of grass before him and marveled at the idea that he could run headlong into that green for more than a minute and still not crash into anything. During another break, he threw a ball to Josh and watched his happy flopping, then took his dog to Peet's to practice the girl-watching skills Jennifer had taught him long ago.

May took the ferry to his next eye appointment. In the office, Goodman again stood to the side (to avoid being kicked in the groin) and pushed the needle into May's eye. This time the pain was a bit more reasonably horrific.

"Come back in a week," Goodman said. "I think we'll have our answer then."

May's eye hurt, but he forced it open as he and Josh walked to the Ferry Building. Near the dock, he watched seagulls swoop for dropped popcorn— perhaps the most elegant motion he'd seen—then followed an unusual pattern on the sidewalk he knew would lead to nowhere in particular. Nearby, he saw rows of miniature gray statues lined up along the curb, a single-file army of tiny men who looked ready for battle. He figured them to be parking meters. He walked over to inspect one of them more closely.

The meter felt the way it looked—heavy, metallic, cold, and smooth. Near the top he could see small blotches of irregular color, a darker gray than the rest of the meter. He ran his fingers along these spots; tiny jagged edges rubbed rough against his touch. He knew right away that he was seeing chipped paint. He stared longer at these torn shapes. They looked ugly to him, disorganized and broken, and they gave him a bad feeling. It was the same feeling of disgust he'd had when looking at the bird droppings outside the Graduate, at the fading paint on the eastern side of his house, at the pieces of drab yellow stuffing that coughed up from torn public transit seats. It was the same sad feeling he'd had looking at a homeless person. Soon, he might be blind again. He wouldn't move his eye from the chipped paint at the top of the parking meter.

When May's boat arrived, he turned to the dock and headed for the round tentlike structure he knew would guide him in. He stood on the pier, watching the buoys bobbing and making ripples in the water. When the ferry arrived, he studied how the men grappled it with a pole and secured it to the dock; he wanted to see the workers' every action, and they seemed to move as smoothly as the gulls. He found his favorite window seat and got ready to look at everything.

A week remained before May's big appointment with Dr. Goodman. He continued to ingest and apply the heavy doses of antirejection drugs. Jennifer prayed that he wouldn't need any more injections. One evening, May thought she seemed distraught.

"What's wrong, Jen?" he asked.

Tears began to run down her cheeks.

"I haven't been grateful enough."

"Grateful about what?"

"About your vision. I took it all so much for granted. I was just living my life as if it would be here forever."

"Me, too," May said. "Me, too."

May dove back into his work, spending several days seeking new investors and checking on his grant proposal, for which there was still no word. During breaks he wrestled with his kids, dressed them for bed, and directed them to clean up the mess in their room, which, he warned them, he could still see until further notice. Sometimes, after the boys fell asleep, he lingered in their room to look at the strange Lego buildings they'd constructed and to study the up-and-down motion made by their blankets as they slept underneath.

When the weekend arrived and Jennifer asked if he'd like to attend Wyndham's soccer practice, May grabbed his video camera and popped in a fresh tape. At the field, he followed the action on the camera's large LED preview screen, recording Wyndham's mad dashes to the ball and using the device's powerful zoom feature to pull in details, like the confetti of mud that kicked up when Wyndham slid to make a steal. On Sunday morning, he showed the video to his family, standing inches from the television and pointing out the skill in his shaky cinematography. After that, the family walked to Fluffy's for doughnuts.

Two days later he was due for his eye appointment. He arrived early and used the time to walk the streets and admire San Francisco. When his turn came, a nurse showed him to an examining room. Goodman entered a few minutes later.

"Let's take a look," Goodman said.

He held open May's eyelids with his thumb and forefinger. The touch still reminded May of his boyhood ophthalmologist, Dr. Max Fine, and of the day he first met Goodman in this office, the day Goodman had told him about stem cells and said, "This could work."

Goodman peered through the biomicroscope. He adjusted the machine and looked again. For several seconds May heard nothing but Goodman's breathing. Then he heard him say just two words.

"Oh, my."

May's heart started to pound.

"How's it look, Dan? Can you tell anything?"

Goodman kept looking but said nothing more.

May breathed harder. Why wasn't Goodman speaking?

Goodman pushed his chair away from the instrument.

"I don't use these kinds of words often, Mike. But this is a miracle. The eye is clear. You turned it around. You did it. This is the most dramatic reversal I've ever witnessed. You did it."

May sat motionless. Nine months earlier he had walked from this chair to the mirror, where he'd seen himself for the first time in forty-three years. He looked across the room. The mirror was still there. He stood up and searched for his reflection. He could see a man standing in the distance.

"That guy looks tall," he thought. "That's me."

EPILOGUE

Days after beating the cornea rejection, May set out to conquer Chair Six at Kirkwood, the same black diamond run that had accordioned his limbs when he'd dared to ski it with new vision. This time, he came armed with his new approach to vision: a commitment to integrate his other senses with the visual scene. He zoomed down the mountain, listening as his skis carved the snow, following Jennifer's voice in front of him, ordering himself to let the world come to his eye rather than the other way around. He fell, but far less frequently this time.

A few weeks later, May laid his eyes on Christmas. He'd heard people talk of twinkling ornaments, but it wasn't until he saw the glowing rainbows of dots hanging from his tree and wrapped around neighborhood homes that he felt like he really understood the word **twinkle**. In a department store, he asked his sons why so many people were standing in an aisle. They told him that the people were there to see Santa Claus.

"Where's Santa?" May asked.

"Right there," the boys replied. "He's the guy in the red suit."

May walked slowly toward the red man until

he stood just a few feet away. He remembered Jennifer's cautions against gawking, but this time he stared—at the man's pink face, his round body, his shining red hat. He could see the man's stomach rise and fall as he exclaimed, "Ho ho ho!" but May looked longest at Santa's bushy white beard, a sky's worth of white clouds pressed onto a tiny patch of pink face. His kids were in a hurry to pick out toys, but they didn't rush their dad while he was looking at Santa.

In early 2001, Sendero got word that its latest grant proposal had been turned down. Despite making inroads in shrinking the GPS unit and refining its capabilities, the company was now in serious trouble. Only a major grant could save the business. May and his assistant, Kim Burgess, redoubled their efforts to seek out government money, which they still believed must be there.

On the morning of March 7, 2001, May set out for a checkup with Dr. Goodman in San Francisco. It had been a year to the day since Goodman had removed May's bandages. On the ferry, May saw a mosquito for the first time. He watched it dance like the tip of a symphony conductor's baton, astonished that such busy movements could be so silent.

At the appointment, Goodman pronounced the eye to be perfectly healthy.

"I always aimed for making a year," May said.

"A year is good," Goodman replied. "But we'll always need to check you every few months."

That spring, May was invited to speak to a vision-science class at the University of Minnesota. The students had been assigned the classic studies by Richard Gregory and Oliver Sacks—cases May still hadn't got around to reading. On the airplane, he used his laptop to listen to the stories of Sidney Bradford and Virgil, the subjects of these landmark vision-recovery studies. It was the first time he'd learned anything about any of his predecessors. He could not tear himself away from these men.

The meeting room was packed with students and professors. Straightaway, someone asked May to compare his experience to that of Gregory's subject, Bradford, and to Sacks's subject, Virgil. It struck him, May said, that the essential difference between him and these men seemed to be in the lives they'd led before the surgeries—in who they were, going into vision. "I didn't do it to see," he told them. "I did it to see what seeing was."

In mid-2001, May and Burgess discovered a grant for which Sendero might apply, this one worth more than $2 million, a real long shot. There were none available after that; it was Sendero's last hope. When May and Burgess finished writing, the proposal was the size of the Davis telephone book.

May went back to work, this time negotiating

with a New Zealand–based company called HumanWare. He wanted to put Sendero's GPS software onto that company's BrailleNote, a small and lightweight personal digital assistant, or PDA. The advantages would be profound: lighter weight, better portability, instant-on technology, longer battery life, no laptop required. He was awake early, thinking about such matters, on the morning of September 11, 2001, when he heard radio reports of airplanes crashing into the World Trade Center. The announcer said that flames were shooting from the towers and that people were jumping for their lives. He listened for more than an hour before it occurred to him that he could watch the events on television. He didn't know if he could bear to look at such a thing.

May walked slowly to the television set in the family room, where he pushed the power button and moved his face to within inches of the screen. He didn't need to change channels to find the story. He could see flames bursting out of the sides of the pale towers, the same colored flames doing the same kind of dance he loved to watch in fireplaces. "There are people in there," he thought, and he kept thinking those five words for the next hour, until his legs ached and he had to go sit down on the couch a few feet away, and when he did that the image on the screen blurred. May had long wondered if he would retain visual memories if he were to go blind again. After September 11, he knew that he would.

Two weeks later, the phone rang in May's office. From the kitchen, Jennifer could hear him say, "Are you sure? Are you sure?" Then May walked into the room.

"You're not going to believe this," he told Jennifer. "We got the grant. We got the grant. It's for $2.25 million. We're going to make it."

Jennifer hugged her husband harder than she had ever hugged him before. This wasn't just a grant for Sendero, she told him. It was a grant for the laser turntable and the bun warmers and the talking computers. It was a grant, she said, for him. May called friends and family and organized a night of celebration. When his boys returned from school, he told them the good news—that this grant had been their last chance and that they'd made it.

"When do we get to shave your beard?" the boys asked.

"What did you say?" he asked.

"When do we get to shave your beard?"

Then May remembered. Months ago, when sending in the proposal, he'd told his sons that the grant was so important that if Sendero won it he would let them shave off his beard. His boys had never mentioned the offer after that. But now they stood sober and ready to collect.

"I've had my beard since I came back from

Ghana," May said. "Mommy's never seen me without a beard. It's part of me. I've had it for more than twenty-five years."

"Can I do it first?" Carson asked.

"No, I want to do it first!" Wyndham said.

"This has been a huge day," May replied. "Let's talk about it tomorrow."

The next morning, May walked into his sons' bedroom holding a three-head electric razor.

"Let's do it, guys," he said.

In the bathroom, May knelt on the floor and gave the razor to Carson.

"I don't even know how to shave off a beard," May said. "I think you have to do it slowly. Don't mow like it's the front lawn."

Carson made gentle and rounded strokes on May's cheek.

"I'm making a C for **Carson**," he said. Soon, there was a C on May's cheek.

Wyndham tried for a **W**, but his father's cheek was too small for that. Several minutes later the boys had finished.

"That was definitely mowing," May said.

"You look like an alien!" Carson said. "Let's show Mom!"

The men walked to the kitchen, where Jennifer was making breakfast. She took a look at May and nearly fainted.

"Whoa!" she cried. "Is that you, Mike?"

The boys belly-laughed.

"Oh, my gosh!" Jennifer said. "Oh, my! What happened? Who are you?"

"It's Dad!" the boys exclaimed.

"Well, it doesn't look like him," Jennifer said, laughing. She walked over and smoothed the back of her hand over May's cheek.

"I guess it is him," Jennifer agreed. "Have you seen yourself yet, Mike?"

May realized that he hadn't. He walked back into the boys' bathroom and found himself in the mirror. The dark splotch that had always helped him frame his face was gone, replaced by acres of skin. May had never seen himself without a beard—not even in old family photographs from before he went to Ghana. He stayed at the mirror awhile longer, marveling at the changed face that stared back at him.

Days later, May struck a deal with HumanWare to put Sendero's GPS software on the PDA. The breakthrough was nearly as significant as the grant. Sendero was now positioned to thrive. Sales increased. May hired more people. The company was rolling.

In November 2002, May's dog guide, Josh, died at age eleven. The loss cut May deeply. Josh had crossed the cusp of some of the most important events in May's life: moving to Oregon, the birth and raising of his children, starting Sendero, moving to Davis, gaining vision. More than once he'd saved May from speeding cars that had seemed to come from nowhere. May wondered if his new vision had troubled Josh, perhaps made him feel less necessary than he had in the days when they were an original team, in the days when May was blind. May couldn't face another loss like this one. He told himself he would never get another dog guide.

Since his cornea rejection, May had been taking heavy doses of immunosuppressive drugs. In mid-2002, after consultation with Dr. Goodman, he gradually began to reduce the doses, and in early 2003 he stopped them entirely. This time, his transplant and his eye stayed healthy. He continued to see Goodman for regular checkups.

All the while, May practiced his new approach to vision, integrating his other senses with the visual and building mental libraries of clues to help him identify objects. Instances in which he felt overwhelmed grew increasingly rare. He got faster at recognizing things.

Still, there were regular reminders of the limitations of his vision. In 2003, for example, he made his long-awaited trip to a topless beach, only to discover that he couldn't see much of a woman's chest unless she was wearing a brightly colored bikini top.

"All these years I've dreamed of getting here," he lamented to Jennifer. "Now I need the women to be dressed."

In 2005, after two years of missing the warmth and companionship of a dog guide, May went to the Seeing Eye in Morristown, New Jersey, and got a new one, a golden retriever–Labrador retriever mix named Miguel. Another client had recently returned Miguel because he'd pulled too hard and shown too much initiative. "We'll be a good match," May told Miguel. The two have been together since.

In the summer of 2006, May and Jennifer traveled to London, where they had been invited by Richard Gregory to speak to a gathering of leading academics. The conference room was filled with some of Britain's top vision scientists, psychiatrists, philosophers, ophthalmologists, neurologists, and psychologists. Gregory was eighty-two and emeritus professor of neuropsychology at the University of Bristol. In an introduction, he recalled his famous case study of Sidney Bradford and described May's case; then he opened the floor to questions for May.

May was beaming after the meeting. He told Jennifer that it was remarkable to have been among so many brilliant minds and to be the subject of their curiosity. In the hallway, Gregory tested May on the hollow mask illusion, rotating a large Albert

Einstein example in front of him. To the by-standers, the hollow side of Einstein's face leaped outward, appearing every bit as convex as a real face. May did not perceive the illusion.

Gregory and a few of the other scientists took May and Jennifer to dinner at London's oldest Indian restaurant, where their discussion lasted well into the night. After that, Gregory invited the Mays to be his guests at the fabled Athenaeum Club, which counted among its past members the Duke of Wellington, Charles Darwin, Charles Dickens, and one of Gregory's old professors at Cambridge, the philosopher and mathematician Bertrand Russell. They talked about their lives in the club's library. After midnight, Gregory drove the couple back to their hotel in Hyde Park in his hybrid Toyota Prius. May and Jennifer thanked Gregory and wished him a good night.

"That man is alive," May said as they walked into the hotel.

The years since May beat his cornea rejection have been busy ones for many of the important people in his life.

In 2002, Jennifer May and her friend Penny Lorain formed their own interior design firm, Lorain & May, which specializes in all facets of residential and commercial design. Jennifer oversaw the expansion and redesign of the Mays' home, where she continues to raise the couple's two sons, and where Mike May continues to run Sendero Group.

Shortly after her son's surgeries, Ori Jean May moved from Florida to Chico, California, about a hundred miles from Davis. In 2005, at age seventy-seven, she cracked a vertebra in her lower back. Doctors said that they could repair it, but that such surgery for a person of her age carried with it the risk of heart attack and stroke. "It's a quality-of-life issue," they told her. "If you don't opt for the surgery the pain probably won't worsen, but it won't improve, either. You'll just live with it." To the surprise of none of her children, Ori Jean decided to undergo the surgery, which was successful. She continues to live in Chico, as do all four of May's siblings.

Dr. Daniel Goodman continues to practice corneal and refractive surgery in San Francisco. He still sees May every three months for checkups, and the two meet occasionally for dinner or a ball game.

Bryan Bashin is currently a consultant to businesses and individuals, often working in the area of job development and coaching. He continues to monitor advances in the science and technology of vision restoration but has decided to put off his own surgery until the required immunosuppressive drugs are made less risky and the surgery itself becomes less disruptive of daily life. "I'm still open to the idea," he says, "but for me, the time and the science still aren't quite right yet."

Ione Fine has continued to test May inside and outside the fMRI scanner; there have been no changes in the results. In 2003, she published a paper on May's case, "Long-term Deprivation Affects Visual Perception and Cortex," in the journal **Nature Neuroscience.** She expected it to prove interesting to colleagues. On the day the paper was published, Fine was attending a small conference in rural northern California. Her cell phone began to ring and did not stop for hours. Mainstream media from all over the world wanted to know more about May's story. Fine spent the day standing on a nearby hill—the only place she could get cell phone reception—describing the strange visual world in which her subject lived. When her phone battery died she borrowed replacements from colleagues who owned the same model.

Based on her work with May, Fine received a five-year grant to study long-term visual deprivation and sight recovery. She was thirty-two years old, much younger than the average first-time grant recipient. The work also led directly to a professorship in the department of ophthalmology at the University of Southern California. She married longtime boyfriend and fellow vision scientist Geoff Boynton in 2003.

In 2006, Fine and Boynton accepted professorships in the psychology department at the University of Washington. She continues to test May in an effort to further understand how and why parts of his visual cortex changed their representations after he went blind.

During a routine physical exam in 2006, May's family physician found a discolored spot on his chest. In past visits, such spots had not worried the doctor. This time, the man said, "This isn't good, Mike."

The doctor snipped a sample from May's chest to send for testing. A week later, he called with the results.

"It's malignant. You need to come in right away."

In the office, the doctor applied a topical anesthetic and cut away the rest of the spot. He explained to May that such skin cancers were common among adults over age fifty, and that so long as they were detected and removed early, as this one had been, they usually posed no further danger.

"I took cyclosporine for a long time," May told the doctor. "I always wondered if this day was coming."

The doctor said that it was impossible to know whether the cyclosporine had caused the cancer. But he did not rule it out.

At home, May told Jennifer the news. Since the spot was so small and could not be felt, they would need to be vigilant in watching for others.

"Do you think it was the cyclosporine?" Jennifer asked.

"I was really curious about that," May said. "But you know what? In the end, I don't think it matters. In the end, no matter what, I would have done everything the same."

ACKNOWLEDGMENTS

The author is grateful for the help and support of the following people:

Kate Medina, my editor at Random House, who believed in me and understood me from the start. Kate's sense of story and instinct for what matters to people are the products of a beautiful heart. The help she gives a writer in finding and conveying his own heart is a gift that lasts a lifetime.

Robin Rolewicz, editor, for her unwavering support and encouragement, and for her insightful and invaluable reading of my manuscript. Robin was with me every day on this book, and her contributions helped me immensely.

Abby Plesser, editorial assistant, who read my work, cheered me on, and made things easy for me.

Gina Centrello, president and publisher of the Random House Publishing Group, who has made Random House a true home for me.

Sally Marvin, my friend and the best publicist in the business. I can't imagine making these journeys without her.

Thanks also at Random House to: Dennis Ambrose, Rachel Bernstein, Nicole Bond, Sanyu Dillon, Sue Driskill, Kristin Fassler, Megan Fishmann, Paul Kozlowski, Ruth Liebmann, Marty McGrath, Elizabeth McGuire, Katie Mehan, Gene Mydlowski, Tom Nevins, Peter Olson, Allyson Pearl, Jack Perry, Thomas Perry, Bridget Piekarz, Lydah Pyles, Kelle Ruden, Carol Russo, Stephanie Sabol, Carol Schneider, Erich Schoeneweiss, Beck Stvan, Bonnie Thompson, David Thompson, Claire Tisne, David Underwood, Jaci Updike, Andrew Weber, Don Weisberg, and Amelia Zalcman.

Flip Brophy, my literary agent at Sterling Lord Literistic. I feel privileged to have joined forces with her and am so lucky to know that she's by my side.

Mike May invited me into his home and his life. For two years, he sat for countless hours of interviews and was unwaveringly thoughtful and frank in his answers. Mike included me on business trips, doctor visits, family outings, Labor Day cookouts, and skiing weekends. He picked up the phone at every hour to answer my queries. And he was patient with me. I spent weeks asking him to recall the most minute details of his early vision, and pushing him to describe every moment of certain experiences; he never rushed a single answer or asked me to move things along. An author could not hope to work with a brighter subject, finer gentleman, or nicer guy.

Jennifer May was equally generous with her time and forthcoming in her answers. Not only did she forgive my intrusions into her family, she made me feel at home for the long stretches I spent away from my own home. Carson and Wyndham May were cool with me borrowing their dad for whatever time I needed him.

Bryan Bashin, a genuinely kind man with a wonderful mind. Some of the most interesting conversations I've ever had came over dinners with Bashin in Sacramento.

Dr. Daniel F. Goodman of San Francisco, who carved time from a busy schedule to discuss May's case, the technical aspects of stem cell and cornea transplants, and the emotions a doctor feels when he has helped a person to see.

Richard Gregory, Emeritus Professor of Neuropsychology at the University of Bristol, who spent time with me in England explaining the critical role of implicit knowledge in human vision, and recalling his landmark 1963 case study of Sidney Bradford. No one has ever explained science to me more clearly or with as much passion and joy. It is impossible to know Richard Gregory and not wish oneself a fraction as engaged with the world and ideas as he is.

Dr. Ione Fine, without whom I could not have hoped to understand the brain's role in vision or May's singular case. Fine is exceptionally smart, and she also possesses that rarest of skills—the ability to explain complex concepts in ways that come alive for the layperson. It was never surprising, even when she was describing neural architecture, to know she was the daughter of a renowned children's book author.

Professors Geoff Boynton at the University of Washington, Donald MacLeod at the University of California–San Diego, Steven Shevell at the University of Chicago, and Alex Wade at the Smith-Kettlewell Eye Research Institute in San Francisco, who helped me understand vision science; and Dr. Ali Djalilian, Assistant Professor of Ophthalmology at the University of Illinois at Chicago, and Dr. Edward J. Holland, Director of Cornea Services at the Cincinnati Eye Institute, who taught me about corneal epithelial stem cell transplantation. It was thrilling to learn from all of them.

Thanks also to: Dr. Mike Carson, Kim Casey, Fiona Morrison-Cassidy, Ori Jean May, Nick Medina, Mark Pighin, Sheila Randolph, Ron Salviolo, and Diane Slater.

Elliott Harris and Robert Feder of the **Chicago Sun-Times** and author Jonathan Eig have read my writing and have been my sounding boards for years. Richard Babcock of **Chicago** magazine gave me a wonderful opportunity and made me a better writer. Jonathan Karp began my journey into books; his instinct for story and character continues to resonate with me.

I cannot adequately thank David Granger and Mark Warren at **Esquire.** I think differently about writing, manhood, and friendship from knowing them. I will never forget how passionately Mark believed in the Mike May story. I will always remember how Mark and David believed in me. Thanks also to Peter Griffin, Tyler Cabot, and Victor Ozols at **Esquire.**

Elizabeth Gabler and Rodney Ferrell at Fox 2000 Pictures, who connect with the spirit of my work and are two of the loveliest people I know; Gil Netter, a true friend and superlative producer at Fox; Bruce Rubin, a beautiful man and writer who reminds me often about what matters most; and Jonathan Liebman and Kassie Evashevski at Brillstein-Grey Entertainment, for their faith and support.

Two of the finest writers I know—Ken Kurson and Annette Kurson—reviewed and critiqued my manuscript. Ken is my best friend and his encouragement was inspirational. Annette taught me to write and continues to do so, not just through words but through a special sensitivity to the world. Jane Glover reviewed the book with the same sweet heart I've known since we were kids. Thanks also to Rebecca, Steve, Carrie, and Anna Kurson, and to Larry, Mike, and Sam Glover. And the memory of my dad, Jack D. Kurson, the best storyteller I've ever known. I still hear his stories in my dreams.

Dr. Steven Tureff, and Robert Gassman, Lynn Gassman, Lauren Freedman, and Mike Collins have been blessings to me and my family—I can never thank them enough. Thanks also to Steven Beer, Randi Valerious, Brad Ginsberg, Jane Thompson, David Shapson, Bill Adee, Seth Traxler, Dori Frankel Steigman, Ray George, and Daniel Meyerowitz; and to Mitchell Lopata of Lopata Design for his beautiful illustrations.

I couldn't hope to write without the love and support of the Wisniewski family—Kazimiera, Eugeniusz, and Paula. They are my family and I love them.

Finally, thanks to Amy, Nate, and Will Kurson. They are my true loves and inspiration. I have never known a heart like Amy's, nor a greater champion. For more reasons than I could hope to list, this is her book as much as it is mine.

A NOTE ON SOURCES

I spent hundreds of hours over two years interviewing Mike May: at his home in Davis, California; alongside him during his business trips to Chicago, Washington, D.C., Sacramento, San Francisco, London, Los Angeles, Kalamazoo, and the Kirkwood Ski Resort in the California mountains; and by telephone and Internet during his travels to Europe, Australia, New Zealand, and Central and South America.

Jennifer May granted me dozens of hours of interview time, both at her home in Davis and by phone. Carson and Wyndham May popped in and out of interview sessions to add memories of the year in which their father gained vision. I interviewed May's family, friends, and teachers to learn about his life.

Human vision—and the brain's role in it—is a massively complex subject. It was explained to me in person by Dr. Richard Gregory in England; Professors Ione Fine, Geoff Boynton, and Donald MacLeod in San Diego; Dr. Alex Wade at the Smith-Kettlewell Eye Research Institute in San Francisco; and Dr. Steven Shevell at the University of Chicago. I benefited greatly from the textbook **Sensation and Perception** (sixth edition) by E. Bruce Goldstein, published by Wadsworth; I can't remember reading a textbook at once so engaging and educational. For the role of knowledge in vision, I read Richard L. Gregory's books **Eye and Brain: The Psychology of Seeing** from Princeton University Press, and **The Intelligent Eye** from McGraw Hill, as well as his monograph "Knowledge for vision: vision for knowledge" from Philosophical Transactions of the Royal Society. V. S. Ramachandran's **A Brief Tour of Human Consciousness: From Imposter Poodles to Purple Numbers** from Pi Press provided a lively primer in the miracle of the brain.

Sight recovery after a lifetime of blindness is extraordinarily rare. For accounts of those cases (the first dates back about a thousand years) I relied on M. Von Senden's hard-to-find book **Space and Sight** from Methuen & Co., and Alberto Valvo's equally rare pamphlet "Sight Restoration after Long-Term Blindness: The Problems and Behavior Patterns of Visual Rehabilitation," from American Foundation for the Blind. For the case of Virgil, I read Oliver Sacks's beautiful article "To See and Not See," originally published in **The New Yorker** and taken from his book **An Anthropologist on Mars,** published by Vintage Books. I learned the case of Sidney Bradford from Gregory's seminal paper, "Recovery from Early Blindness: A Case Study," written with Jean Wallace and published in the "Experimental Psychology Society Monograph

No. 2," and from interviews I did with Gregory in England.

I came to understand the technical and scientific details of May's own case through extensive interviews with Fine, Boynton, Wade, MacLeod, and Dr. Daniel F. Goodman. Invaluable to me was Fine's groundbreaking paper "Long-term Deprivation Affects Visual Perception and Cortex," published in **Nature Neuroscience,** volume 6, number 9.

The revolutionary and complex stem cell surgery that restored May's vision was explained to me by Dr. Edward J. Holland, director of Cornea Services at the Cincinnati Eye Institute and professor of clinical ophthalmology at the University of Cincinnati; Dr. Ali Djalilian, assistant professor of ophthalmology at the University of Illinois at Chicago; and by Dr. Goodman, the ophthalmologist who performed the operation on May.

ILLUSTRATION CREDITS

Page 338, inverted face photographs, courtesy of the author

Page 347, Shepard Tables, courtesy of Dr. Roger Shepard. First appeared in **Mind Sights** by Roger N. Shepard, published by W. H. Freeman and Company, New York, 1990.

Pages 354, Chaplin mask, courtesy of Richard L. Gregory

Page 355, "Terror Subterra," courtesy of Dr. Roger Shepard. First appeared in **Mind Sights** by Roger N. Shepard, published by W. H. Freeman and Company, New York, 1990.

Page 359, turtle fossil, courtesy of John P. Adamek, EDCOPE Enterprises, Fossilmall.com

Page 360, fish fossil, courtesy of Denise Neville

Page 361, strange tool, courtesy of the author

Page 362, stem cell slide, courtesy of Dr. Tung-Tien Sun

Page 364, cats in baskets, illustration by Lopata Design

Page 369, occlusion, illustration by Lopata Design

Page 369, relative height, illustration by Lopata Design

Page 370, cast shadows, illustration by Lopata Design

Page 370, eight balls, illustration by Lopata Design

Page 371, dolphins, Marc M. Ellis, www.h2opictures.com

Page 372, mountain range, courtesy of Free High Resolution Photos, www.pointie.com/free_photos

Page 373, railroad tracks, courtesy of the author

Page 373, texture gradient, courtesy of the author

Page 374, shape from shading, illustration by Lopata Design

Page 375, windmill, Marc M. Ellis, www.h2opictures.com

Page 379, elephant, side view, courtesy of David Shapson

Page 380, elephant, rear view, courtesy of David Shapson

ABOUT THE AUTHOR

ROBERT KURSON earned a bachelor's degree in philosophy from the University of Wisconsin, then a law degree from Harvard Law School. After working as a features reporter for the **Chicago Sun-Times** and **Chicago** magazine, he moved to **Esquire** as a contributing editor. His award-winning stories have also appeared in **Rolling Stone, The New York Times Magazine,** and other publications. He lives in Chicago and can be reached via the Internet at www.robertkurson.com.